Citizens of the Kingdom

Publications of the Finnish Exegetical Society
Edited by Jaakko Hyttinen

Cover design by Jaakko Veijola

ISSN 0356-2786
ISBN 951-9217-38-X
ISBN 3-525-53622-4

Vammalan Kirjapaino Oy 2002

PUBLICATIONS OF THE FINNISH EXEGETICAL SOCIETY 83

TALVIKKI MATTILA

Citizens of the Kingdom

Followers in Matthew from a Feminist Perspective

The Finnish Exegetical Society in Helsinki
Vandenhoeck & Ruprecht in Göttingen
2002

Acknowledgments

When I started research on Matthew in an effort to break new ground toward a plausible feminist approach, I could not foresee the change this project was going to bring about in my own life. It was not only an exegetic investigation leading to an academic degree, but also included a process of inner transformation that irrevocably changed my whole existence and way of thinking.

I was introduced to feminist theology by Professor Kari Syreeni (Uppsala), who encouraged me to adopt this approach in my own dissertation. As my supervisor during these years of research, he has been unfailingly generous with ideas, enthusiasm and time. I owe him my deepest gratitude for his continuous support and encouragement.

This study is part of *The Gospels as Stories* research project in the Department of Biblical Studies at the University of Helsinki with Professor Syreeni as the head of this project. I also warmly remember the other members of this project: Outi Lehtipuu, Arto Järvinen, Petri Merenlahti and Raimo Hakola.

I spent the academic year 1996-1997 in London as a visiting student in Heythrop College. My supervisor there was Bridget Upton (PhD, Lecturer in New Testament) whose sharp eye and clarity of vision helped me further with my thesis. It was my privilege to participate in Professor Graham Stanton's postgraduate seminar in King's College and to discuss Matthew with him. I thank them both for their advice and encouragement.

I think, with special gratitude, of Sister Jennifer Dines (PhD, Lecturer in Old Testament in Heythrop College) who helped me in many ways, first to enter the college and then to make my life comfortable and inspiring in London. She introduced me to the Catholic Women's Network in London. This group of women (and some men) hold vigils in front of Westminster Cathedral praying for women's priesthood in the Catholic Church and celebrate women's liturgies once a month. The celebrations and discussions with these warm and wonderful women taught me that feminist theology is not just theory, but very much flesh and blood in the Catholic world.

I am deeply indebted to Professor Heikki Räisänen (Helsinki) who, more than once during these years, has taken the time to read my manuscript and to offer valuable and incisive comments. At a later period of the process, Docent Petri Luomanen, a Matthew scholar himself, pointed out many ways to improve my text. I also thank Docent Risto Uro and Professor Turid Karlsen Seim (Oslo) for their valuable insights and suggestions. I am grateful to all of them, even if I haven't always followed their lead. Sister Renée Brinker has done a marvellous task in revising my English. I thank her warmly for the arduous work she did in the last moments of this process. Whatever mistakes remain are due to my own ignorance and negligence.

During this research process I received financial support from *The Research Unit for Early Jewish and Christian Culture and Literature*, of which the project *The Gospels as Stories* is a part. This unit is one of the Centers of Exellence at the University of Helsinki. I have also been supported by a grant from the Emil Aaltonen Foundation.

Very special support, always unreserved and loving, came from my parents, Helmi and Kalervo Mattila, who did not live to see this project finished. With love and gratitude I dedicate this book to their memory.

During these years of research, there have been a number of people, my children, my sister, friends and colleagues, people who supported me, as well as those who opposed, and many others who all, in their way, have been part of this process. I am grateful to all of them for what I have learned. Life has been generous to me.

January 2002

Table of Contents

1. Introduction

Discipleship in the modern ecclesiastical context often conveys a schizophrenic message to women. In its original context in the Second Testament Gospels, the word refers to the twelve, or perhaps more, men who traversed Palestine with Jesus in the first century CE. Discipleship in the Gospels denoted a master-student relationship, which is familiar in both the Jewish world and Hellenistic environment. As such, it is a thoroughly patriarchal system.

Patriarchy, of course, is about power, and one way of exercising power is through naming.[1] Discipleship, as defined in patriarchal terms, excluded women – and many men as well – leaving them undefined and nameless. Nevertheless, some feminist scholars insist that discipleship encompasses women, that the women who were part of Matthew's narrative or the other Gospels are to be seen as disciples. Between the lines, they say, we can detect a true discipleship of equals.[2] This hermeneutic strategy implies that the women who, though not called disciples in the Gospel narratives, are included in the same category as the character group of 'disciples' by modern interpreters. This would incorporate women into what was originally a male group.[3]

When I began working on this theme, I was inclined to agree with this line of thinking.[4] I have, however, slightly modified my views, and in the present thesis I have adopted a more inclusive interpretative strategy, which at the same time seems more ideologically plausible in the contemporary context. Since society has begun to value women on their own account in today's world, why should we not grant the women in the Gospels the same right? Jesus' disciples in Matthew's narrative are undeniably men. Defining women followers through them narrows the perspective of a following to a single limited group while in Matthew

---

[1] For power as naming and describing reality, see Isherwood and McEwan 1993, 97.

[2] Especially Schüssler Fiorenza 1983. Also Wainwright 1991; Dines 1993; Ricci 1994, 179-192.

[3] The word 'disciple' is never used of a woman in the Gospels. Only once in the Second Testament is it connected to a woman, namely in Acts 9:36.

[4] In my article about women and disciples in Matthew's Passion narrative I came to the conclusion that women *are* disciples in substance even if they are deprived of the *name* disciple (Mattila 1999, 178-179).

there are other kinds of followers as well. Is it not possible to define the followers of Jesus in Matthew's narrative in such a way as to do justice to *all* characters – women and men alike – who respond affirmatively to the message of Jesus?

Trying to find a wider context for all who followed Jesus in one way or another, I soon realised that following Jesus meant being a member of God's kingdom, which is the key to Matthew's Gospel in many ways. All the followers share equally in this membership. One question then arises: what kind of power relationships existed in this kingdom of God, and how were they expressed among the insiders? The kingdom of God, the different manifestations of power, and the character groups in Matthew's narrative are the elements from which I have tried to form *an alternative definition of Christian following.*

One predecessor in interpreting Matthew from a feminist perspective is Elaine Wainwright, whose analysis[1] was divided into two parts[2]: on the one hand, a redaction-critical analysis, which aimed at historical clues about women in Matthew's communities, and on the other hand, a literary analysis. Since my own interests do not centre around the historical reconstruction of ancient women traditions, this research does not deal with that aspect. Instead I have chosen a literary perspective, comparing different character groups in order to find a more inclusive perspective – inclusive in the sense of including all, not only emphasising women. I have seen the texts more as narratives and less as historical evidence of the past.

Feminist scholars, as we shall see later on, are sometimes very keen to prove the existence of a period in Christian history when women and men were truly equal. This has demanded reading 'against the text' and the resulting 'proof' has not been unanimously accepted. Those involved in searching for this kind of equality too readily make a connection with the status of women today and attempt to inculcate their 'findings' into the mainstream of their denominational beliefs. Unlike society at large, many denominations have not accepted the equality or authority of women. These groups and their male leaders defend their policy by using the social order of the ancient world as a norm, and some feminist

---

[1] Wainwright 1991.

[2] For her it was really a three-part solution as in the third part she tried to answer questions concerning women traditions in Matthew's community. The analysis, however, was done in two parts.

theologians have gone along with this, following the same misleading reasoning.

Historical research is important in order to uncover the facts about women of the ancient world (in different social, religious and geographical contexts) so that we can become more aware of the roots of our heritage and oppose unacceptable treatment in our modern world. Another question entirely is what we are now building on the foundation of these ancient texts. Feminist ideology in all its manifestations opposes injustice, inequality and oppression – whether past or present – and therefore, any text that is used to legitimise injustice today needs to be challenged. This involves, primarily, efforts to find alternative readings to oppressive texts, and then the courage to reject those texts that cannot be reinterpreted.

In patriarchal systems, power is connected to the ability to get things done.[1] It is limited, competitive and used as a means of authority, control, and domination where, by definition, political, economic and domestic power is held mainly by men. This kind of 'power-over' implies a system of hierarchy and subordination. Such is usually also the case in the master-disciple relationships. Feminist ideology envisions a different concept where power is relational.[2] It is not control over others, but being-in-relation-with, 'power-with'. I claim that the feminist way of understanding power is useful in depicting the nature of the kingdom in Matthew's Gospel. The followers of Jesus in Matthew belong to the realm of relational power-with.

However, the situation is not that simple. The term 'kingdom' itself implies domination and hierarchy, which are anathema to any feminist perspective. Matthew's kingdom also includes hierarchical features that surface at various points in the narrative, showing that power-over extends its expressions inside the kingdom as well. Matthew was not able to escape his own time and conventions. Further, if the kingdom in Matthew itself includes indications of both hierarchical and relational power systems, the followers necessarily represent both as well. This of course leads to further questions concerning the feminist interpretative strategy. If Matthew and his environment were stuck in the patriarchal society, what does it mean to our modern world?

---

[1] Kramarae and Treichler 1985, 351.
[2] See McBride 1996, 182-183; Heyward 1996, 52-53.

2. Background and Preliminaries

2.1. Feminisms

2.1.1. What is Feminism

More than forty years ago, Simone de Beauvoir in her book *The Second Sex* was seeking an answer to the question: What is a woman? She maintained that woman is always defined in relation to the male. "He is the Subject. He is the Absolute. She is the Other."[1] She claimed that the terms 'masculine' and 'feminine' are used symmetrically only as a matter of form, but this is not the actual relation. Men represent both the positive and the neutral while women represent the negative, defined by limiting criteria, without reciprocity.[2] This kind of polarized structure emphasises the separation between the two sexes and assumes no relationship between them. Also, if women are seen as something different from men, isn't this an implication that all women are alike![3] In the contemporary world, especially among the postmodern feminists, this implication has been seriously questioned. The difference, for instance, between women in Latin America or Asia on the one hand, and women in Europe and North America on the other, has been acknowledged to be greater than the one between men and women on these respective continents.

Feminism is in reality a wide field of co-operating and competing approaches and nowadays it would be more appropriate to speak about feminisms. Pluralism and heterogeneity are the code words. What is common to all feminisms is first of all the resistance to all forms of male

---

[1] de Beauvoir 1988, 16.

[2] de Beauvoir 1988, 15.

[3] In feminist criticism, one debatable point has been 'essentialism', which has been defined to mean that all women in the world have some common aspects in their being and these aspects are due to biology and thus inevitable. (See, e.g., Morris 1997,10) Women's biology and 'feminine' features are generalized and thus the basis for subordination of women.

dominance of women.[1] A critique of patriarchal reality and the need for a change are at the core of every feminist approach.[2]

Focusing on women characters in the Bible or in early Christian literature does not make the research feminist. The basic element of the whole enterprise lies in the process and direction of the study. We can imagine a line at one end of which we have a more 'impartial' approach, the goal of which is to gain more knowledge about ancient history and women who are part of it. This work is not always considered feminist. At the other end of the line, we have an approach motivated by 'empowerment', one of the central concepts in feminist theory, refering to a relational process, a transformation to openness, growth, and change.[3] This kind of work prioritises change over strictly objective research. Therefore, *feminism* always includes an ideological commitment, whereas *female studies* concentrate on women on a more objective basis heading primarily towards knowledge rather than automatically to a change.[4] As I call my approach a feminist perspective I commit myself to transformation. The next question would then be, what does this transformation process mean in practise?

Feminist literature uses several concepts and terms to describe the process of change. The following list forms no order or hierarchy, but

---

[1] Gerda Lerner divides feminism into two different directions, making a distinction between *Women's rights feminism* and *Women's emancipation feminism*. (Lerner 1986, 236-237) The women's rights movements demand equal participation for women in the status quo and want to give women an access to the rights men have in the society. Women's emancipation is a goal with more temporal and spatial latitude: freedom from oppressive restrictions imposed by sex; self-determination and autonomy. Women's emancipation seeks not only justice in the political and social status quo – as is the goal in women's rights feminism – but liberation from all injustice against women, both past and present, public and private, collective and individual.

[2] Accordingly, Katharine Doob Sakenfeld has defined feminism as "a contemporary prophetic movement that announces judgement on the patriarchy of contemporary culture and calls for repentance and change". (Sakenfeld 1985, 55). Still another definition comes from Pam Morris who says that feminism is a conscious ideology that fights against such conscious ideologies that prioritise masculine authority and power (Morris 1997,13).

[3] Heyward 1996, 52-53.

[4] It is necessary to make a distinction between the terms 'female', 'feminine', and 'feminist'. 'Feminism' describes a political commitment to the struggle against all forms of patriarchy and sexism, 'femaleness' is a matter of biology and 'femininity' a set of culturally defined characteristics. Being female does not mean the same as being 'feminist'. See Moi 1989, 117, 120-122.

illustrates the multiple character of this kind of interpretation. All these goals can exist simultaneously. The connected attributes are only suggestive and sometimes overlapping, and they exemplify the different ways of focusing on the type of change the feminist strategies may look at:

- liberation – the political goal
- conscientisation – the individual goal
- inclusion – the ecclesiastical (communal) goal
- revision – the historical goal

From a feminist point of view, the Bible authorises the struggle for liberation of women and other marginal groups. First, however, the Bible itself must be liberated from the androcentric interpretations that have been used as a means of subordination. It must also be subjected to historical revision, a process that feminists believe can be inclusive and liberating.[1] The liberation is both political (cf. the basic communities in Latin America) and individual, the latter happening through conscientisation.[2] Conscientisation is a transformation process that takes place internally and leads to growth, which can in turn lead to further political action. Inclusion refers not only to gender, but also to questions of race and class. Liberation, revision and conscientisation ideally lead to a perfect inclusion where no one is excluded or held up as a norm to others. A truly feminist reading is *critical* in exposing the factors that make genuine inclusion difficult or impossible, and in liberating the reader from accepting oppressive structures embedded in the texts. It is also *constructive* in that it creates inclusive interpretations where they have traditionally not been found.[3]

---

[1] Wainwright 1991, 29-32 counts liberation and inclusion as the key characteristics of her feminist critique.

[2] Conscientisation is a transformation process that is happening in a woman. A woman starts to think and shape things differently, which again changes her behaviour and way of life. See Bartky 1975, 425-426. For Bartky the feminist consciousness is bipartite. On the one hand it is consciousness of victimisation, on the other, consciousness of the possibility of enormous personal growth (430-432, 437-438).

[3] In feminist theory the two goals of the research have often been defined as 'critique' and 'construct' where 'critique' is the critique of the existing research that has been done, and 'construct' includes new insights and theories. See for example Gunew 1990, 23,29.

It is of course evident that constructive solutions are not always possible. Feminist interpretations sometimes ignore this fact and try artificially to construct positive answers where they do not exist. Biblical texts include passages that offend the standards of the modern woman and what we really need is courage to criticise and abandon them if necessary. Still, the twofold perspective creates new possibilities for women: Traditionally oppressive texts can and must be read in a new way whenever possible. This encourages women to see themselves as a part of an inclusive community where new traditions can be created.

Feminism, as I see it, is thus a political[1] view with a twofold task. Since gender difference is seen as the basis for structural inequality, the first task is to understand the mechanisms that maintain that inequality. The second task is to try to change these mechanisms.[2] Judith Fetterley has put it very aptly: "At its best, feminist criticism is a political act whose aim is not simply to interpret the world but to change it by changing the consciousness of those who read and their relationship to what they read."[3]

2.1.2. The Object of Feminist Critique

The object under critique is often referred to as 'patriarchy', the definition of which is not unanimously accepted. The word itself comes from the ancient Greek and Roman legislation where the male head of the household had legal and economic power over women and other men in his family.[4] In modern feminist usage, the concept has gained a more general meaning of male dominance over women and children in the family, over women in society in general, or of an institutionalised system

---

[1] 'Political' is again something that in the feminist world can be dealt with in very different ways. As the understanding of 'power' is relational, so also politics can be defined in a related sense. For Hannah Arendt, political action means *gathering together in the common world in order to begin something new,* which concerns the world between us; the world between us is really the only thing we can share with each other. For more see Arendt 1958, 177-178 and Parvikko 1997, 16-18 who has studied Arendt's thinking.

[2] Morris 1997, 9.

[3] Fetterley 1978, viii.

[4] According to Gerda Lerner, the system is even older dating from the third millennium BCE. (Lerner 1986, 239).

of male dominance.[1] As the map of dominance and control is much more complex in reality than the hierarchy between men and women, the German feminist exegete, Luise Schottroff, has widened the definition to include men and women on both sides: those who dominate and those who are dominated. According to her, patriarchy is "the many men and few women of the elite who directly or indirectly exploit the poor...They are the many women and the few men who suffer from this system but who participate in sustaining and upholding it."[2] This factors out to a system wherein some elite women subordinate non-elite men, but elite women are never equal to elite men.

Therefore, the basic problem is not 'the women's issue' – although the problem concerns more women than men – but a social system consisting of entrenched hierarchies. This system has affected the cultural symbolism and religious expressions of ancient societies, including the Jewish and Christian traditions. God is the male head of the Earth just as a man is the head of his household. One of the main tasks of feminist theology has been the critique of this theological model and a turn toward egalitarian relationships of women and men.[3] Elisabeth Schüssler Fiorenza has suggested redefining patriarchy as a neologism 'kyriarchy', which means 'master-centred'. This expression embodies the critique against the hierarchical power models of the androcentric world. 'Patriarchal' means the rule of the father, 'kyriarchal' the rule of the master or the lord. This shifts the emphasis to a dividing line between those who own and those who are owned, between superiors and dependents. Kyriarchal power does not operate in gender alone, since the power structures include race, class, culture, and religion.[4] Since the kyriarchal/patriarchal system is also characterised by dualism, one of the goals of feminist theology is the abandonment of this dualism in favour of holistic structures.[5]

---

[1] Lerner 1986, 239; Brooten 1980,57.
[2] Schottroff 1995, 20
[3] See e.g. Lerner1986, 231-241; Radford Ruether 1996, Staumberger 1991, 321-323.
[4] Schüssler Fiorenza 1992, 114-117, 123; eadem. 1994, 13-18.
[5] Dualism refers to a system where two (or more) objects are related in a binary opposition to one another. Within feminism, dualism is understood as a relationship of domination. The basic dualism is between God and the material universe, which is followed by dualism of mind and body. For more see Jantzen 1990 and Boss 1996.

In this thesis I have adopted the concept 'patriarchal/kyriarchal' in its wider sense as shaped by Schüssler Fiorenza. The term includes elements of subordination other than merely those between genders, with particular emphasis on the hierarchical model and power structures. I do not presuppose that women are always victims, or that patriarchal gender systems are similar everywhere.

Thus, feminism is not only about women. The perspective has widened to include criticism against all kinds of hierarchies and all injustice. I prefer the term 'kyriarchy', because the critique against domination is a wider cause for the struggle on behalf of all who are subordinated and oppressed.

2.1.3. Women's Experiences as the Basis?

Feminist theories have been developed through the 'experience' of women. The roots of the tradition, then, are in experience, while the continuous experience in turn renews the tradition.[1] In conventional theologies, there is a generic 'man' who is the norm for theological reflection and whose experiences mirror those of most men. Feminist theology demands the inclusion of women's as well as men's experience, which means perceiving theology in a new light.[2]

What is meant by women's experience or experience in general? On the physical level, women's bodily experiences include menstruation, birthing, and lactation, but a closer investigation denies the validity of assuming these functions as universally female. Not all women give birth, and not even all women menstruate. On the historical level, seeing women's experiences leads to a dead end as well. In different cultures and different times, women's experiences, both individual and as part of the social-cultural structures, are dissimilar. Strictly speaking, there exists no

---

[1] See also Räisänen 2001, 251-252: "This means that religious thought develops in a process in which traditions are time and again interpreted in the light of new experiences, and vice versa: experiences are interpreted in the light of traditions."
[2] Radford Ruether 1983, 13; eadem. 1985, 111-113.

such thing as 'women's experience'.[1] Furthermore, I would question the idea that the experiences of women and men – apart from biological ones – are so unlike. The differences between women from two different cultures or two different ages can be greater than those between a man and a woman from the identical culture or the same historical period. Still, taking a living tradition as the basis of theology and research is a valuable starting point if it includes both men and women.

2.1.4. The Problem of Equality

A distinction that needs to be considered is an understanding of the *difference* and *complementarity* between the sexes.[2] Ivan Illich has dealt with this by connecting his economic theory to an understanding of gender as a historical category.

For Illich, gender is something other yet more than sex, but not in the same sense as in gender studies in general. His definition is a distinction in behaviour, a distinction universal in vernacular cultures. "It distinguishes places, times, tools, tasks, forms of speech, gestures, and perceptions that are associated with men from those associated with women. The association constitutes social gender, because it is specific to a time and a place."[3]

Illich calls it vernacular gender and says that it always reflects an association between the dual, local, material culture and the men and women who live under its rule. This social polarity is fundamental and never the same in different cultures.[4] Illich contrasts the vernacular gender to economic sex, which he sees as genderless. He connects each term to different kinds of societies: gender to pre-industrial society, and

---

[1] See also Stenström 1999, 27. Critique against experience as the basis of feminist research also challenges the so called "standpoint feminism". (For different epistemologies within feminism see Harding 1986, 24-29.) Differences between women make it impossible to suppose any common standpoint.

[2] De facto the word *sex* points to the biological while *gender* is connected to the social and the cultural which are bound to a certain time and a certain place. Graham 1996, 78 says that gender "denotes the nature of our experience as women and men, female and male, feminine and masculine: the origins and attributions of these categories, and their implications for all aspects of individual and corporate life."

[3] Illich 1983, 3.

[4] Illich 1983, 4.

sex to industrial capitalist society.[1] What is noteworthy in Illich's analysis is the relation he sees between economic discrimination of women and the gender construct itself: "Economic discrimination against women cannot exist without the abolition of gender and the social construction of sex."[2] An industrial society imposes assumptions that both sexes are made for the same work, perceive the same reality and have the same needs. Both parties live under the relationship of competition and can be regarded as genderless. In a pre-industrial world of vernacular gender, men and women do not compete for the same work; here, according to Illich, an ambiguous complementarity prevails. It is not equality or egalitarianism, but the mutual interdependence that sets the limits to struggle, exploitation, and defeat. According to Illich, vernacular culture represents a truce between genders.[3]

For Illich, the relationship between men and women is different in the pre-industrial world of the first century and the industrial world of the 19th century. Both are patriarchal in the sense that men dominate women, but the manner and essence of domination have changed. Therefore, egalitarianism cannot mean the same in ancient and modern societies.

Whatever we may think about Illich's view of complementarity, it is important to note differences in the relationship between man and woman in ancient societies, and in that of the society we now live in. Complementarity is a problematic solution if it is taken to mean that neither of the parties is 'whole' by her/himself. But if it is applied in the sense of accepting different perspectives in one unity, it is acceptable and useful. It would be naive to presume that patriarchal ideology purposely underlined women's subordinated position. However, early Christianity was shaped in patriarchal contexts where women were, using modern standards, generally unequal with men. The whole concept of equality as

---

[1] Illich 1983, 3, 9,12. His starting point is the economic discrimination of women in modern industrial society, and he sees this discrimination as threefold. First, women earn less than men in paid, taxed, and officially reported jobs. Second, in the unreported economy, women are involved in work for which no legally recognised salary is paid, no social security accrues, and where activities may be remunerated in kind. Women are also unequally excluded from certain sectors of the 'unreported economy' and are unequally bonded to others. Thus, women are discriminated against in both the reported and unreported economies, and also in the sector of shadow work. (50-53)
[2] Illich 1983, 13.
[3] Illich 1983, 178.

we understand it now, is an anachronism if applied to women and men of the first century. On the other hand, women's position in ancient societies varied greatly. Some upper class women and widows in larger cities could achieve a certain degree of independence compared to peasant women. The real problem is the invisibility of women in historical records. We simply do not know enough.

2.2. Feminist Perspectives in Biblical Interpretation

The Hebrew Scriptures and the Second Testament writings are not just ancient texts that interest scholars. The Scriptures as a whole also form an authoritative, canonical basis for Christian churches, and they are repeatedly acknowledged to be 'the word of God'.

For centuries the Bible has been a means of control and power, and its authoritative position in churches has maintained unjust structures and kept women subordinated to men. The tension that women have experienced through the authority of the Bible and the oppressive message it includes in some parts, has led many women in biblical scholarship to search for alternative interpretations. The basic question is whether women's subordination and oppression are so irrevocably part and parcel of the Christian tradition that they cannot be released from it.

2.2.1. Brief Historical Overview

The history of feminist interpretation of the Bible[1] has usually been acknowledged to start with Elisabeth Cady Stanton's pioneer study, *The Woman's Bible*, a two-volume work, published in the United States between 1895-1898 as a collective revision of twenty women. The head

---

[1] Throughout the centuries, there have always been women who have been interested in the theological issues and from time to time, have been able to produce their own views and visions about the biblical passages concerning women. For details, see, for example Radford Ruether 1998. However, feminist theology and biblical interpretation emerged first in the 19th century in the midst of the Women's Right's Movement in Europe and in the United States. For a survey of this history see for example Wacker 1995, 3-33; Bass 1992, 6-12; Brown Zikmund 1985, 21-29; de Swarte Gifford 1985, 11-33; Schüssler Fiorenza 1993, 117-128.

of this committee was Elisabeth Cady Stanton, who by that time was a notable theorist in the women's movement. Since according to her, one cause of women's oppression was the Bible, the committee re-translated and then gave a commentary on each passage that dealt with women. Stanton had invited distinguished Hebrew and Greek scholars to join her committee, but they refused to contribute because they were "afraid that their high reputation and scholarly attainments might be compromised by taking part in an enterprise that for a time may prove very unpopular."[1] Therefore, there were no theologians or biblical scholars (such women did indeed exist then) on her committee, and the commentary did not cover the continuous text, but concentrated on certain texts that at the time were used to legitimate women's inequality.[2] This work was very much a child of its own time, born in the middle of the political struggle for women's equal rights in society. The main interest was not in the exegetics but in the effects these chosen texts had had for centuries on the Christian tradition. An effort was therefore made to change these traditions by giving new interpretations.

It took several decades until the next start of feminist biblical interpretation emerged in the 1970s, first in Europe[3] and then in North America.[4] The spread to all continents of the world has been rapid, and now the multiple voices of European women, North-American white women, African-American feminists, and African, Latin-American and Asian feminists form a chorus of different voices. There are also Jewish feminist voices, and clear denominational tones among Christian feminist scholars. A few examples from these diverse and vast sources will illustrate the pluralism.

Elisabeth Moltmann-Wendel's book, *Ein eigener Mensch werden: Frauen um Jesus,* was the first German feminist monograph to be published.[5] It takes up some of the women characters in the Second

---

[1] Cady Stanton 1972(1895/1898), 11.

[2] For more about Cady Stanton see Cady Stanton 1971 (1898). See also de Swarte Gifford 1994, 52-63.

[3] The history in German-speaking countries is well reported in Wacker 1995, 7-33.

[4] Bass 1982, 6-12.

[5] Moltmann-Wendel 1991, first published in 1980. The history of women's contributions to biblical history is, of course, as long as the history of Christianity. Elisabeth Gössmann has discussed women's biblical readings before modern feminism back to the Middle Ages in her article "History of Biblical Interpretation by European Women" (Gössmann 1994, 27-40). However, women's traditions are still not to be

Testament, and with the help of church history, legends, and pictures, follows their trajectory in Christian history. She is able to draw alternatives to the traditional images of these women. In 1994, Luise Schottroff published a feminist social history of early Christianity, *Lydia's Ungeduldige Schwestern*.[1] She and her husband belonged to a group of biblical scholars who adopted a social-historical approach to biblical interpretation. In her feminist social history, as well as in her earlier publications[2], she believes that it is possible to reach beyond the androcentric text to the life of ordinary, non-elite women in Roman patriarchal society. She focuses on ordinary women in the first century, their work and everyday life. German feminist theologians, especially Schottroff, but others too, are very sensitive to German history during World War II and the post-war period, and issues concerning anti-semitism and life 'after the holocaust' are central to their work.[3]

In North America, Elisabeth Schüssler Fiorenza is a notable, prolific feminist biblical scholar whose hermeneutics will be discussed later in this work. Her writings[4] have been and no doubt continue to be a source of inspiration to many students within feminist theology and biblical scholarship.

---

considered as feminist interpretation.

[1] Translated in 1995 as *Lydia's Impatient Sisters*.

[2] *Befreiungserfahrungen: Studien zur Sozialgeschichte des Neuen Testaments* (1990). Selection of essays from this book was published in English by the name *Let the Oppressed Go Free: Feminist Perspectives on the New Testament* (1993). Note also "Auf dem Weg zu einer feministischen Rekonstruktion der Geschichte des frühen Christentums" in *Feministische Exegese: Forschungserträge zur Bibel aus der Perspektive von Frauen* (1995, 173-248).

[3] Radford Ruether, *Nächstenliebe und Brudermord. Die Christlichen Wurzeln des Antisemitismus* (1978); Schottroff and Wacker (eds.) *Von der Wurzel getragen. Deutschsprachige christlich-feministische Exegese in Auseinandersetzung mit Antijudaismus* (1995); Reinhartz, "The New Testament and Anti-Judaism: A Literary-Critical Approach" (1988, 524-537); Plaskow, "Anti-Judaism in Feminist Christian Interpretation" (1994, 117-129)

[4] Among others: *In Memory of Her: A Feminist Theological Reconstruction of Christian Origins* (1983); *But She Said. Feminist Practices of Biblical Interpretation* (1992); *Jesus Miriams's Child Sophia's Prophet* (1994).

The pioneering work in feminist hermeneutics and interpretation was originally carried out by white European and North American women.[1] Gradually, African-American and Hispanic women in North America criticised this kind of feminism as not being sufficiently interested in the questions of race and class, and they distanced themselves from what they called a white feminist approach by calling their own approach *womanist* (African-American) or *mujerista* (Hispanic).[2] African black women[3], Latin-American[4] and Asian women[5] have also created their own specific approaches starting from their own cultural and social contexts. Thus,

---

[1] Europe, North America and Australia (Elaine Wainwright) form the wider Western context that will mainly be referred to in this work, because that is my own contextual location. It is worthwhile to note, however, that the European feminists – theologians as well as exegetes – come mainly from the northern parts of Europe. The traditionally Roman Catholic areas, like Spain, Italy and France are less interested in feminist theology. About European feminist discussion in the 1990's, see Radford Ruether 1998, 202-207.

[2] The context of their respective interpretations is the experience they and/or their foremothers have had of slavery, survival and liberation. For African-American interpretations see Schüssler Fiorenza 1994, 6-7; Baker-Fletcher 1993, 41-51. And for Hispanic Isasi-Diaz 1994, 86-94.

[3] Teresa Okure is one of the major representatives of the African biblical feminists. She is a Roman Catholic sister in Nigeria and a professor at the Catholic Institute of West Africa. The starting point in African feminism is strongly contextual. Women's situations in African culture and society, and women's positions in African churches are compared with situations in the Gospels, and conclusions are made concerning contemporary life. The contemporary world determines the method; historical questions are less important (Okure 1994, 77-82).

[4] The reading of the Bible in Latin-America is also done in the context of life experience: coming closer to one's daily life, which implies different kinds of experiences. The perspective of the reading is that of the poor, and among the poor are also women who are marginalised because of their sex. See Tamez 1988, 173-180.

[5] In Asia, Christianity is a minority religion and the different readings – both feminist and liberation theological in general – are born in the context of dialogue between the religious traditions. I shall name here only one, a Chinese biblical scholar Kwok Pui-lan, who has received her doctorate in the United States and also currently works there. In her book, *Discovering the Bible in the Non-Biblical World* (1995), she has created a multi-dimensional reading that combines the ancient tradition of the East with the Christian tradition of the West, and the insights of feminism and Third World Theologies. She proposes 'dialogical imagination' as a new approach to biblical interpretation. The Bible is set in a larger multi scriptural context of Asian cultural and religious traditions. For further information see Kwok 1995, 4-19, 101-116. For other examples of Asian feminist interpretation see Lehtiö 1999, 76-78.

feminist biblical scholarship has grown to cover all the continents and gone in many directions.

As my own specific context is in the Western tradition, the literature referred to in my work comes mostly from the northern and western parts of Europe, North America and Australia. But as a Finnish exegete from Helsinki University, my thinking has been, both unconsciously and consciously influenced by this milieu.[1] As a Roman Catholic woman, I share the pain of the inferior status of women in my own church and therefore, the women's issue goes beyond an academic question; it became a mission for me.

2.2.2. Hermeneutic Strategies

For nearly 2000 years, the book we call the Bible, a collection of ancient texts, has been normative in the Christian churches. With awareness that the Bible is a major cause for much of the oppression women experienced in their churches, they adopted different strategies to survive within their respective traditions.[5] The most extreme, but also in fact the most logical, reaction is *rejection*. The Bible is abandoned and the whole Christian tradition with it. From this point of view, the whole Christian tradition is corrupt and useless. The supporters of this view concentrate on ancient female cults and on the matriarchal heritage of prehistoric times.[6] This

---

[1] During the last two decades, Finnish biblical scholarship has taken an interest in women. The major representative of women studies has been professor Raija Sollamo who has published articles and has been a tireless spokeswoman for women's issues both in her church and in the faculty. In 1992, as a result of her work as a teacher, she published a book of articles about biblical women (*Naisia Raamatussa:Viisaus ja Rakkaus*). Several of the contributors in this book had been members of her seminar on women in the Bible. Characteristic of Finnish biblical work on women is that the coeditor of this book, Ismo Dunderberg, as well as some of the writers, is a man. One of them, Antti Marjanen, has studied the history of the early Christian women and wrote his doctoral thesis about Mary Magdalene as well as articles about early Christian women.

[5] For an overall description of main strategies within feminist biblical interpretation the best articles are Middleton 1990 and Osiek 1985.

[6] The most prominent representative of this attitude is Mary Daly (Daly 1973 and 1979). According to her, the Bible – and the whole of Christianity – were not only distorted by patriarchy, but represent the ideology of patriarchal domination itself and are therefore rejectable. See also Hampson 1990.

attitude has been criticised as a new dualism: male is evil while female is good, forming a hierarchy which is the reverse of the one feminism is struggling to eradicate. It also indicates disconnectedness to a real past.[1]

Other strategies do not cut themselves off from the Christian tradition, most of them admitting that the Bible is a product of its own patriarchal time, in which patriarchy was a way of maintaining order.[2] Some scholars wish to eradicate distorted traditions and return to the original practises that were innately good. Others wish to transform the patriarchal traditions. The division used here was introduced by Carolyn Osiek[3], whose broad understanding of feminism includes all ways of affirming the dignity of women.

One hermeneutic strategy is the extreme opposite of rejection, *loyalism*, where the essential validity and goodness of the biblical tradition as the Word of God is acknowledged. The Bible is 'the ultimate expression of God's authority' and it can never be oppressive. The problems are always seen to be in the interpreters, never in the text itself.[4] In practice, loyalism looks for positive texts about women to counteract pivotal texts used against women.[5] Existing texts are reinterpreted or the 'forgotten texts' that give a positive view of women are exhumed.[6] This choice can, however, be considered conservative, and in some sense apologetic and not feminist at all[7], but Carolyn Osiek reminds us that it is usually based on the sound use of exegetical methods.[8] Sakenfeld, on the other hand, stresses the possibilities of this approach by emphasising

---

[1] For critique see Osiek 1985, 98; Radford Ruether 1983, 230.

[2] Tolbert 1983, 122; Osiek 1985, 104.

[3] Osiek 1985, 93-105. This is the division also used by Wacker 1995, 34-45. – I include four strategies from Osiek. Originally there are five as Osiek starts with the rejectionist alternative as number one.

[4] Osiek 1985, 99-100.

[5] For example 1 Cor 14:34 against 11:5 or 1 Tim 2:12 against Titus 2:3.

[6] Osiek 1985, 99; Sakenfeld 1985, 57-58; Trible 1984, 3. Osiek also mentions another form of loyalist hermeneutics, namely acceptance of "traditional argument for order through hierarchy as datum of revelation but one sorely in need of transformation from within because of its abuse by imperfect human instruments". (100)

[7] Wacker 1995, 36.

[8] Osiek 1985, 100. Conservative evangelical Christianity in Britain has created an alternative that could be classified as loyalist. It rejects nothing in the Bible, but all texts can be explained in the light of the role of 20th century women. (Middleton 1990, 232).

the diversity of the biblical testimony concerning women. Because there
are positive biblical texts and traditions to be recovered, there is no need
to abandon the Bible as totally patriarchal. The reinterpretations,
however, are far from universally accepted, and texts that cannot be
evaluated positively by women's standards will be retained.[1]

Revisionist hermeneutics offer another alternative. In this approach,
historical and social factors in traditions are separable from the
theological content, and therefore, new traditions can evolve. In practice,
this means that the historical sources are reinterpreted as much as possible
to include women and what is known about women's contributions in
history. 'Reading between the lines' is applied in order to find the
positive role of women in the ancient sources.[2] However, one can still
question the one-sided view of presupposing only a positive tradition.

Phyllis Trible is considered a notable representative of revisionism.[3]
She has applied the method of rhetorical criticism to stories describing
women as victims of heinous crimes, even murder and rape, in order to
recover neglected history and remember these women. Her intention is to
retell stories about women so as to make today's patriarchy repent.[4]
Critics of Trible have contended that when the text is separated from its
socio-cultural context, no direct critique against the culture it represents
can be made, and that the patriarchal and androcentric views are not taken
seriously.[5] Nevertheless, if attention is concentrated on the ideological
construct of the text using feminist rhetorical criticism, the authority of
the patriarchal readings, as well as the notion that the texts are transparent
reports about the past, are challenged.

The third alternative is *sublimationist hermeneutics*[6] where the
'Other', the feminine, operates on its own principles and is totally distinct
from those of the male realm. Using sublimationist hermeneutics,

---

[1] Sakenfeld 1985, 58-59.

[2] Osiek 1985, 100-101. Tolbert 1983, 122-123 names this perspective as 'the remnant
standpoint'.

[3] Sakenfeld 1985, 62; Wainwright 1991, 17-19; Tolbert 1983, 122 n 22. Tolbert also
additionally includes E. Struthers Malbon's article "Fallible Followers: Women and
Men in the Gospel of Mark" in revisionism.

[4] Trible 1983, eadem 1984.

[5] Schüssler Fiorenza 1983, 20-21; Osiek 1985, 100-101; Wainwright 1991, 18-19.

[6] Wacker 1995, 41 uses the title *Hermeneutik des "Ewig Weiblich"* and describes it as
a matriarchal world view.

femininity is considered superior to masculinity. In practice, this means a search for the feminine in biblical symbolism.[1] This alternative seems to somewhat overlap the rejectionist attitude, even though it sets out to find feminine imagery *in* the Bible. Its major defect is the neglect of a socio-historical dimension and a tendency towards dogmatism.

The fourth alternative is *liberationist feminism*, which proclaims that the central message of the Bible is *human liberation*. The larger context is liberation theology in general, liberation from patriarchal domination, leading to partnership and equality among all humans. The oppression and subordination of women are seen as a part of larger political, economic, social, and theological relationships of dominance-submission. Accordingly, the main message of the Bible is interpreted as human liberation, which is the meaning of salvation.[2] The main representatives of this option are Letty Russell and Rosemary Radford Ruether, both of whom have created a theological perspective that functions as a norm according to which the texts are organised and prioritised.

According to Russell, the Bible must be liberated from one-sided, white, middle-class male interpretation as well as from abstract and doctrinal interpretations that take the narratives out of their social and historical contexts and metamorphose them into timeless truths. The Bible must be read from the perspective of the oppressed to reconstruct a history of the losers.[3] The interpretative key for Russell is the witness of scripture to God's promise; partnership in the "mending of creation", by restoring the partnership of human beings within themselves, with one another, with God, and with nature. The Bible is not just a collection of narratives from the past, a prototype, but also "a memory of the future", open to new life.[4]

Rosemary Radford Ruether emphasises the human experience and reads the Bible from the perspective of the poor and the oppressed, as other liberation theologians do. The oppressed and the poor are not just women. Women's experience in particular is the starting point for her critical theological principle of "the full humanity of women". Everything that affirms the humanity of women is redemptive, everything that does

---

[1] Osiek 1985, 101-102. The scholars within this direction are focusing on topics like Israel as a bride of God, or Mary as the virgin-mother.
[2] Osiek 1985, 103.
[3] Russell 1985(1), 12.
[4] Russell 1985 (2), 139.

not is rejectable. She goes even further towards inclusive humanity: No group must be made the norm of humanity, not men, not white people, not Christians. She insists a correlation between the feminist critical principle and the prophetic-messianic tradition in the Bible.[1] For Radford Ruether, the biblical message of liberation is visible in 'the prophetic-messianic tradition' which, according to her, is to be understood as a critical perspective through which the traditions of the Bible are continuously evaluated in a new context. For her, the biblical principle of prophetic faith parallels to a feminist judgement of the unjust structures in society. The goal of this liberation is the full personhood of women, full humanity. It is not just the goal, but a feminist principle in itself.

Osiek criticises this view for its narrowness. The prophetic tradition is limited to Exodus, to the prophets in the Hebrew Scriptures and to Jesus. Osiek points out that it likens revelation and authority, rejecting as non- revelatory everything that does not fit its own narrow criterion. It is a very weak basis for forming a 'canon within a canon'.[2] While I agree that the criterion itself may be problematic, I maintain that rejecting oppressive texts in the Bible is a logical and brave choice.

Furthermore, the correlation between the feminist critical principle and the prophetic-messianic tradition does produce an evaluative tool for modern readers. In my opinion, we should not dismiss it as too narrow, but rather accept it as *one* strategy while creating others parallel to it. It may not be possible to find one all-embracing idea, but it is possible to create smaller tools in order to open alternative interpretation of oppressive texts. While the prophetic-messianic tradition is not applicable to every book of the Bible, other kinds of correlation can be used to release true meanings. My own idea in this thesis is to develop Radford Ruether's strategy by demonstrating that the kingdom of God and the feminist idea of power as relational are, in several respects, compatible in Matthew's Gospel.

I would add to this list a fifth alternative[3], which in a sense is included in Osiek's liberationist perspective, but which deserves to be mentioned on its own. This is the *reconstruction model* where the main

---

[1] Radford Ruether 1985, 111-118. See also Tolbert 1983, 122.
[2] Osiek 1985, 104.
[3] This is number 3 in Tolbert 1983, 123. Also Wainwright 1991, 21 separates this as 'theological/reconstructionist'.

interest is not in the canonical scriptures and their interpretation, but in reconstructing biblical history, so as to prove that women had more importance in the shaping of history than the canonical writings acknowledge. The major representative of this option is Elisabeth Schüssler Fiorenza, who has created a feminist model of biblical interpretation which consists of four stages. For her, feminist interpretation begins with an ideological suspicion that biblical texts and their interpretations are androcentric and serve patriarchal functions. The model continues with historical reconstruction as a form of remembering. This means "reintegrating women and other marginalised people into history as agents and at the same time to write biblical history as the history of women and men." Remembering is followed by proclamation or theo-ethical assessment, which means that patriarchal texts are not to be proclaimed as the Word of God, merely as words of men. As a fourth point, the texts need to be actualized with a creative imagination by retelling the biblical stories from a feminist perspective.[1]

Schüssler Fiorenza has created a hermeneutical centre which is called 'the women-church' (*ekklesia gynaikon*). It has been defined as a liberation movement of self-identified women and women-identified men in biblical religion. The goal is women's religious self-affirmation, power, and liberation from patriarchal alienation, marginalisation, and oppression.[2] For her, patriarchy is not a theoretical world view of androcentrism, but a socio-political system and social structure of graded subjugation.[3] The 'women-church' aims to emphasise the visibility of women in biblical religion. For Schüssler Fiorenza, the hermeneutical centre is a dialogical community of equals, based on the ideal of the Greek *ekklesia*, a public assembly of free citizens. The gathering of the women and men struggle equally for liberation from patriarchal oppression in society and in religion.

Schüssler Fiorenza's model has gained an established position within feminist interpretation. She has defined the revisionist alternative as interpretation that concentrates on women and tries to find all the information possible about women in biblical writings. Her

---

[1] Schüssler Fiorenza 1990, 15-22; eadem. 1992, 52-57. As an example of her model, she gives an interpretation of Luke 10:38-42.
[2] Schüssler Fiorenza 1985(1), 126. For women-church also eadem. 1990, xiv-xvii, 1-22.
[3] Schüssler Fiorenza 1990,5; eadem. 1985(1), 127.

reconstructionist position is somewhere between loyalism and revisionism in Osiek's division. She defines her goals as research into the forgotten traditions about women, and a critique against the androcentric interpretation that for centuries has hidden the original meaning of the texts. The presupposition is that the text in itself is not misogynist.[1] The strength of the model is in its consideration of both the historical context and the situation of the modern community where the text is valued as something more than mere history. The weak point lies in her historical interpretation, and her reconstruction has received a fair amount of criticism.

Schüssler Fiorenza does not view the biblical texts as reflections of reality. According to her, the reality, about which the text is silent must be found through clues and allusions hidden within the text.[2] She regards the texts as theological interpretations, argumentation, projections, and selections rooted in patriarchal culture. The texts not only reflect their patriarchal context, but at a deeper level, suggest the discipleship of equals as well as women's leadership. Therefore, the reading of such texts has a twofold purpose: First the texts must be evaluated historically in terms of their own time and culture and then assessed theologically in terms of a feminist scale of values.[3] The goal is to reconstruct early Christian history as women's history and at the same time to sort texts according to their degree of correspondence with feminist theologies. Her view of history, as written today for our own time, denies value-neutrality. She further stresses that historical discourse requires public consciousness and discussions of one's values, interests, commitments, presuppositions and socio-political position. "The past is not a continuum of given facts that we can rediscover by mere objective observation, but it discloses itself to us only if we put specific questions to it."[4] According to her, early Christianity was an egalitarian reality that can be verified through those traditions and texts, which like the tip of an iceberg, indicate a possibly rich heritage, now lost to us, and allow us "a glimpse of the egalitarian-inclusive practice and theology of early Christians".[5] Schüssler Fiorenza melts everything through suspicion. This approach

---

[1] Schüssler Fiorenza 1992, 21-24.
[2] Schüssler Fiorenza 1983, 41.
[3] Schüssler Fiorenza 1985(2), 56-57.
[4] Schüssler Fiorenza 1985(2), 52-53.
[5] Schüssler Fiorenza 1985(2), 59.

clearly posits losing the reality of the social and cultural context of the very time meant to be reconstructed. She wants simultaneously to reveal the suppression of women in biblical times and to seek Christian affirmation of women through the same analytical process.

Lone Fatum, a Danish exegete, has criticised this methodological approach by saying that "it is like wanting to eat your cake and have it." She contends that its hermeneutical consequence is a faulty methodology which only produces a utopian vision and wishful thinking. According to Fatum, this can stop critical questioning and consistent analysis and therefore "instead of deconstructing with critical consistency to the bitter end where androcentric values and patriarchal strategies can be fully unveiled and analytically exposed, it stops half way and chooses to (re)construct a pattern of utopian values which may serve as an affirmation of Christian women. Deconstruction becomes reconstruction and the hermeneutical difference between the two is blurred by apologetic endeavours."[1]

Schüssler Fiorenza seeks powerful women in biblical times and she uses the Second Testament texts as models in a modern context for the liberation of women. In this method, the real historical context is at least obscured if not forgotten. She wants to make women historical subjects they have never been and is really replacing androcentrism with gynocentrism. There is not necessarily anything wrong in seeking Christian affirmation of women, but methodologically this cannot be done by means of historical-critical analysis.[2]

I agree with Fatum that the social reality as it reveals itself in the text must be taken as androcentric. The women in the texts must not speak with our voices or bear our images.[3] However, Schüssler Fiorenza is right when claiming that the text is not reality and tradition is not history 'as it really happened'. We are very much involved with the rhetoric,

---

[1] Fatum 1992, 264. Fatum also sees that feminist suspicion has limits: some texts, some fundamental beliefs, some presuppositions about freedom and equality are above suspicion and taken for granted.

[2] Fatum 1992, 266 sees behind all this the current dilemma of feminist exegesis, an obsession, as she says, that feminist theological insight and experience of spirituality have to be authorised by Scripture, legitimated by canon, or at least by canon within the canon. Feminist theological apologetics seem to run the risk of ending up as a self-fulfilment of wishful feminist thinking or as a gynocentric mythology.

[3] Fatum 1992, 265.

theological argumentation and the selective mind of the biblical author. The context is undeniably patriarchal. The Bible is written by men; it originated in a patriarchal society, and has been preserved and interpreted mostly by men. However, as the Bible has empowered women to struggle against oppression, the affirmative task is a reality as well. Even if no egalitarian communities existed in the first century, the Bible narratives include characters and teachings that are not in accord with the patriarchal structures. I find my own sympathies somewhere between Schüssler Fiorenza and Fatum. The early Christian reality was not in any way uniform and there is no reason to expect otherwise as far as women are concerned. Each text should be approached without presuppositions about egalitarianism or oppression. Egalitarianism and/or oppression by modern standards should not be read into the historical analysis.[1] Still, the task is not easy, as the texts have legitimised a great deal of injustice and oppression. We should also remember the long history of using these texts as a negative implement to justify inequality.

All these strategies cover a large area of the feminist field of interpretation. The general problem is that there are so many different approaches to the subject that not all the factors that contribute to the interpretation fit in smoothly. The critique of reality within the biblical area can be focused as much on the patriarchal structures in the society of the first century as on the male bias in 20th century interpretations. Furthermore, Third World feminists' critique of white Euro-American feminism is as pressing a problem within feminism as the fight for inclusive language in translations of the Bible in the Western environment. The historical context and research as such, and the process of making the ancient texts meaningful for modern women, are inter-related, making the chart of biblical feminisms multi-dimensional and pluralistic.

---

[1] That every interpretation should be seen as a dialogue grounded in experience see Tolbert 1983, 119; Wainwright 1991, 34.

2.2.3. The Diversity and Complementarity of Methods

The feminist approach in biblical studies has not developed any new methods, but takes advantage of already existing ones.[1] The historical-critical methods have been joined more recently by many others that approach the ancient texts from the perspective of linguistics, sociology, literary criticism, history of religions, and psychology, to name only some. This means that the research broadens and differentiates in order to answer questions concerning the history behind the texts as well as questions on the text itself or the ideological interpretations insinuated by the reader. The questions asked determine the method(s). This is also the situation within feminist interpretation.

Those with *historical interests* concentrate on questions concerning women in the Bible or concerning ancient Jewish, Greek, and Roman women in general. Here the distinction between *female* studies and *feminist* historical interpretation is relevant. The latter does not necessarily record history only as women's oppression by men, but, with the help of rhetorical analysis or social history, focuses on women as historical agents, and on their resistance against patriarchal oppression. Women's historical experience needs to be unearthed and rewritten. The questions must highlight the everyday life of women in biblical times, the life of women belonging to different races and classes, women's capability to read and write, etc.

One of the salient facts to emerge from historical research in general is that the interests of the community that produced the narrative are not the same as those of the historians. Rhetorical analysis may reveal that the emphasis given in the narrative can be more a device for driving home the views of the author/editor than a reality expressing the convictions in the communities for whom the text is written. The editing work points to problems and discussion within the community or the communal tradition where the redactor comes from, not unanimous beliefs within it. Historical studies also reveal the possibility of different theological traditions existing simultaneously. All these points have proven valuable

---

[1] For a thorough treatment of different methods as used in feminist exegese see Wacker 1995, 61-79.

to feminist research.[1] A feminist way of observing history is as a network of parallel lines, not a set of hierarchical layers. In this way, the delineation of women's lives becomes visible, as do those of other groups of 'nobodies'.[2] In this sense, the historical approach is essential in feminist research as it recognizes the possibility of 'many truths' existing at the same time. This approach avoids rigid, dogmatic thinking and tries to bring out the forgotten story lines of ordinary people and their contribution to history.

In the *literary approach*, the text is considered the centre of a communication process. The focus can be on different elements of this communication event: the author, the reader, the text or the context. In the feminist approaches[3] – especially but not exclusively – in the Third World, the Bible is considered more as 'a story' than history as such. This is a sound reminder that the Bible is also 'a sacred book', a source of empowerment and inspiration, not only history. The literary-critical methods applied to Second Testament studies have been primarily narrative criticism and reader-oriented approaches.[4]

Narrative criticism investigates the elements of the narrative – settings, characters, plot, and rhetoric as a network of relationships. The critics differentiate between a real author and an implied author and between a real reader and an implied reader. From a feminist point of view, the issues of interest are the ignored women characters and women imagery.[5]

Reader-response critics highlights the effects of the text on the reader. Feminist reader-response criticism points out how gender, class, and race affect our reading. *Immasculation* defines a phenomenon where women as readers and scholars are taught to think like men, to identify with a male point of view and to accept the male system of values.[6] As a

---

[1] Fander 1994, 205-224 has listed these and several other advantages of the historical-critical work from a feminist point of view.

[2] Lappalainen 1990, 79.

[3] About feminist literary criticism see Struthers Malbon and Anderson 1994, 242-244.

[4] For example *The Postmodern Bible* by The Bible and Culture Collective introduces several new "criticisms" like reader-response criticism, structuralist and narratological criticism, post-structuralist criticism, rhetorical criticism, psychoanalytic criticism, feminist and womanist criticism and ideological criticism.

[5] Struthers Malbon and Anderson 1994, 247.

[6] Fetterley 1978, xx.

defence, the female reader must refuse assent, and start a process of exorcising the male mind that has been implanted in her, in a word, she must become a resisting reader.[1] This process involves re-visioning, seeing with fresh eyes, transforming the text for the use of feminism. Reading as a woman implies that the reader resists the ideological implications in the text and the logic of the narration in order to find an alternative reading that also gives space to women. The point of view in the narrative, the masculine perspective (cf. a male 'I' who tells the story), invites the female reader to adopt the male ideology that is integral to it. This also needs to be actively resisted. Because 'men' have been the norm, their writings and descriptions have been accepted as 'the truth'. Moreover, in men's works, women are often described as stereotypes: as a seductress, as a mother or a virgin, as a perfect woman (pure and submissive), as a witch.[2] When women become conscious of the immasculation, they can resist it, and read the text in a feminist way. Here is another instance of the twofold task of reading: the critique against immasculation and the new transformed way of using the same text.

In historical analysis, the distance between the text and the reader is not necessarily bridged, though the distance is recognized. In her biblical hermeneutics, Sandra M. Schneiders claims that this historical gap can only be overcome as we realise that the text is a dynamic medium rather than a static object. She emphasises the continuity between the past and the present, and points to Ricoueur's theory of oral discourse becoming written by undergoing three fundamental changes.

Firstly, the discourse is sheltered from destruction by the written word. Secondly, it is cut loose from its author and attains a relative semantic autonomy as a text. Thirdly, the text transcends its own psycho-sociological conditions of production and can be decontextualized and recontextualized.[3] This means that the text not only has meaning in the

---

[1] Fetterley 1978, xxii; Struthers Malbon and Anderson 1994, 251.
[2] See Morris 1997, 23-48.
[3] Schneiders 1989, 7. As an example Schneiders gives the American Declaration of Independence, which was written in the patriarchal slave culture of 18th century America. When the white, property-owning, free adult males wrote that "all men are created equal" they certainly did not mean the equal rights or dignity of children, non-whites, the landless, slaves, or females. In successive periods of American history this declaration has been decontextualised, which means that it has been separated from its

time and place it originated, but it has its own future. Schneiders particularly elaborates on this third point. She claims that the world of the Second Testament as text is the world of a Christian discipleship structured by the paschal mystery of Jesus. "The real referent of the text that is normative for the Christian community of all time, is not the experience of those first Christians, but the experience that is made possible for a reader by the text."[1] Further, she maintains that it is not merely an isolated critical reader, but the Christian community as such that is capable of reading the text "through ideologically critical eyes".[2]

Schneiders' argumentation reveals a positive response to the question of how a historically oppressive text can also be liberating. She calls her theory a 'hermeneutics of transformation'. The historical world behind the text was a patriarchal world, but the world projected by the Second Testament is the world of Christian discipleship. "The semantic autonomy of the text means both that it escapes from the limitations of author's intention and that it transcends the historical world from which it emanated. But it also means that the text itself can generate an effective history which is constitutive of the effective historical consciousness of subsequent readers."[3]

Schneiders' central point is the paschal mystery of Jesus. It is the Christ, not the historical Jesus, that is the key to the interpretation. In my opinion, from this perspective, the history of ancient society is not taken seriously and the oppressive structures escape defining. Also, the understanding of the text presupposes a Christian mind set. Furthermore, it is questionable to assume that the text itself could generate its own history. Nevertheless, there is a sound core to Schneiders' thinking. The biblical text is not only a document from the past; it can also be, and indeed has been, recontextualised in the later phases of history. What is needed is a balanced process that takes into consideration the historical context from which the text originated and the text as it is in the modern reader's hands. The interpretation, however, should take into consideration as much as possible the time and the place of the text, the

---

own psycho-sociological conditions of production and recontextualised in the struggle for the emancipation of the slaves, suffrage for women, civil rights for blacks and the inviolability of children.

[1] Schneiders 1989, 7-8.

[2] Schneiders 1989, 8.

[3] Schneiders 1989, 8.

principal concerns of the author and the community behind the text. Sharon Ringe compares the interpretation process with a conversation: first we have to know something about the conversation partner in order to know where s/he comes from. In a conversation there are always at least two partners; it is a dialogue. But even if we listen sensitively and carefully, we understand through our own experience, and we probably perceive, at least partially, something other than was intended. This is also the situation when reading biblical texts. The history, culture and society of the reader influence every reading effort and produce questions concerning the text.[1]

When biblical scholars refer to literary analysis, they sometimes point to a combination of methods. Narrative criticism applied to the gospels is combined with other methods, such as redaction criticism[2] or sociological inquiry[3]. This is commendable because the gospels by their nature are not just literary fiction.[4] If they are examined only as texts without anchoring them to their historical context, there remain more unanswered than answered questions. The historical and cultural backgrounds are essential for understanding.[5]

I have also taken advantage of this plurality of perspectives. My main interest is in the narrative, but I have related my interpretation to the historical realities. I am not looking for specific historical traditions behind Matthew's narrative, rather I try to locate the texts in their contemporary setting by considering the kind of traditions and facts that were involved in shaping the final form. This does not, however, prevent searching for new meanings in the texts from a modern perspective, in this case by taking advantage of feminist interpretative strategies. The

---

[1] Ringe 1992, 1-2. For Ringe this interpretation is "active reading".

[2] Wainwright 1991.

[3] For example Barton 1994, where he approaches his texts from four different angles: form criticism, redaction criticism, sociological approach and literary approach.

[4] See Merenlahti and Hakola 1999.

[5] A model within feminist criticism that in a sense combines the historical and the literary is Schüssler Fiorenza's "a critical feminist rhetorical model" that "seeks to articulate feminist interpretation both as a complex process of reading and reconstruction and as a cultural-theological practice of resistance and transformation. To that end it utilizes not only historical and literary methods, which focus on the rhetoric of the biblical text in its historical contexts, but also storytelling, role-play, bibliodrama, pictorial arts, dance, and ritual to create a 'different' historical imagination." (1992, 40).

literary approach allows the text to have its own values which are not necessarily the same as in the ancient society. The values of Matthew's narrative can in fact challenge those of his contemporary environment, maybe even his personal values.

2.3. My Choice of a Feminist Perspective

My special interest in asking ideological questions concerns the power system reflected in the Matthean story. A feminist way of describing power distinguishes between the hierarchical system on one hand and reciprocal relationships on the other. Some feminists[1] have termed these two as power-over, and power-with.[2] Power-over[3] is associated with the

---

[1] See Starhawk 1990, 8-20; Heyward 1982 and 1989; McBride 1996 and Heyward 1996. Also Russell discusses the feminist paradigm of authority and replaces the authority of domination with authority as partnership. Reality is interpreted in the form of a circle of interdependence. In this way "experience, tradition, biblical witness, and intellectual research enrich each other in a rainbow of ordered diversity, in a synergetic perspective of authority in community." (Russell 1985[2], 143-146)

[2] Starhawk considers these different types of power to be rooted in different modes of consciousness and world views. The consciousness associated with power-over involves estrangement; it is disconnected and fragmented, and the relationships between the separate objects within it are described by rules and laws. It presupposes that it is possible to find rules for everything as well as for all relationships, and that the ability to control these rules and relationships exists. Human beings have to earn their value, or it must be granted to them. Power-over enables one person to make decisions for others and to use control (Starhawk 1990, 9-14). According to Carter Heyward, power itself – outside any particular context – is not positive or negative, but using power *over* others is evil whereas using power *with* others is good (Heyward 1989, 191).In power-with relationships, persons are valued according to how they affect others. Heyward makes a distinction by noting that power-with seeks to empower all persons in a relationship, whereas power-over empowers only a few and disempowers others. Thus, power-over is connected to hierarchy. It is limited, competitive, and used as a means of authority, control, and domination. Power-with is something that forms no hierarchy, because it exists between equals. It is not power to command, but to influence, to suggest and to be listened to. The feminist way of understanding power as power-with underlines relatedness. "We come to this world connected, related, to one another..." (Heyward 1989, 192) and "[m]utuality is sharing power in such a way that each participant in the relationship is called forth more fully into becoming who she is – a whole person, with integrity. Experientially, mutuality is a process, a relational movement. It is not a static place to be, because it grows with/in the relationship. As we are formed by mutuality, so too does the shape of our

patriarchal system where it is exerted as authority, might, control, force, and aggression, while power-with is a social power, the influence among equals. Alternatively power-over can be imaged as a triangle and power-with as a circle.[1]

In the present study as well, power as understood in a feminist sense as power-with, is opposite to any kind of hierarchy and domination that characterise a patriarchal system. The power materialises in a mutual relationship, and it is a process rather than a state of possession. In the same way, authority in a feminist sense benefits this process, that encourages and empowers growth.[2] In this work I shall look for signs of power-with in the texts examined, and hope to set them against the patriarchal power-over. In this way, it will be possible to challenge the models of hierarchy and domination that for centuries have been legitimising the hierarchical structures of the church.[3]

As for my personal location in the feminist field, I would consider myself a practical feminist whose primary interests involve the understanding and use of the biblical texts in a modern context. The difficulty, as I see it, is that any one strategy is not applicable to all texts. Some of the texts can be re-interpreted, while some are irrevocably patriarchal and therefore rejectable. Each text must be open to its own questions and strategies. Therefore, I shall not commit myself to any of the strategies outlined above, though I willingly admit the influence of Radford Ruether and Schüssler Fiorenza.

---

mutuality change as our lives-in-relation grow."(Heyward 1989, 191)

[3] Starhawk 1990, 9-10 also distinguishes a third kind of power, *power-from-within* which sees the world itself as a living being, a world where one thing shape-shifts into another, where there are no solid separations and no simple causes and effects. Persons do not have to earn value and the immanent value cannot be rated or compared. As this relates more to personal development than relations between persons, it is not a relevant referent to the relationships between the characters in Matthew's narrative.

[1] Isherwood and McEwan 1993, 85-86.

[2] Heyward 1989, 73-75.

[3] See also Stenström 1992, 26; Isherwood&McEwan 1993, 83-86; Heyward 1996, 52-53.

The analysis presented in the latter part of this study will focus on Matthew's Gospel[1] in its final form with the primary thrust on feminist ideology. Therefore, the strategy in this thesis involves two factors. 1) The study must be anchored in the real world of biblical patriarchy (in which the women of this time are embedded).Any effort that singles out only references that present positive paradigms and solutions for women and ignores all uncomfortable passages, is doomed to fail. It would be just as futile, however, to picture women of that time as wallowing in misery – as, for example, liberated women of today would be if transported into that world. Every interpretation must be grounded on unbiased historical research. This involves not presupposing that women's equality or women's oppression will be found in every passage dealing with women. Each passage should be considered in its own right. Interpretations of texts originating from different communities, environments, and cultural contexts must allow for different solutions reflecting gradations between total misery and total affirmation as understood by modern women's standards. On some points, we have to admit uncertainty. 2) The next step is to evaluate the knowledge we have gained so as to reveal it to the modern community. The standards of evaluating should reflect the fact that some of the texts are unquestionably considered normative in the modern Christian world, the conviction that all humans are to be treated as equals and the growing consciousness of the world as a global multi-faith community. Historical and modern, critique and construct, oppression and affirmation – whatever the two elements are called – must be present in a strategy that calls itself truly feminist.

Thus questions rise from two different perspectives. The first viewpoint is the women stories in the Gospel, i.e. stories where women figure as characters. I do not automatically anticipate that women will be found inferior or superior to men in any systematic way.I therefore do not ignore the patriarchal structures of the ancient society. Even if women are part of the patriarchal social structures and inevitably subordinated to men, they can have egalitarian power with them. Their responses and

---

[1] I shall use the traditional name 'Matthew' as a simple way of referring to the redactor of the Gospel. By this I am not taking a stand for his identity. I shall also use the masculine pronoun 'he' when referring to the redactor as I see no grounds for suspicions that 'Matthew' might have been a woman.

actions can create their own space of relational authority. The literary approach complemented by a consideration of relevant historical or social-historical data may or may not give clues for further work. My second concern is to find an interpretation that is reasonable from modern women's perspective. Hence, there will be an evaluation of feminist interpretations and choices of emphasis, as well as discussion of the issues that have been treated in prior feminist scholarship.

After the stories including women have been analysed, woman characters will be compared with other character groups that respond positively to Jesus, such as the disciples and the crowd.

My interest is not so much in the patriarchal ideology of the environment of 'Matthew' as in the textual and ideological reality he creates in his narrative. What kind of values does it include? The values of the narrative are not necessarily the same as in the patriarchal environment in which Matthew produced his work. The points he emphasises are not necessarily views of the communities he writes to; they could be attitudes he wants them to adopt. Furthermore, a narrative is a form open to different interpretations in different cultures and environments. Therefore, whatever Matthew may have meant with his narrative in his time may not be understandable to his modern readers, even as later generations may have interpretations that would not have been understood in his environment. Hence it is possible to contend that the central values of a feminist ideology are compatible with the ideological atmosphere of the Gospel. I claim that the Gospel of Matthew is in fact about the Kingdom (cf. Mt 24:14), and that this Kingdom is the key to the Gospel's ideology. I intend to show that it is possible to create a new definition for Jesus' followers as equal 'citizens'[1] of the kingdom, all of whom express different aspects of the following, but nevertheless are truly equal among themselves. This inclusive definition makes women and male disciples equal parts of a unified group of followers.

---

[1] I use the word in a modern sense only as a descriptive image. No deeper theological or philological meaning is intended.

3. The Gospel of Matthew

3.1. Feminist Research on Matthew

The earliest feminist readings of Matthew were published by Janice Capel Anderson. In her 1983 article[1] she focused on gender in Matthew's narrative and discussed the symbolic function of gender. She did not make a historical evaluation, but used a purely narrative perspective. In 1987, she published another article that dealt with Matthew's infancy narrative.[2]

A detailed work about the infancy narratives, both in Matthew and in Luke, was Jane Schaberg's *The Illegitimacy of Jesus: A Feminist Theological Interpretation of the Infancy Narratives* (1987). Her thesis is that both of the birth narratives imply that Mary's conception is not a miraculous virginal conception. According to Schaberg, the texts imply that the virginal Mary was seduced or sexually assaulted. Jesus was an illegitimate child and Mary's conception was a human conception.

Elaine Mary Wainwright's dissertation in 1991 was the first feminist monograph on Matthew. Her work encapsulated the women characters in the Gospel and she applied both literary and redaction-critical methods in order to find inclusion within the text and inclusion within the formation of the text. In other words, her aim was to restore the stories of women to the biblical texts as well as to reconstruct the history of early Christianity as an inclusive history.[3] In her work she shows that women appear in the narrative as faithful followers of Jesus. She claims that women's stories were preserved among the women in the Matthean community. In the final redaction, however, women's tradition was embedded and hidden in the context of patriarchal leadership. To find this tradition, therefore, the text must be read 'against the grain'. Finally, she approaches questions concerning the 'real world' of Matthew's

---

[1] Anderson 1983: "Matthew: Gender and Reading"
[2] Anderson 1987: "Mary's Difference: Gender and Patriarchy in the Birth Narratives". In 1994, she published a monograph *Matthew's Narrative Web* which is not mainly a feminist orientated work, but will also be referred to during the analysis.
[3] Wainwright 1991, 38.

community, claiming that Christian households were voluntary associations where leadership and participation were possible for all, including women and slaves. She returned to these themes in an article on Matthew in the feminist commentary *Searching the Scriptures*[1].

The first feminist commentary since Cady Stanton's early work, was published in 1992 and titled after her work. This volume, *Women's Bible Commentary*, includes Amy-Jill Levine's article on Matthew. The article, like others, focuses only on selected parts concerning women and therefore gives no overall view of the Gospel. Levine has also written on Matthew's story about the haemorrhaging woman (1996).

In a German feminist commentary (1998), Martina Gnadt made an interesting contribution to the interpretations of Matthew's narrative. Her point of view involved the contrary position of Matthew's community vis-à-vis the *Pax Romana*. Here again her article dealt only with certain parts of the Gospel.

The feminist work done on Matthew is not abundant; Mark and Luke have been more popular.[2] Apart from Wainwright's work, there are no interpretations of Matthew as a single entity. Melzer-Keller writes about Jesus and the women in the synoptic tradition.[3] In Matthew she concentrates on the women characters around Jesus, on the parables with women in them[4] and Jesus' view of marriage. The articles in the feminist commentaries focus only on the passages concerning women. What will be needed in future are feminist assessments of other passages in the

---

[1] Searching the Scriptures (ed. by E. Schüssler Fiorenza) is a two-volume publication where volume I concentrates on the methods and approaches within feminist interpretation and volume II offers a commentary on early Christian writings. What is notable is the breadth of the selection beyond the boundaries of the books of the Canon.

[2] As the pericopes about women in Matthew are in most parts dependent on Mark and have parallels in Luke, feminist literature concerning these Gospels or isolated pericopes in them will be referred to as well. Examples of such works are the discussions about the Syrophoenician woman (a Canaanite in Matthew's parallel) by Ringe 1985, Kwok 1995, 71-83 or Mark's women characters in general Kinukawa 1994. Schüssler Fiorenza 1983 starts her monograph by discussing the anointing scene in Mark and Struthers Malbon 1983 and Dines 1993 write about discipleship in Mark. Seim 1994 has written about women in Luke.

[3] Melzer-Keller 1997: She deals with all the synoptics, including the Q source separately, and ends with the question of tradition in the communities, and the historical Jesus.

[4] The parable of yeast (13:33) and the parable of ten virgins (25:1-13).

Gospel, as well as their relationships within different parts of the Gospel. This work is a minor step in this direction.

3.2. The Original Context of the Gospel

As the date and location of the composition of the Gospel are not the issue in this study, I shall rely on the commonly held views in Matthean scholarship. It is widely accepted that the redaction of the text in its final form as a revised and extended version of Mark probably took place between 80-90 CE.[1] For the location, the majority vote for the possibility of Syria or even Antioch, though it is impossible to know for certain.[2] One major reason for choosing Antioch is the Matthean quotations in the letters of Ignatius, who was the bishop in Antioch in the second century CE.[3] A viable argument against Antioch is the connection Paul had to this city. It is well-nigh impossible to conceive Jewish and Hellenistic Christianity co-existing in the same city without any notable traces.[4] The evidence is so scattered that no place can be named for certain. This complicates the historical analysis of the Gospel as we cannot uncover the social setting of the Gospel apart from what the text itself supplies.

The writer of the Gospel remains anonymous as well. The earliest tradition from Papias in the second century connects the Gospel with the apostle Matthew (9:9-13, and in the list of apostles 10:2-4). Opponents of this opinion point out that an apostle who was an eyewitness would

---

[1] Meier in Brown and Meier 1983, 45 dates the Gospel 80-90 CE. Luz 1989, 93 says 80 CE; Strecker 1971, 36 says 90-95 CE; Stanton 1992, 380 says between 80 and 110 CE, though within this period rather earlier than later. Bredin 1996, 98 says 80-90 CE; Syreeni and Luomanen 1997, 219 dates around years 90-100 CE.

[2] For various opinions see e.g. Meier in Brown and Meier 1983, 15-27; Viviano 1979, 533-540; Davies and Allison 1988, 138-147; Luomanen 1998,275-277. Luz 1989, 92 makes a choice for a large Syrian city whose *lingua franca* was Greek. Stanton 1992, 380 says that it is not even possible to assume that Matthew was written in an urban setting.

[3] See e.g. Meier in Meier and Brown 1983, 24.

[4] Luomanen 1998, 276. Luz 1989, 91 has not seen this as an impossible situation because there could have been several house churches in a large city.

hardly have used Mark's material as his source.[1] Another tradition sees the author as the scribe in verse 13:52.[2] All agree, on firm grounds, that the author was Jewish.[3]

The historical position of the Matthean community in the history of religion, offers contending opinions as well: inside Judaism[4], within those recently parted from Judaism[5], and finally within the Gentile community[6]. These contentions reflect the situation in early Judaism. Rabbinical Judaism was only emerging. The early Christian communities were originally part of Judaism but these Jewish communities accepted Gentile adherents to their faith. The first missionaries, such as Paul, started their work in the local synagogues. Matthew, too, aspired to be faithful to the Jewish heritage believing that the law could not be abrogated. Jesus himself was entrenched in Jewish history. The promises to the Gentiles (28:16-20) widen the promises of God. The hostility against the scribes and the Pharisees has been interpreted as evidence that the recent parting of the ways was still an acute problem.[7] As nothing can be claimed with certainty, it is best to be content with the assumption that Matthew was writing to communities, who though formerly inside Judaism, were in a process of drifting apart, and in the prevailing circumstances of conflict, were creating their Christian identity. The forming of this new identity was influenced not merely by the separation from the Jewish community, but also by internal conflicts.[8]

---

[1] Hagner 1993, lxxvii thinks that the apostle Matthew is "probably the source of an early form of significant portions of the Gospel." The editing was then being done by disciples of the Matthean circle.

[2] For a thorough treatment on the issue of authorship see Davies and Allison 1988, 7-33; Syreeni and Luomanen 1997, 219-221.

[3] Davies and Allison 1988, 33; Syreeni and Luomanen 1997, 221.

[4] Saldarini 1994, 1; Gnadt 1998, 483

[5] Stanton 1993, 124; Luomanen 1998, 264, 274-275.

[6] Strecker 1962, 15-35; Trilling 1959, 215.

[7] Stanton 1992, 382-383.

[8] Stanton 1992, 385-386 considers the Matthean communities as a sectarian group. He calls the Matthean community 'new people', meaning neither Jews nor Gentiles, but something new. Syreeni and Luomanen 1997, 226-227 point to conflicts between different groups inside the community. For Gundry 1982, 5 Matthew's problem is the mixed church, true and false disciples living side by side. Gnadt 1998, 484-486 sees conflict in the context of the Roman empire, for the community had only one Father and Authority in God and this caused problems with respect to the Roman authorities.

An additional question on this topic arises from a widely held
assumption that the communities in early Christianity consisted of house
churches.[1] It seems improbable that Matthew was writing to an individual
one community (that would have been very small), but rather to several
communities.[2] Whether these communities were within close range of one
another (forming a coherent group) or whether the audience Matthew had
in mind formed a looser connection is not clear. He could have written his
Gospel to be copied and spread around. This, of course, makes it even
more difficult to filter out facts about his own community through the text
itself. We can make deductions about Matthew's own priorities and
intentions, but how well they mirror the practises in the communities he
was writing to cannot be verified. The most we can say is that he wrote
to communities within the Jewish Christian heritage who were on their
way from Judaism to a new identity as Christians.

3.3. The Narrative of the Gospel

As a narrative, the Gospel of Matthew follows a roughly chronological
order from the birth of the protagonist, through his baptism and ministry,
and on to his passion and resurrection.[3] Christopher Smith has recognised

---

[1] Schüssler Fiorenza 1983, 175-184; Meeks 1983, 75-77; Stambaugh and Balch 1986,
138-140. See also Osiek and Balch, 1997.
[2] Stanton 1993, 50-51.
[3] Over the years, there have been numerous inquiries into the structure of Matthew's
the narrative. For a thorough presentation see, for example, Bauer 1988. Gundry 1982,
10-11 has suggested that it is best to avoid imposing any structures on Matthew; the
redactor did not think in terms of fixed arrangements. One of the classic cornerstones
has been B.W. Bacon's pentateuchal theory of the Gospel containing five 'books', five
discourses after the fashion of the Mosaic Pentateuch. (Bacon 1930). The second
model is from C.H. Lohr (1961) who also based his model on the fivefold formula and
developed Bacon's model towards a chiastic outline. The third discourse, chapter 13,
is the centre of the narrative around which the others are chiastically grouped.
(Referred from Davies and Allison 1988, 60. Luz 1989, 36 calls this a centre model).
The third alternative comes from J. D. Kingsbury who divides the Gospel in three parts
by using the formula in verses 4:17 and 16:21 ('Ἀπὸ τότε ἤρξατο ὁ 'Ιησοῦς) as the
argument. Kingsbury does not take much notice of the contents of the narration, the
gap between the second and the third chapter, nor the change that happens in the
narration. The passion history does not start in chapter 16, it is only anticipated.
(Kingsbury 1975 [1], 9-10). A fourth alternative is Michael Goulder's lectionary

a unifying theme – other than Jesus' life – that can be seen in the text, the Pentateuchal theme.[1] This theme functions as a glue between the different parts of the Gospel and also explains the structural patterns. His literary outline of the Gospel groups the Gospel around five 'books'.[2] Each of them begins with a narrative and concludes with a discourse, and he claims that each of them develops a specific theme related to the meaning of the kingdom. The genealogy is considered a prologue, and the passion narrative a conclusion. For Smith, the Gospel of Matthew is 'this gospel of the kingdom' (14:14)[3] and the 'five books' each deal with one aspect of this kingdom. What is problematic in Smith's model is the relegation of the genealogy and the passion narrative to the margins, as prologue and conclusion. To my mind, both these sections reveal as much about the kingdom as the other 'five books'. The first book – the introduction if you like – in fact forms a unity larger than genealogy alone, as the birth of Jesus and the infancy narratives are clearly a part of this section rather than the next.

The protagonist of the narrative first enters the scene in Chapter 3. In Chapters 1-2, his background has been verified through the genealogy, and his otherworldly origin is revealed in his irregular birth and escape from death. In the beginning of Chapter 3 the narrative starts to move in a more 'ordinary' world. The function of the first two chapters is to prepare the reader for Jesus' ministry and his final mission. In the same way, the shift in expression is visible in the passion and resurrection

---

hypothesis, according to which the Gospel was composed in accordance with an annual weekly lectionary cycle and therefore forms a liturgical structure (Goulder 1974). This is rejected by Luz 1989, 41.Matthew's Gospel consists of narrative parts and speeches. Narrative critics like Powell make a distinction between the book's compositional structure, which belongs to redaction criticism and the plot structure in narrative criticism. He does not seem to find the inclusion of the speech sections troublesome in the narrative (Powell 1992[2], 343-344). Syreeni and Luomanen make a distinction between the paradigmatic and the syntagmatic structure in the Gospel, and recognize a problem that remains between the narrative sections and the discourses. For them, each alternative is important in its own way. (Syreeni and Luomanen 1997, 205). For a thorough discussion about Matthew's overall plan see Syreeni 1987, 75-87.
[1] He follows Bacon. See the previous note.
[2] Smith 1997, 540-551. The five 'books' are The Foundations of the Kingdom (1:18-7:29), The Mission of the Kingdom (8:1-10:42), The Mystery of the Kingdom (11:1-13:53), The Family of the Kingdom (13:54-18:35) and The Destiny of the Kingdom (19:1-24:46).
[3] Smith 1997, 549.

narratives, where the events of the first two chapters reach their counterpart and explanation. The correspondence between the beginning and the end[1] can be visualized as follows:

Ch.1: Jesus' birth	Ch 27-28: Jesus' death
Ch1: prophecies fulfilled	Ch 28: new promises
(Looking back)	(Looking forward)
Ch 1: irregular conception	Ch 28: resurrection
Ch 1: Jesus comes to the world	Ch 28: Jesus goes to heaven
Ch 1: the name Immanuel	Ch 28: promise of continued presence
Ch 1: named women mentioned	Ch 27-28: named women present

These pairs indicate the correspondence. The pair 'irregular conception and resurrection' confirms the notion that the beginning and the end form a different story from the intermediary narrative describing the story of the ministry of Jesus. Irregular conception and resurrection point here to the expressions of a transcendental reality that frame the narrative of the earthly ministry of Jesus. Both the frames and the fivefold narrative in between are related to the kingdom. 'The Kingdom' is the story in Matthew of which the narrative of Jesus is only a part.[2]

Accordingly, I shall outline the narrative as follows:

INTRODUCTION: 1-2

Narration: 3-4	Discourse: The sermon on the Mount 5-7
Narration: 8-9	Discourse: Mission 10
Narration: 11-12	Discourse: (Parables of) Kingdom 13
Narration: 14-17	Discourse: Community 18
Narration: 19-23	Discourse: Eschatology 24-25

PASSION AND RESURRECTION 26-28

---

[1] For a structural parallel between the beginning and the end, see also Brown 1994, 1302-1304 and Davies and Allison 1997, 640 and 656 who further point to the actions of Joseph on behalf of a helpless Jesus in both sections.
[2] See Genette 1980, 27 for the definitions of story and narrative.

The literary structure allows space for the ordinary and the extraordinary. In the narrative of Jesus' ministry, the ordinary and the extraordinary are interwoven. The ordinary, contemporary society with its built-in hierarchy started to encroach on the extraordinary, the kingdom.[1] No conflict need occur, rather a tensile co-existence.

The events in the narrative form several *storylines*.[2] The main storyline in Matthew is about Jesus.[3] However, the story itself is about the kingdom which includes the intertwining of Jesus' character and his message. The kingdom storyline exceeds the Jesus narrative of the Gospel. The story of the kingdom continues in Jesus' followers.

But there are subsidiary storylines in the narrative that delineate other characters, such as the disciples or the Jewish leaders. I intend to follow one of these minor storylines, that of the women characters, which entails reading against the natural flow of the narrative; the women in Matthew's Gospel are separate characters and in the course of the narrative have no causal connection with each other. Seeing the women characters as forming a storyline of their own means thus tracing the female thread of the narrative. From a modern reader's perspective, this is a reasonable, natural method to redress the influence in the story telling, especially since all the major characters in the narrative are male.

In the Gospel, the events start with the birth of Jesus and end with his death and resurrection. But the *temporal boundaries* extend beyond the story itself – in Chapter 1 to the history of Israel, and at the end, to the indefinite future. Matthew very firmly locates the story of Jesus in the

---

[1] The ordinary and the extraordinary are understood here as running throughout the narrative side by side. The extraordinary is more evident in the frames. The narrative of the kingdom points beyond the ordinary world. Matthew uses the old Jewish concept when trying to explain the true meaning of the life and person of Jesus. Hereby I am not pointing to any ontological problems, merely to Matthew's way of telling his narrative.

[2] Rimmon-Kenan 1983, 16. Events in a story-line are connected to each other by chronological succession or causality. A 'plot' has been defined as a narrative of events arranged by causality, while a story is a narrative with chronological succession (Forster 1963, 82). Causality has been argued to be a strong principle in a reader's mind, so much so that s/he creates it when it is not explicitly stated. It is easy to agree with this especially when dealing with the Gospels that otherwise are often interpreted as a collection of isolated units.(Abrams 1971, 69; Chatman 1978, 45-46).

[3] For Kingsbury 1988(1), 11 Jesus is "God's supreme agent who is in complete accord with God's system of values." God is also 'a major character' in the Gospel.

history of Israel.[1] The connection to the First Testament is also frequently present in references to the fulfilment of the prophecies. This theme of promise/fulfilment has also been seen as a means by which the narrative is plotted temporally.[2]

In general, the temporal plotting is twofold. First, there is the continuity of events in the order the narrator wanted to present them, not necessarily in the order they occurred.[3] Events can be explained in the course of the narration by referring to something that has happened before in real time. In literary theory, allusions in the narrative that point to the occurrence of past events are called 'analepses'.The counterparts of analepses are 'prolepses' where the event is told prematurely.[4] 'Mixed analepses' refer to events prior to the narrative, which continue in the plot of the story, while 'mixed prolepses' begin in the narrative and continue after it.[5]

The mixed prolepses and analepses in Matthew relate the story of Jesus and the kingdom to the history of Israel on the one hand, and to the events subsequent to Jesus' death and resurrection on the other. Two kinds of mixed prolepses have been detected in Matthew's narrative. First, there are references to the church as it exists in the post-resurrection period after the story itself has ended. The second type is concerned with the rejection of Jesus by Israel. For example, in verse 27:25, the Jewish people *and their children* accept responsibility for Jesus' death. The mixed prolepses clearly indicate the continuity between the story of Jesus and that of his followers. Thus, the prolepses are a means to connect the

---

[1] Brown 1977, 59.

[2] Howell 1990, 111-112.

[3] For difference between *story time* and *discourse time* in narrative theory, see for example, Powell 1993, 36-37.

[4] Genette 1980, 40.

[5] Genette 1980, 49; Powell 1993, 37. There are also such things as internal and external prolepses. The former happen within the story, such as the passion predictions (in Matthew 16:21, 17:22; 20:17) and the latter point to the historical events within temporal boundaries after Matthew's story, such as the prediction of the destruction of Jerusalem and the temple. Culpepper 1983, 64 also names eschatological prolepses which refer to events "When the Son comes in Glory".

plotted story with the reader.[1] Also, the story of the kingdom is extended beyond the boundaries of the narrative. In the birth narrative and the genealogy, Jesus is connected to the expectations of the past, while the story of the kingdom extends its influence to a time after the narrative; for example, to the communities to whom Matthew is writing. The story of the kingdom is a larger entity, in which the narrative of Jesus is set.

A further important element to consider relates to the *characters*. In narrative-critical theory, characters are understood as constructs that have been created by the implied author.[2] This author has provided the characters with certain qualities and actions in order to either tell or show something about them. The characters are the people who perform the action in the narrative.[3] One way of defining the characters has been through the number of traits they have. 'A trait' is defined as a personal quality that persists over a part, or over the whole of the story.[4] The classic division is between 'flat' and 'round' characters. The 'flat' characters are usually built around a single idea while 'round' characters are complex, developing and many-sided. Later, the concept of a 'stock' character was introduced; this character with a single trait performs a perfunctory role in the story.[5] According to this theory, Jesus and the disciples in Matthew are usually considered to be 'round' characters.[6] Matthew's portrayal of the disciples is less negative than Mark's, but still not totally positive. Several times, the disciples claim to understand, or the story reports their understanding, but Matthew indicates that they sometimes did not. It is true that many of Mark's critical comments have been removed, whereas Matthew reports Jesus' criticism and rebuke. Matthew seems fond of describing them as 'those of little faith'.[7]

Of the individual characters Peter is one of the few, along with Jesus himself and John the Baptist, who have their own story line in the

---

[1] Howell 1990, 102-103. Howell also sees sayings like 5:17 which present Jesus as the eschatological fulfiller of the law, as mixed analepses. It is the life and teachings of Jesus which function as the dynamic expression of God's will in Matthew's story. The question of how Jesus fulfilled the law still remains open.

[2] For the theoretical background see Powell 1993, 51-58.

[3] See Abrams 1971, 69.

[4] Chatman 1978, 125.

[5] For 'flat' and 'round' characters see Forster 1963, 75-85, for 'stock' characters Abrams 1971, 93. See also Powell 1993, 54-55.

[6] Kingsbury 1988(1), 19; Powell 1993, 55.

[7] Cf. Edwards 1985, 47-61.

narrative. Peter is primarily a 'round' character. His strengths and weaknesses are portrayed, especially in his role as spokesman for the disciples, but in the end, he does not seem to develop fully. He appears in Matthew only in relation to Jesus. Furthermore, Peter's whole story line is limited to scenes and dialogues with Jesus.

Meanwhile, the women mostly fulfill the roles of 'stock' characters. They usually appear only once, their actions are told from one angle only, and from the story's point of view, they are only representative of 'real people'. In most cases, they do not speak. It has been argued that Matthew did not preserve the words of the dialogues between Jesus and the people he healed because he wanted to underline Jesus as the centre.[1] On the other hand, reported words exchanged between Jesus and some individuals exist. The comparison between incidents with and those without dialogue also reveals something about the characters. In other words, characters can also be evaluated by the things that are *not* told. Lack of names, lack of actions, lack of words can define the character. There are two ways of informing the reader about the characters: telling and showing.[2] Showing means that the characters speak or act for themselves or other characters respond to them. In Matthew, showing is the main vehicle used to describe the women characters, but showing also includes hiding women's presence or contribution in the course of events, or silencing their words.

However, 'flat', 'round', and 'stock' types are static ways of describing the characters. A more dynamic way is to see the characters in a continuum. At one end is full complexity, and at the other end, characterisation around a single trait. There can be an infinite number of degrees between the poles.[3] Women in Matthew are usually closer to a single trait than real complexity. Paradoxically, simplifying their character can reveal more nuances. However, the accumulation of the traits of Matthew's women does not present a portrait of any individual woman character. More than adding up material, it is necessary to describe the nature of their connectedness with Jesus, as this connectedness is the uniting bond between them.

---

[1] Theissen 1983, 178-179.
[2] See Powell 1993, 52-53.
[3] Cf. Rimmon-Kenan 1983, 41.

The last area to be considered is the *setting*. The context of the events, the scene where everything happens, is an integral part of understanding the narrative. Nothing happens in a vacuum. The settings have different functions in the narrative and they can be defined as spatial, temporal, and social.[1] One of the most important divisions of space is *inside/outside*. The boundary markers in the text also express division. Being inside might imply security, a private sphere, while being outside can imply risks and public life.[2] The place where women are, where they act as characters is significant.

The haemorrhaging woman approaches Jesus in the crowd. She is outside the domestic boundaries, which is not the usual place of women in that time. The awakening of the ruler's daughter happens inside, in the domestic area. The Canaanite woman, a Gentile, is told to come (ἐξελθοῦσα) to Jesus. This episode also happens outside.[3] The episode with the mother of Zebedee's sons (20:20) seems to happen on the road while Jesus and his followers are going up to Jerusalem. It indicates that there were also women among the group that walked with him. Later on, this mother is found under the cross (27:56). She was among the itinerant followers right up to the end. The anointing woman performs her deed inside the house while Jesus is having a meal. The women beneath the cross are outside at the site of execution, which in itself could be considered risky at the least.

3.4. The *basileia* in Matthew

Point of view in the narrative can be defined in many ways, and the questions regarding the values or ideology of the narrator belong to this area. For Matthew, the point of view is thought to be 'thinking the things of God' as an evaluative perspective.[4] Jesus is doing the things of God, proclaiming the things of God. It has been interpreted that since Jesus himself embodies all the values and virtues the disciples are called to

---

[1] Thus Abrams 1971, 175.
[2] Bal 1985, 45-46.
[3] In contrast to Mark where the dialogue with the Syrophoenician woman happens inside the house.
[4] Kingsbury 1988(1), 37-38. Cf also Edwards 1985, 47-61.

accept, he functions as a model for discipleship in Matthew.[1] This conclusion – which is no doubt correct – misses a relevant point in the course of the narrative. Though the major story in Matthew is not the Jesus story but the kingdom, to which he points, the Gospel contains several subsidiary themes about those who follow Jesus. Matthew has put much effort into stressing the continuity of the events narrated with the time following those events. The reader exists in the time between the resurrection and the parousia, and from this position is called to identify her/himself with the characters in the narrative as they confront Jesus. The characters are representative of different attitudes towards the kingdom of which the narrative of Jesus is a part.

From a feminist point of view, the 'kingdom' imagery in both the First and the Second Testament, especially in the synoptic gospels, shows itself profoundly patriarchal with God imaged as a king, a judge, or a father. Jesus rules as the king of this new kingdom in Matthew's narrative which unfolds as a story about how people either accepted or rejected this kingdom and its king.[2] However, the qualifications of the kingdom as expressed in the narrative, and conventional expectations concerning power hierarchies are turned upside-down.[3] The essence of the kingdom turns out to be something other than hierarchical domination and monarchical power. The 'kingdom' itself is not what the patriarchal language would lead one to believe it is.

In some feminist interpretations the expression *basileia* has become a central term seen in opposition to patriarchy[4] and the dominant culture.[5] Schüssler Fiorenza considers the *basileia tou theou*, which was common to other prophetic movements of the time, a central symbol of the Jesus movement. It referred to God's sovereign rule, and therefore served as an opposition to the Roman empire. Fiorenza uses the transcription *basileia* because it preserves the ambiguity of the word and is capable of several theological meanings at the same time.[6] Wainwright sees the elements of

---

[1] Howell 1990, 18.
[2] So also Kingsbury 1988(1), 11-13.
[3] Carter 1994, 211-214 has made this evident. For him the new structure of the Christian movement is a challenge to the existing hierarchical and androcentric pattern. An anti-structure opposes the hierarchical structures.
[4] Schüssler Fiorenza 1994, 92-94.
[5] Wainwright 1991; eadem. 1995.
[6] Schüssler Fiorenza 1994, 92.

conflict and tension between the *basileia* (which Jesus preached about and the Matthean Gospel proclaims) and the existing dominant culture. She regards the tension as especially visible in questions of ethnicity and gender.[1]

Both writers see the kingdom, the *basileia*, as a concrete entity in opposition to the dominant culture. Instead of seeing it in opposition, I prefer to consider the *basileia* in Matthew as a larger story beyond Matthew's narrative that expands the boundaries of the ordinary world. On the one hand, the life of Matthew's communities could be included in the *basileia*, just as the life of Jesus was included. On the other hand, patriarchy posed a danger to its development. This does not mean that in the contemporary world of Matthew, the *basileia* would not be an example of values and conduct, but it would be an example that is not always so easy to follow.[2]

Henceforth, the Greek word *basileia*[3] will be used to distinguish between a power-over structure (kingdom) and a power-with structure (*basileia*).[4] As I understand the *basileia*, it points to values and attributes – often expressed in the form of a metaphor or a parable – that are essential to understanding, but is never equivalent to these. Each image and metaphor reveals one corresponding aspect of the *basileia*, but no definition adequately covers the whole of it. The *basileia* in Matthew is expressed from several angles using several images and metaphors.[5] All of these are like peep-holes through which we see a fraction, but never the whole.

---

[1] Wainwright 1995, 635-637.

[2] Carter 1994, 214 speaks about an alternative existence and identity that makes it possible to remain in touch with the society. "In the midst of, in opposition to, and as an alternative to, hierarchical structures, disciples are to live in households of unity and mutuality."

[3] Schüssler Fiorenza 1994, 92 points out the difficulty of translating this concept because it can mean kingdom, kingly realm or empire. She uses the translation 'commonweal'.

[4] The problem involves language. In English, as well as in Greek, the term includes 'king'. In Finnish, 'valtakunta' or Swedish,'rike', the problem is less relevant. The problem is, of course, the same in both Greek and English.

[5] Uro 1996, 75-78 follows Perrin and understands the kingdom as a "tensive symbol"where there are several referents for the symbol which can never be exhausted by anyone of them.

Matthew refers to the *basileia* in different ways. Notable expressions are ἡ βασιλεία τῶν οὐρανῶν, which is particularly common in Matthew (32 times in Matthew alone) or ἡ βασιλεία τοῦ θεοῦ (of 64 appearances in the NT only 5 are found in Matthew). Matthew also mentions εὐαγγέλιον τῆς βασιλείας three times (the expression occurs only in Matthew), and λόγος τῆς βασιλείας (once, only in Matthew). Matthew uses the expression οἱ υἱοὶ τῆς βασιλείας twice, once referring to the heirs of the *basileia*, the Jews (8:12), once in the context of a parable referring to those who are inside the *basileia* (13:38). This symbol clearly retains the connotations of Jewish views of God's reign. Jesus' sayings and parables situate the *basileia* both in the present and in the future.[1] In the narrative, on the one hand, the followers are already inside the *basileia*, but on the other hand, they also enter it in the eschatological future (see 25:31-46).

In Chapter 25, the deeds that are the criteria for entering, themselves belong to the values of the *basileia*. Only those who have already accepted these values are able to carry out those deeds. The conflict is not really a conflict. The deeds are also such that the high and mighty of the world would not consider them worth while doing.

Jesus' last discourse before he headed towards Jerusalem (18:1-35) transparently deals with the situation in the Matthean communities.[2] It also reveals something essential about the relationship between the followers and Jesus. The passion for power is clearly a problem that calls for treatment in the narrative. The overarching problem is 'Who is the greatest in the *basileia*?'[3] Jesus answers the question by taking a child as a model. "Unless you turn around and become like children, you will never *enter* the *basileia* of Heaven. Whoever humbles himself and becomes like this child *will be the greatest in* the *basileia* of Heaven."

---

[1] So also in Beasley-Murray 1987 which is a very thorough work on the subject in all the Gospels, not only Matthew.

[2] Luomanen 1998, 231. According to Perrin 1976, 63-64 the *basileia* in Matthew's time is not equivalent with the Matthean community, this identification first takes place in the fourth century.

[3] Adding the *basileia* in the question is Matthean, in Mark (9:33-37) the question was only who is the greatest.

Being childlike is both the passport into as well as the standard for those already inside. 'The little ones' are closest to God (18:10).[1]

The absence of a ranking order in the *basileia* is opposite to the gradations of a hierarchy, and the ideal conduct expected is contrary to the conduct of the ordinary world. A shepherd leaves the flock in order to search for one lost sheep. In the same way, a member (a brother) of the community must be looked for and forgiven. Forgiveness is what is expected of those inside. Jesus' parables show the misplacement of the question of greatness. The little ones, weak, and defenceless must be taken care of and valued. The parables of the mustard seed and of the leaven (13:21-33) point to the value of the small and the seemly insignificant.

The same applies to the rich. It is hard for a rich man to enter the *basileia* (19:23-24)[2], and the *basileia* is worth more than any riches (13:44-45). The passport requires giving up everything, not only possessions, but families and friends as well. The new family – members of the *basileia* – substitutes for the biological bonds (12:46-50) and the essence of the new family is being subsumed in the will of God. An alternative existence confutes the hierarchical structures and embraces the care for others.

On the one hand, as will be obvious during the analysis, the *basileia* itself embodies a certain tension. The story of a *basileia* whose would-be king is the protagonist of Matthew's narrative is bound to the history of Israel and to God. The coronation is the death of the king, and the resurrection is the starting point of the reign. It is, unfortunately, in eschatological promises to his male adherents that the hierarchical structures emerge.[3] On the other hand, the narrative and discourses within

---

[1] There are different opinions about who 'the little ones' really were. Trilling 1959,92 for one, is of the opinion that this referred to a minority group in Matthew's community. Schweizer 1981, 238 interprets them as disciples and equates them with those 'weak in faith' (cf. Romans 14; 1 Cor 8:7-10). Luomanen 1998, 237 sees here a general title for the disciples. Syreeni 1999,138- 141 discusses at length the 'little ones' who had a counterpart in the concrete world, which are but dimly seen through their narrative representations. Their personality is not solved through the information of the narrative.

[2] See Carter 1994, 144-145. Jesus calls here to create an alternative social existence of mutual care which is not based on hierarchy.

[3] Cf. 20:20f and the promise that the twelve will sit on twelve thrones and judge the twelve tribes of Israel (19:28).

the frame story (after the infancy narrative and before the death of Jesus) reveal the credentials required for the kingdom and set Jesus as the criterion for entry. The literary, the mythological, and the eschatological as well as the historical and the hierarchical are all different aspects present in Matthew's *basileia* narrative. All this points, not to a coherent definition but to several perspectives, to something that is indefinable.

Hierarchical structures in Matthew's communities are discernible in the Gospel along with his *basileia* vision that includes no hierarchies and value differences. Both the historical perspective and the one that expands beyond the time are simultaneously present. Tension arises in the course of the narrative due to the mind set of these two opposing structures.[1] The tension even extends inside Matthew's view of the *basileia* as he acknowledges the hierarchy in the eschatological promises given to the disciples (19:28). Matthew himself is unable to surmount the structures of his contemporary world.

A similar tension is visible in Paul's letters. I do not intend to enter Paul's world, but it is noteworthy that he experiences the same tension and difficulty when depicting Christian life. He seems to respect the patriarchal order in which women are subordinate to men (1 Cor 11:1-16; 14:33b-36[2]) while in another context, he boldly proclaims: "As many of you as were baptized into Christ have clothed yourselves with Christ, there is no longer Jew or Greek, there is no longer slave or free, there is no longer male or female; for all of you are one in Christ Jesus" (Gal 3:28). The same difficulty in expressing the new within the old is visible both in Matthew and in Paul.[3] The subversive order of the new existence also surfaces in Paul who in 1 Cor 1: 28 says: "He has chosen things without rank or standing in the world, mere nothings, to overthrow the existing order."[4]

It should be obvious now that a central understanding of the *basileia* in Matthew is compatible with the feminist understanding of 'power'. Common features are rejection of all kinds of domination, emphasis on

---

[1] Also Fredriksen 1988, 36-42 assumes 'a double context': the historical setting of the narrative and the 'true' context, the divine realm of light beyond.

[2] For discussion about the possible interpolation and other interpretations, see for example Wire 1995, 186-187.

[3] For difficulties in interpreting Paul from feminist point of view, see among others, Schottroff 1993, 35-59; Wire 1995, 153-195.

[4] The translation is according to The Revised English Bible.

the relatedness and connection between people, and the care of others as all are dependent upon one another. Therefore, the *basileia* draws close to the ideology of feminism. One problem that arises in Matthew's description of the *basileia* is the hierarchical images which are counter to feminist ideology. Nevertheless, the emphasis in the text on the subversive concept is so compelling that its usefulness for modern feminist interpretations is justified.

Therefore, by connecting the characters who follow Jesus, the story of the *basileia* and the vision of relational power in feminism, it is possible to challenge the traditional view of holding up the male disciples as the models for Christians of later generations. Even if Matthew himself was stuck in the patriarchy of his own time and culture, he opened the door to envisioning changes.

4. Women's Story Line in Matthew

4.1. Women in Matthew

Women are not abundantly present in Matthew. There are no major female characters in this Gospel and scarcely any uniting bond among the women. The main characters next to Jesus are the disciples and his Jewish antagonists, all of whom are men. From this perspective Matthew's narrative seems androcentric and faithful to the patriarchal structures of the society in his time.

If one isolates women in Matthew's narrative, the overall impression is that he has taken over the Markan material, changed and abbreviated it.[1] He has not introduced any new stories about women and the only Markan pericope missing is the story about the widow's mite (Mark 12:41-44), where the woman is not really a character – more like an object or item in Jesus' teaching. This vignette appears in Luke (Luke 21:1-4) as the only text concerning women common to Mark and Luke, but missing in Matthew. Matthew's fidelity to the Markan text would indicate that women were not among Matthew's primary focuses of interest. This is quite different from Luke, who has added material about women to his narrative, such as the story about the son of the widow of Nain (Luke 7:11-17), the healing of a crippled woman on the Sabbath (13:10-17), and even Martha and Mary, who are not in the gallery of characters in Mark and Matthew.

The following material concerning women is common to all three synoptic gospels:
* The cure of Simon's mother-in-law (Matt. 8:14-15 par.)
* The woman with a haemorrhage/ the ruler's daughter (Matt. 9: 18-26 par.)
* Jesus' mother and brothers (Matt. 12:46-50 par)
* The anointing woman (Matt. 26:6-13 par.)

---

[1] It has been noted that the peculiarly Matthean interpretation in general is recognizable by two main characteristics, namely his way of adding speech material on the one hand, and abbreviating the narrative part on the other. The latter particularly concerns the miracle stories. See Held 1961, 155-156.

The versions of these pericopes differ in each gospel, the incident of the anointing so much so that it is worth questioning if Luke's story really is a parallel. Moreover, women stand out in the passion narrative at the cross and tomb in every gospel. The identification of these women and the course of the narrative differ in details, but there seem to be grounds to regard these stories as unanimous witnesses to the presence of women in the context of Jesus' death and resurrection.

Material common to Matthew and Mark, but missing in Luke[1], is the story about the Syrophoenician woman (a Canaanite in Matthew) and the women story in the context of the beheading of John the Baptist. In the latter, the 'wicked' queen Herodias and her daughter, who are presented as accomplices in John's death, appear.

Still, there is material concerning women which is peculiar to Matthew. First, there are the names of four women in the genealogy. These women are not really characters in Matthew's narrative, but the memory of their stories is part of Matthew's infancy narrative. Mary in the birth narrative (Chapters 1-2) has a parallel in Luke, but Luke's and Matthew's contributions differ considerably. In verse 20:20, the mother of the sons of Zebedee (two disciples in the inner circle) asks for benefits for her sons. In Mark, the sons ask for these themselves. This mother is mentioned twice, but only in Matthew. The reference to Pilate's wife in the passion narrative is also a Matthean innovation.

When considering women characters *in toto* and women mentioned in Matthew, a conspicuous common feature is the lack of names. The only ones named are the women at the cross and tomb, Mary in the birth narrative, the foremothers in the genealogy, and Queen Herodias. Otherwise, the women are identified in terms of their nationality (Canaanite), male relatives (Peter, the ruler, Jesus, Pilate, Zebedee) or the disease they suffer (haemorrhage). Some of these means of identifications have been taken over from Mark, but in some instances Matthew has altered Mark's material. The lack of names implies the lack of identity in the narrative, and shifts the focus away from the character to what she represents. The Twelve, on the contrary, are carefully identified by their names (10:2) and stories about the named disciples, Peter, James, and John, are repeated.

---

[1] See Ringe 1985, 154 about Luke's decision to omit the story.

Continuity cannot, unfortunately, be linked to any woman character because none of them has a story line of her own. I intend to observe *women* characters to draw a portrait of how women are treated in this narrative. They will not be traced as one character, but instead placed in a continuum to form a profile. Reference will be made to those parts of the narrative in which no women characters appear as they provide a context in which the women episodes are read.

The basic question in this thesis concerns the following of Jesus; therefore, the pericope of John the Baptist's death is excluded even though it includes women characters, namely Herodias and her daughter. These women are negative characters, flagrantly opposed to the message of the *basileia* and, as such, comparable to the Jewish leaders. The presence of malevolent women in the narrative attests that not all women are followers and that the division between those who follow and those who impede is not due to gender. In that sense, Herodias and the daughter are even necessary characters in the narrative. My analysis includes, however, only the positive characters: women in chapter 4 and men in chapter 5.

The pericope 12:46-50 where Jesus' mother and brothers come to talk with him has been excluded because it deals primarily with Jesus' relationship to his followers rather than to his mother[1] who is, in fact, not even a character in this episode, rather a device in Jesus' teaching.[2]

Furthermore, I have taken the liberty to include the birth narrative even though it is not directly connected to 'following'.It clearly involves aspects of the *basileia* that are relevant to the essence of 'following'. The women in the genealogy and their stories, implied in the text, are as essential to understanding the *basileia* as the women in the company of Jesus. Eventually, the following of Jesus is inseparable from an understanding of the *basileia;* and an understanding of the *basileia* leads to the 'following'.

The episodes and women in this analysis are therefore:

---

[1] For a parallel conclusion in John, see Dunderberg 2002, 269: "The fact that no brother of Jesus is mentioned by name in John could indicate that the beloved Disciple is introduced in John in order to disqualify not a certain "brother" of Jesus, but more generally *all* current attempts to seek authority with claims to the membership of Jesus' family."

[2] The pericope is referred to on page176.

The birth story (1-2)
Peter's mother-in-law (8:14-15)
The haemorrhaging woman / The ruler's daughter (9:18-26)
The Canaanite woman (15:21-28)
The mother of the sons of Zebedee (20:20-23 and 27:55-56)
The anointing woman (26:6-13)
Women at the cross (27:55-56) and at the tomb (28:1-10)

The main issues in each of the above passages are the interaction between the characters (conflict or dialogue in the broad sense), as well as the power relationships and the connection to the *basileia*, the central reality in Matthew's narrative. In Matthew, the *basileia*, the kingdom of heaven/ the reign of God is simultaneously a Jewish symbol and an image of power. As Matthew is writing his narrative to Jewish-Christian communities in the Roman empire, different ideological controversies can be inferred, including the ideological controversy between the reign of God and the reign of Rome[1]. Another controversy is between different ways of understanding power structures, in the *basileia* on the one hand, and in the structures of the developing communities on the other.

The following analyses are divided into two sections. First, I have followed the text itself and treated the questions that are relevant from the viewpoint of women characters. Second, under the title 'feminist critique and construct', I have taken up prior issues in feminist literature and considered their credibility and usefulness. The illustrative benefit of this division may be an excuse for overlaps on some issues. I have also sketched the power relationships of the characters in respect to the *basileia*.

4.2. The Birth Narrative (1-2)

4.2.1. Women Characters

Section 1:1–2:23 forms an introduction to the ministry of Jesus. Here the author[2] wants to reveal the background of his protagonist so that when the

---

[1] See Gnadt 1998, 483-484.
[2] I refer to 'Matthew' as author. However, I do not take any stand as to whether he really wrote the narrative, edited it, or was a redactor.

story begins, the reader is well informed of Jesus' real identity. The birth narrative in Chapters 1 and 2 and the passion and resurrection narratives in Chapters 26-28 frame the account of the ministry of Jesus and locate his life both in a broader historical context, giving it continuity and a mythological dimension.

A. Women in the Genealogy

The story begins with a narrative commentary in the form of a genealogy leading up to the time of Jesus. People connected to Jesus are not only those who follow him; the connections to the *basileia* before his ministry are also relevant and form the first pearls of the string that continues throughout the Gospel. The genealogy is followed by the story of Jesus' birth where the chief actor is Joseph. In Chapter 2 this individual event is put into a broader context, both historically and as a part of expanded reality. The Magi come to honour the baby Jesus, which leads to the massacre of the innocent by Herod. Joseph and his family flee to Egypt, and after Herod's death, they come back and move to Nazareth. All these events are guided by dreams given to Joseph. The characters besides Joseph are the Magi, Herod, and the chief priests.

The genealogy serves as proof that the promises of the Hebrew Scriptures have been fulfilled in Jesus. The title of the genealogy – βίβλος γενέσεως[1]– identifies Jesus as 'Jesus Christ, the son of David, the son of Abraham'. These three designations in the very beginning describe the intentions of the author. Χριστός is clearly a messianic title in Matthew (cf. 2:4; 16:16,20; 22:42; 24:5,23; 26:63,68). The genealogy points to the fulfilment and continuity of the messianic hopes of the Jewish people. υἱοῦ Δαυὶδ demonstrates the emphasis on proving that

---

[1] For Beare 1981, 64 and Davies and Allison 1988, 149-150 this is the title of the whole gospel, for Haapa 1969, 16-17 and for Hagner 1993, 9 the title of the genealogy and for Luz 1989, 104 the title of the prologue including the birth narrative (Ch 1) and for Kingsbury 1988(1), 40, 43-45 as far as 4:16. For a thorough treatment of the problem see Waetjen 1976, 205-230. Hill 1972, 74 suggests that something more is implied, meaning a new era for humanity and the world.

Jesus qualifies as the Davidic Messiah[1]. υἱοῦ' Αβραάμ has been seen as referring to Jesus as the Saviour of all nations.[2] Through David's royal line (verse 6 clearly entitles David 'king'), Jesus, as the Messiah, continues the history of Israel. But the cognomen 'son of Abraham' merely tells the reader that Jesus is a Jew. The promises to Abraham expand into the blessing to the Gentiles through his descendants, i.e. the Jews. Brown considers the genealogy a demonstration of God's providence.[3] In any event, the main point is not to give a biological record of Jesus' forefathers or foremothers, but to lay out a cross-section of Israel's history. As such, the genealogy presents Jesus both as the final stage in the salvation history[4], and in continuity with the history of Israel.

At the same time, the genealogy contains some ambiguous points besides the descent from Abraham. Jesus is described here as an heir to

---

[1] Brown 1977, 67; Albright and Mann 1984, 5. Davies and Allison 1988, 156-157 point to the dialogue with the synagogue, who looked for the arrival of *ben Dawid*. The title is used nine times in the Gospel: 1:1,20; 9:27; 12:23; 15:22; 20:30,31; 21:9,15. (Cf 3 times in mark and none in Q). The title can be seen as the most characteristic appellation of the earthly Jesus in the Gospel of Matthew.

[2] Brown 1977, 67-68. Davies and Allison 1988, 158.

[3] Brown 1977, 68.

[4] The genealogy is divided in three sections of 14 generations. There are, however, problems with regard to 'mathematics', historical names and omissions. How did the author compose this genealogy? According to Brown 1977, 67-70 he took two already existing genealogies, adapted and combined them and thus created a Matthean genealogy with its own theological emphases. One list covered the pre-monarchical time and had similarities with genealogies in 1 Chr 2 and Ruth 4. The other list was a popular genealogy of the house of David and its popular circulation may explain its errors and omissions. Brown sees that the evangelist noticed that the first list as well as the monarchical section of the second consisted of fourteen generations; so he added Joseph and Jesus to the last part, thus producing a genealogy of the pattern 3 x 14 generations. - Davies and Allison 1988, 165-166, 186 do not accept this theory, but see in it a more complicated process. The evangelist may have had at his disposal two existing genealogies of monarchical and post-monarchical descendants of David. These he adapted as well as 1 Chr 1-3, knowing the traditional reckoning of fourteen generations from Abraham to David. To be true to the pattern of 3 x 14 he had to omit four names of the monarchical period, and add at least two to the post-monarchical one. Still, despite his saying that there are 14 names in each period, if we start the last period from v. 12, we get only 13 generations. See also Luz 1989, 107. – Albright and Mann 1984, 4 suggest that Matthew follows the LXX I Chronicles; the omitting of the three kings is due to a scribal error (homoioteleuton). The present genealogy is from an editor assimilating Matthew's list into the LXX record.

a very respectable pedigree. He is a son of David, a son of Abraham, very honourably established in a religious context, and also of royal blood. Nevertheless, despite the ancestry, Joseph and Mary seem to belong to the common people.

The genealogy has a carefully ordered structure, a patrilineage of Jesus, with thirty nine repetitions of the pattern male δὲ ἐγέννησεν male. Sons are born to and for the male, while women are invisible. This kind of genealogy functions as a legitimation.[1] However, this patrilineal structure of the genealogy is broken five times by including the names of five women.[2] The first four initial breaks are

ἐκ τῆς Θαμάρ (3:1)
ἐκ τῆς Ῥαχάβ (1:5a)
ἐκ τῆς Ῥούθ (1:5b)
ἐκ τῆς τοῦ Οὐρίου (1:6)

It was not very usual to mention women in Jewish genealogies, although there are exceptions.[3] With regard to the First Testament genealogies, Tamar and Bathsheba occur in 1 Chr 1-3, while Rahab and Ruth do not. All four women come up in the beginning of the genealogy, the first three in the first part of the pattern, and the fourth right after, in the beginning of the second part. The women form no structural pattern inside the genealogy, which implies that they are not mentioned merely as representatives of women, but that their identity is what counts.

The fifth break in verse 16 includes Mary, not simply as the mother of Jesus, but in a totally different form by defining Joseph as τὸν ἄνδρα Μαρίας ἐξ ἧς ἐγεννήθη Ἰησοῦς. Joseph is mentioned only as the husband of Mary, not as the father of Jesus, as would be expected from the previous breaks in the genealogy.

There are other breaks in the pattern. Verse 2c and 11 also mention 'brothers'. Verse 6 inserts a comment that David is 'a king'. The exile is mentioned twice (11 and 12). These breaks serve merely as narrative

---

[1] Luz 1989, 108. About the different functions of genealogies see Johnson 1988,77-82
[2] Weren 1997, 291-292 notes the order of names. First there are the names of the fathers, then of the sons and, only in the end, of the mothers.
[3] Gen 11:29; 22:20-24; 35:22-26; 1 Chr 2:18-21,24,34,46-49; 7: 24. – Cf. Johnson 1988, 153. Luz 1989, 107 considers the possibility that their names are due to Matthew.

comments and the main interest concentrates on these five women. Why, in the first place, are women mentioned at all in the genealogy that otherwise is so true to the patrilineal structure? Why these women? Is there a connection between these four women from Jesus' prehistory and his mother? The genealogy in fact ends with Joseph, so where does Mary come in? This is a genealogy of Joseph, not of Jesus. For possible answers to these questions each of these women will be considered separately.

The first woman mentioned is *Tamar* (Gen 38), the Canaanite wife of Er, who was a son of Judah. When Er died without an heir, his brother Onan married Tamar according to the law of the levirate; when he too died without a child, Tamar was sent home to her father to wait until the third brother grew up and could marry her. When Tamar noticed that her father-in-law, Judah, did not intend to give his third son to her as a husband and would thus deprive her of the right to have children, she took the matter into her own hands. She disguised herself as a harlot in order to seduce Judah and became pregnant. Despite her duplicity, she was within her rights. It was Judah whose behaviour was against the law of the levirate.[1] This law protected the childless widow within the patriarchal society.[2] To understand this, the roles of women in the patriarchal times of the First Testament must be considered. She really had only two possibilities: either to be a virgin in her father's home, or a faithful, childbearing wife in her husband's home.[3] A married woman without a child was in a very awkward position. Unmarried girls in sexual relationships, or married women committing adultery, however, were more severe threats to the system. Death was the penalty for illegal sexual relationships (Deut 22).[4] However, the story relates that because she was disguised as a harlot, Tamar was not condemned. From all accounts, what happened between Tamar and Judah seems to have been an everyday occurrence. But as a daughter-in-law who was pregnant, she was accused of harlotry and condemned to death by her father-in-law. Niditch states:

---

[1] Deut. 25:5-6

[2] In the First Testament patriarchal narratives one sees a society in which the young married woman's role is to bear children. The identity of women depends on their bearing their husbands' children. Niditch 1979, 144-145.

[3] The third problematic category involved widows who, in patriarchal times, came under their sons' protection.

[4] Niditch 1979, 146.

"Certainly the OT discourages such illegal unions, as is indicated by a formal expression of the law at Lev. 19:29; yet once a girl is not seen in the role of daughter, virgin, and nubile woman, she is in effect, outside the rules. Prostitutes seem to have an accepted, outcast place in society."[1] Accepted and outcast seem to be attributes that are contradictory, but if we consider Tamar's situation, it is obvious from the narrative that being a prostitute was an accepted role for a woman *outside* the family structures. Inside the family, the patriarchal codes were strict and such behaviour condemnable. Judah claimed that Tamar was his third son's betrothed, and thus condemned her because of her harlotry. But Tamar's action rose from the conviction that Judah was not going to let her marry his third son, and because of her farsightedness – she could prove who the father was – the death sentence was overturned and Judah was forced to admit that she was more righteous than he. The ending of the story is strange. The reader is left with the impression that Tamar continued the line of Judah, but she was not reincorporated into the family through marriage. She remained outside the family structure. The situation can be described as 'legitimated illegitimacy'. Tamar's children from Judah are considered Judah's legitimate sons (Gen 46:12).[2]

Rahab (Jos. 2; 6:22-25)[3] is described as a harlot, but her profession is of little importance in the story, which concentrates on her action on behalf of the Israelites.[4] Joshua had sent two spies to Jericho whom Rahab sheltered in her house. In return, the Israelites saved her life and the lives of her relatives when they captured the city. What is noteworthy is that she is a Gentile, a foreigner, who through betrayal of her own people is incorporated into the history of Israel. The story portrays her as an independent individual, living alone in her house (verse 18), without any family or relatives living with her; and she acts independently, without consulting anyone. Her status as a prostitute is not condemned in the story, nor is the reason why the spies came to her house explained. As previously pointed out, prostitutes had an accepted status outside the

---

[1] Niditch 1979, 147.

[2] Schaberg 1990, 23.

[3] In the tradition, there is no mention anywhere of Rahab as the mother of Boaz. According to the First Testament chronology, there are almost two hundred years between Rahab and Boaz. In the Talmud, Rahab is said to have been the wife of Joshua. Cf. among others Davies and Allison 1988,173; Schaberg 1990, 25.

[4] Josephus regards Rahab as an innkeeper. Ant. V:5-15.

patriarchal structures. In early Christian tradition, she is described as a heroine of faith.[1] Questions have been raised about the exact identity of Rahab. The difference in Greek spelling and dating difficulties (the biblical Rahab in Jericho lived two hundred years before Boaz) have led to debates on whether the Rahab mentioned here really is to be identified with the Rahab of Jericho.[2] In spite of the problems, most scholars see these women as one and the same, so this will also be assumed here.

The story of *Ruth* is about three women, three childless widows, each of whom makes independent choices. The main character is Ruth, a Moabite, who makes the choice to leave her own country and follow her mother-in-law. She is an independent woman, who makes a commitment to follow another woman, but in the end is incorporated into the patriarchal family. The radicalism of her decision is comparable to the story of Abraham. But whereas Abraham is told to answer the call of God, Ruth follows her own feelings in what she thinks is the right thing to do. Whereas Abraham was accompanied by his wife and other possessions, Ruth is all alone.[3] She can only be considered a very unusual woman. As Phyllis Trible has said: "Not only has Ruth broken with family, country, and faith, but she has also reversed sexual allegiance. A young woman has committed herself to the life of an old woman rather than to the search for a husband, and she has made this commitment not "until death us do part" but beyond death. One female has chosen another female in a world where life depends upon men. There is no more radical decision in all the memories of Israel."

In order to find possible connections between the four women in the genealogy, we must also take into consideration that in Ruth's case there may have been some irregularity in her sexual behaviour. This depends on how the story of Ruth uncovering the feet of Boaz and laying herself there (Ruth 3) is interpreted. Was this a description of sexual intercourse between them? It remains speculation; but at all events, Ruth took the initiative to get what she wanted. She acted on the advice of her mother-

---

[1] Cf. James 2:25; Hebrews 11:31; 1 Clem. 12:1. - Hanson 1978, 53-60 looks for an emphasis on repentance in the story of Rahab, and thus also in connection with Tamar and Bathsheba.

[2] Quinn 1982, 225-228 has argued that the *Rachab* in the genealogy should not be identified with the harlot Rahab of Jericho. Brown 1982, 79-80 argues the opposite; they are probably the same.

[3] Williams 1982,86; Trible 1983, 173.

in-law, so in this case there were two women making planing and acting together independently, even if the result was an incorporation into the prevailing patriarchal system.

The fourth woman who makes a break in the genealogy is not mentioned by name but is designated as τοῦ Οὐρίου. *Bathsheba* was the wife of the Hittite Uriah, but she herself was probably not a Hittite.[1] The story of adultery between David and Bathsheba in 2 Sam 11 lays the guilt entirely on David. Bathsheba's possible guilt is outside the focus of the story.[2] On the other hand, even if Bathsheba's guilt is not explicitly mentioned, it can be assumed from the story. She most certainly had her reasons for coming to bathe in a place where David would see her while walking on his roof. But the story itself is very plain and blunt. First adultery, then murder. Bathsheba personifies passivity in the story, quite unlike Tamar, Rahab or Ruth who took matters into their own hands. The fact that Bathsheba is not mentioned by name, but as the wife of Uriah, reminds the readers of the sin of David who in this genealogy is titled 'a king'.

The fifth break does not follow the same pattern as the four preceding ones. It mentions Mary as the mother of Jesus, but not in the way one expects from what is previously said. Joseph, who really is of Davidic, or even, Messianic genealogy, is not the father of Jesus. He is the husband of Mary, to whom Jesus is born. Birth belongs clearly to the female sphere, to Mary only.[3] However, the genealogy as such stresses the importance of the Davidic ancestry of Joseph. The problem seems to be to prove that the birth of Jesus is at the same time Davidic through Joseph (which means that the child qualifies as the Messiah) yet derived

---

[1] See Bredin 1996, 96-97. According to him, Bathsheba was a Judahite.

[2] Berlin 1983, 26-27 points out that Bathhseba's role in the story is entirely passive. She is taken as a part of the plot, an object. This is why her guilt of adultery is not even considered. The whole attention in the story is on David. Berlin sees Bathsheba as an 'agent', a performer of an action necessary to the plot. "The plot in 2 Sam 11 calls for adultery, and adultery requires a married woman. Bathsheba fills that function. Nothing about her which does not pertain to that function is allowed to intrude into the story." Blomberg 1991, 145 reads Bathsheba's adultery "more like the rape of an innocent victim".

[3] The tension that appears in the verse has developed other variants of reading which tend to make it more specific that Mary was a virgin. 1:18-25 has influenced 1:16. For the detailed analysis of the different variants see Brown 1977, 62-63. Waetjen 1976, 216 sees the tension or ambiguity of the verse to be the intention of the author.

only from Mary.[1] If Joseph is not the father, the whole genealogy is meaningless. The birth narrative that follows solves the problem by adoption. Joseph adopts Jesus as his son by giving him his name.[2] Davidic descent is transferred through legal paternity. The genealogy of Joseph becomes the genealogy of Jesus. It seems that two different traditions are combined here: the fact that Jesus is the son of David through Joseph's acknowledgement, and the son of God through Mary.

Why are the four women from the Hebrew Scriptures mentioned in the genealogy? Is there meant to be a connection between Mary and them? Several efforts have been made to explain this and I shall consider these next.[3]

B. The Problem of Irregularity

The four women might be regarded as sinners and their presence would thus emphasise the role of Jesus as the saviour of sinners.[4] Tamar seduced her father-in-law, and Rahab was a prostitute. Bathsheba committed adultery with David. Ruth may have put Boaz in an awkward position, when she laid herself at his feet.[5] This theory is criticised for associating women, sexuality, and sin.[6] Against this explanation, it must first be noted that God blessed these women's actions and their conceptions in the respective narratives.[7] Second, the four women were not sinners according to the Scriptures. With Ruth, it is most uncertain if she sinned

---

[1] According to Aejmelaeus 1987, 468, the trouble to prove Joseph's Davidic ancestry belongs to the time before the faith in the virgin birth was prevalent.

[2] Aejmelaeus 1987, 468; Schweizer 1981, 9; Räisänen 1969, 65. Räisänen's solution is that for Matthew, Jesus is the Messiah despite the virginal origin.

[3] Most of the explanations make attempts to see the common denominator either among the four women or between them and Mary. Heil 1991(1), 544 notes the differences between the women.

[4] Brown 1977, 71. This explanation originates from Jerome.

[5] Note Josephus Ant.V: 328-331: the stress to prove the innocence of Ruth.

[6] Among others, Weren 1997, 288.

[7] Anderson 1987, 188 points out that God has the power of life and death including control of the womb. God did not withhold conception; instead these women's unusual actions promote the patrilineage of the Messiah. See also Trible 1983, 34-35 about the stories of Sarah, Rachel and Hannah. Control of the womb belongs to God only, who closes and opens wombs in judgement, in blessing and in mystery.

with Boaz, and even if she did, that was not the focus of the story, and of no importance. The story of Tamar recognises that she was right, while it was Judah who wronged her (cf. Gen. 38:26). Rahab, though mentioned as a harlot by profession, is also portrayed in the story in a positive way. Bathsheba's guilt of adultery was, as previously noted, outside the focus of the story, and it may be implicitly assumed she was not condemned because she was the mother of Solomon.

The point could not be that these women were sinners. If there had been a need to emphasise Jesus as the Saviour of sinners, there would have been no reason to pinpoint *women*. On the contrary, there are already several male ancestors – for example Judah and David, whose sins would well cover this emphasis. As for Mary, there is no connection between her and the other women from this point of view, unless it was the evangelist's purpose to forestall the later accusations of the Jews; that Jesus was an illegitimate child of Mary. These other women would have been included to point to exceptional women in Israel's history who, in spite of irregularities, were otherwise highly esteemed.

This is the explanation of Edwin D. Freed. According to him, both the genealogy and the birth narrative are written in reply to the charge of illegitimacy. Matthew's defence of Mary's pregnancy could be readily understood by the Jewish Christians. He does not deny the charge of illegitimacy. Freed writes: "Matthew justifies the behaviour of Mary in the same way Jews had come to justify – even extol – the conduct of the four women mentioned in the genealogy. Mary is included with those four women as a paragon of virtue."[1] Weren's solution echoes that of Freed. According to the former, the later rabbinical traditions that made the First Testament women examples of morality were already circulating in Matthew's time and "Mary plays a role already played before by Tamar, Rahab, Ruth, and Bathseba." For Weren, history is accomplished through the efforts of women, and the Hebrew Scriptures include material to prove this.[2]

An examination of the preceding views ignores many basic questions. First, the charges as well as the Jewish interpretations referred to here, derive from a much later time than the Gospel, and nothing certain can be ascertained as to an earlier circulation in some form in

---

[1] Freed 1987, 6.
[2] Weren 1997, 305.

Matthew's environment. Furthermore, nothing in the genealogy nor in the birth narrative suggests that Mary's pregnancy is the result of her taking matters into her own hands and defending her rights as Tamar or Ruth or Rahab did. What is the behaviour that must be justified? Even if we consider the active participants, the First Testament women, as positive examples, Mary remains passive: all is happening to her not by her. I consider the above explanations highly unlikely. At this stage I reject the theory that the women of the genealogy were sinners. (The question of illegitimacy as such will be discussed a little later.)

The second explanation notes that the four women were foreigners, which reflects an interest in the salvation of the Gentiles.[1] Tamar and Rahab were Canaanites, Ruth a Moabite, and Bathsheba might have been a Hittite. Their nationality precludes any connection to Mary, who was not a foreigner. As in the previous explanation, this too overlooks the fact that the Gentiles mentioned in the genealogy should be women. On the other hand, it is not at all clear that the Jews of the first century would have regarded these women as foreigners. In post-biblical Judaism, Tamar and Rahab were regarded as proselytes. Brown asks how the Gentile Christians (among the ancient readers) would understand the two women's proselyte status, because the Gentile Christians did not have to become proselytes to Judaism.[2] Bredin, on the other hand, sees Matthew's community as a background, where debates about attitudes towards Gentiles still prevailed. Bredin is of the opinion that Matthew brought these women to the genealogy (and mentioned Abraham) to defend the Gentile mission against the Davidic tradition. The mention of Tamar, Rahab, Ruth, and Uriah recalled righteous Gentiles.[3] The question of the Gentile mission was relevant in Matthew's community and the mentioning of these three women and Uriah, as well as Abraham, might have been intended to include associations in favour of the Gentiles. However, I still have doubts whether the purpose was to emphasise these women as Gentiles.

---

[1] Haapa 1969, 18; Schweizer 1981, 9; Gundry 1982, 14-15; Luz 1989, 110; 9; Bredin 1996, 110-111; Räisänen 1992, 48. Earlier Räisänen 1969, 59-60 has supported the idea of divine choice which connected the four women and Mary in the same line. Mary too was chosen by God to fulfil God's plans.

[2] Brown 1977, 72-73. See also Brown et al 1978, 79-80.

[3] Bredin 1996, 110-111.

These two explanations have stressed the contrast between Mary and the First Testament women. The third explanation includes Mary with the four women of the genealogy by pointing out that there is something extraordinary or irregular in these women's union with their partners, and that, at the same time, they showed initiative or played an important role in God's plan and, thus becoming instruments of God's providence.[1] This explanation with its two dimensions is certainly the most interesting one so far. First, it is the explanation which also takes Mary into consideration and sees the four women as foreshadowing her role. The first part of the explanation notes something unusual in these women's relationships with men. Tamar seduced her father-in-law, who had wronged her, and she became pregnant and thus part of the lineage even though Judah did not marry her. It is more difficult to adapt this theory to Rahab. The only irregularity that comes to mind was the fact that she, at least before her incorporation into the history of Israel, was a prostitute. Ruth's union with Boaz was perhaps irregular because she was not a Jew, and unusual in that the initiative was on Ruth's side. Bathsheba had an adulterous union with David, but it was still their son who became king after David. It strains credibility, however, to see any similarity between these four women and their unusual relationships with their partners and Mary and her betrothal. The irregularity here seems to equate with both of the previous alternatives: being 'a sinner' in anomalous sexual relationships or being a Gentile, an irregularity in the Jewish patriarchal society.

The other aspect of the explanation emphasises the women's personal initiative or their role in God's plan. Tamar, Rahab and Ruth were clearly independent women who showed initiative and took responsibility for their own lives. Bathsheba, however, is seen in the Hebrew Scriptures in a passive role, while David is the chief actor; as for her role in God's plan, she can be seen only as the mother of Solomon, in the role of reproduction. Bathsheba is clearly in a different category from the other three and it might be good to look at the question from another angle, which would include all four anomalies in the same theory.

---

[1] This is the explanation Brown 1977, 73-74 chooses. So also Filson 1967, 52; Räisänen 1969, 59-60; Albright and Mann 1984, 6; Hagner 1993, 10 and Beare 1981, 63 who also points to the possibility of their being foreign. Hill 1972, 74 suggests their presence points to a lack of convention in the processes of divine providence leading up to the strange event.

Up to now, the question has been: what is the common denominator among these four *women*? In the fourth break, however, it is Uriah who is mentioned, not Bathsheba. Mark Bredin's explanation, cited above, has already changed the focus from Bathsheba to Uriah. Uriah is a positive figure in the story, he is faithful to his commission, but he becomes the victim of David's sin. He is clearly a man with a mind of his own when he refuses to obey David, and in this respect he is comparable to Tamar, Rahab, and Ruth in independence. This is the line Amy-Jill Levine chooses as her solution, where Judah, the king of Jericho, David, and Boaz are taught the lesson of higher righteousness by Tamar, Rahab, Uriah, and Ruth. Each one of them acted against the social mores of their times in order to further God's purposes; in this respect they foreshadowed Jesus, not Mary.[1]

It is difficult to see how these breaks with the persons from the First Testament – women or a man – would foreshadow Mary. Brown suggests that the four women were chosen as foreshadows of Mary due to the combination of a scandalous or irregular union and divine intervention through the woman.[2] As pointed out before, the irregularity, even if it exists, is not comparable to Mary and the four women, nor is the nature of the intervention. God's direct intervention is not even present in the First Testament stories.

On the other hand, Mary is not seen in the narrative as an independent woman of initiative as are Tamar, Rahab, and Ruth (or Uriah); her role is nearer to that of Bathsheba as a passive means of reproduction. If we change Bathsheba to Uriah, the similarities vanish totally. It would seem to me that the four women (or three women and Uriah) are not meant to be foreshadows of Mary.

The next proposal comes from M.D. Johnson. He assumes a Jewish polemical debate over the ancestry of the Messiah. The fate of these First Testament women divided the Jewish tradition, as they had an important role in later Jewish speculation, which was polemical in nature. This is Johnson's reason for why these women were mentioned in the genealogy.

---

[1] Levine 1992, 253. She also points out that these women lived outside normal domestic structures and although they finally were associated with men, this genealogy indicates that marriage is not the prerequisite for righteous action or salvation.

[2] Brown 1977, 74. He reminds us that divine intervention could be seen also in the stories of Sarah, Rebekah, and Rachel, but Matthew did not choose them because there was not anything scandalous about their unions.

On one side of the debate were those waiting for a priestly Messiah, who argued against their opponents by emphasising the 'blots', the four scandalous women of Davidic ancestry. Opposed to them, the Pharisees defended the inclusion of the irregularities of foreign blood and sinful women. Matthew's Jewish or Jewish-Christian readers were aware of this debate in which the four women played a prominent role. Matthew was on the side of the Pharisees and saw that Jesus totally fulfilled the expectations of the Messiah.[1] Against this theory must be noted the lack of evidence for Rahab's role, as she is not connected to the ancestry of David in the First Testament.[2]

It seems to me that searching for only one common denominator among these women is not fruitful. The variety of opinions clearly implies that the answer cannot be a simple one. Each alternative, in its own way, contributes to a plausible explanation. Nevertheless each of them proves inadequate when taken as the sole alternative. The question is not what is shared between the four women and Mary, but what is common between each of them, and what they all separately signify.

Let us consider another perspective. The common facts concerning these four characters from the Hebrew Scriptures include the following elements: Each of the incidents connected to them demonstrated some independence and was in opposition to the social patterns of the time; these characters lived outside normal domestic arrangements (they were unmarried, widowed, prostitutes or separated from wife or husband), and all of them were somehow wronged either by a male or the regulations of the male world. But in every narrative, the wrong was also righted by the actions of men.

All these elements provide foundation for the future in the story. The conspicuous similarities of female gender and the fact that each of these women was somehow outside the normal patriarchal family structure, could be a preparation for a story of a woman in a situation that is not socially accepted, but legitimated later on by the actions of the male

---

[1] Johnson 1988, 176-179.
[2] Davies and Allison 1988, 171. This fact is also acknowledged by Johnson.

world.[1] The common point could be the suspicion of illegitimacy.[2] However, there are still facts that do not exactly fit. Their situations are different. The First Testament women took risks in their own lives and there was no divine intervention. In this respect the comparison to Mary is not plausible. It is possible to replace Bathsheba by Uriah[3] and ask for whom these are people models or to whom do they point? Is it important that they are women, or is the point somewhere else?

In the Gospel narrative, it is important that *Joseph* is proved Davidic. On the other hand, the birth of Jesus in verse 16 is undoubtedly clearly connected to Mary only. The tension is twofold. Up to now, when reflecting on the meaning of these four women in the genealogy, the attention has been focused on Mary because of the female gender, but it must not be forgotten that in Matthew's birth narrative, which immediately follows, Joseph is the chief actor; he is the one who acts against the normal moral pattern of his time and accepts the role of a foster-father. There is every reason to ask whether it is Joseph, and not just Mary, who is the counterpart to the First Testament persons, and who breaks the pattern in verse 16? The main focus is directed on the irregularity in the domestic and social arrangements, in which all these persons from the First Testament, as well as Joseph, were clearly vulnerable in terms of their gender position and independent in their choices of action.

I have already pointed out that describing Jesus as 'the son of Abraham' is somewhat problematic. However, the story of Abraham himself may reveal clues to a deeper understanding. He was a man called by God to turn his back on his old life, take his possessions and family, and blindly go where God would lead him. He is an image of obedience, of 'faith'. To be able to experience the promises of God he had to take risks in his life. In this respect his story also points to Joseph: obedience,

---

[1] Schaberg, 1990, 32-33. The illegitimacy can not be accepted in Ruth's case, which Schaberg herself also notes. Senior 1998, 38 sees these four women as "outsiders" - the incorporation into the lineage of Israel is unusual and this prepares the reader for the account of Jesus' conception.

[2] Blomberg 1991, 147.

[3] The explanation Weren 1997, 292 gives concerning Bathsheba's and Uriah's role in this genealogy is the following: Solomon was not Uriah's son, but David's, as Jesus was not Joseph's physical son. The comparison limps. While David is mentioned in the genealogy, *a passivum divinum* is not so obvious as Weren claims.

and acting out of 'faith' in response to God's command. Many interpretations make particular note of Joseph in the birth history.[1] The name of Joseph serves to remind the reader of the other Joseph in the book of Genesis, who also was a dreamer. In both stories, God reveals his directions through dreams. Joseph is a just man and obedient to God. Ironically, he is proven Davidic according to a genealogy in which the mention of Bathsheba reminds the readers of the sinful act of David himself.

4.2.2. Feminist Critique and Construct

The feminist critique has very forcefully attacked traditional interpretations equating women, sexuality, and sin.[2] Quite interestingly, Corley opposes this attitude by her opinion that the First Testament women are particularly mentioned because they were morally suspect 'sinners'. All five women, Mary included, have one common feature, namely, a bad reputation. The underlying message is that there were numerous sinners among Jesus' followers. Therefore, the genealogy, which includes sinful women, precedes the overall view of 'following'.[3] In considering the explanations of this particular genealogy, moral valuations are not very noticeable; rather the emphasis is on sexual irregularity associated with the First Testament persons. The fact that Mary's conception is described as non-sexual does not mean that sexuality as such is condemned sinful in the genealogy. It is noteworthy that feminist attention has been focused more on Luke's birth narrative than on Matthew's[4] probably because of Mary's central role and her advocacy of the poor and the humble in the 'Magnificat'.

---

[1] Especially Brown 1977, 106-109, 111 who also points to similarities traditions associated with Moses. Also Räisänen 1969, 66, 76 and Luz 1989, 123 emphasise the central role of Joseph in the birth narrative.

[2] Among others, Anderson 1983,9; Wainwright 1991, 64; Levine 1992, 253. Levine notes that in Matthew's time sexuality was not automatically equated with sin.

[3] Corley 1993, 151-152.

[4] See e.g. Schottroff 1993, 158-167; Melzer-Keller 1997, 241-245. In her article about the foremothers and Mary, Schaberg 1996, 158 notes that in Luke, Mary represents the oppressed who have been liberated; but Matthew is primarily about and for males. It is not the story of Mary. But, she adds, by connecting the foremothers and Mary, Matthew implies that salvation history is not "essentially a male enterprise".

From feminist points of view, the central problem seems to revolve around the question of Mary's womanhood; and from that perspective the question of the virginal conception presents a problem.[1] Mary's virginal conception as a non-sexual miracle of motherhood has been considered a slur on all motherhood. If being a virgin and a mother at the same time is an insult, how are we to read these descriptions of Jesus' origin? The feminist responses have either celebrated the female sphere of Jesus' birth, or abandoned the idea of Mary's miraculous virginal conception. These responses indicate different approaches. The historical and biological virginity is a problem different from the metaphorical virginity in the narrative.

A. Celebrating the Female

The first attitude – celebrating the female – is present in Anderson's articles on Matthew and Mary's difference. She suggests the birth narrative to be an attempt "to come to terms with female difference" which, for her, means that, by using the genealogy and the role of Joseph, Jesus is incorporated back into the male world, into the normal patriarchal system. But the tension created by the difference in Jesus' birth remains.[2] God is acting here in a radically new way, which operates outside the male world. For Anderson, the First Testament women serve to prepare the implied reader "for a woman's irregular production of the Messiah outside the ordinary patriarchal norms yet within God's overarching plans and an overall patriarchal framework. The first four women help to celebrate and domesticate female difference and Mary's extraordinary

---

[1] In the mainstream commentaries (written mostly by men) the virgin birth is not problematised. See e.g. Hill 1972, 76; Albright and Mann 1984, 9; Filson 1967, 55; Beare 1981, 66; Gundry 1982,18. However, see Räisänen 1969, 75-76 who says that the idea of the virginal conception in Matthew belongs to Christology only. Matthew has no mariological interests. Also Luz 1989, 127 discusses the problem, but concludes that Matthew's emphasis is not on the virginal conception, but the virgin birth is "rather a conceptual basis which helps him to understand that Jesus is 'Immanuel'.This basis is important because it aids in thinking very concretely that 'God is with us', and to consider it as a *real* acting of God with Jesus in history and not simply as an abstract concept."

[2] Anderson 1983,10.

conception without a male partner."[1] However, the difference between Mary and the four women is greater than the similarity Anderson claims.

Mary's conception of Jesus, as described in the text, is something totally different from any other conception; there is no human male involved in begetting her child, nor is God or the Spirit described as a male progenitor. The manner of begetting is depicted as totally non-sexual. On the other hand, it is clear that the break points not only to Mary, but also to Joseph. Mary is a totally passive figure, the vehicle of reproduction, the womb where the child is conceived. The focus is on Joseph. He is the one who makes the Messiah Davidic; he is the one, who makes the decisions, who receives the divine instructions which he follows. He is the one who gives the child legal status. Everything happens within the boundaries of patriarchy. Joseph seems to normalize the situation.[2] Yet Joseph is explicitly described as the husband of Mary, not the father of the child. The male is excluded from Jesus' conception. Anderson does not discuss the historical nor biological aspects of the event. On a narrative level, only the divine and the female are connected to Jesus' origins. But the male contribution is too easily dismissed by Anderson, since in Matthew's version, Joseph is the actor who steals the scene. The male is in the leading role after all.

Levine suggests that feminine images revolve around the stories of Jesus' conception and birth. The Holy Spirit is grammatically feminine in Semitic languages. Therefore, for Levine "the combination of the originally feminine spirit and Jesus' lack of a human father indicates the restructuring of the human family: outside of patriarchal models it is not ruled by or even defined by a male head of the house."[3] Some caution is needed here: The Holy Spirit does not take the role of the progenitor, male or female, in the narrative and therefore implications of superior power are not well grounded.[4]

Wainwright's interpretation of the women in the genealogy as well as of the narrative of Mary's son, includes a critique against patriarchy.

---

[1] Anderson 1987, 188.

[2] So also Anderson 1987, 186.

[3] Levine 1992, 254.

[4] Senior 1998, 41 stresses here the unique bond between Jesus and God and he says that the Spirit's role "at the origin of Jesus' life is reminiscent of the function of the Spirit in genesis at the beginning of creation (Gen 1:1-2) and it may be that Matthew wishes to suggest thereby that the advent of Jesus is a new moment in history".

The power and the presence of women in Israel's history and in Jesus' birth emphasise the significance of the female. More than that, male and female contributions to Jesus' birth, while different are both significant.[1] Historically, she considers it possible that the kind of tradition that ran counter to the prevailing culture and its androcentric world view was espoused by women in the community "who sought to keep alive the inclusive and liberative vision of Jesus which was in tension with the prevailing culture, especially in their regard." This women tradition has been suppressed in the androcentric perspective of the Gospel and overshadowed by the Joseph tradition.[2] It seems to me that the need to prove the dignity of the female – both for Mary and the women in Matthew' s community – leads to over-interpretation of the text itself.

B. An Illegitimate Conception

Another feminist perspective opposes the idea of miraculous conception altogether. A powerful feminist interpretation of the birth of Jesus is Jane Schaberg's monograph *The Illegitimacy of Jesus*, where she argues that the texts dealing with the origin of Jesus in Matt 1:1-25 (also Luke 1:20-56; 3:23-28) originally were about an illegitimate, not a miraculous virginal conception. According to Schaberg, both Matthew and Luke passed down a tradition they inherited: Jesus the Messiah had been illegitimately conceived during the period when his mother Mary was betrothed to Joseph. At the pre-gospel stage, this illegitimate conception had already been understood theologically as due, in some unexplained way, to the power of the Holy Spirit. While both evangelists themselves presupposed of an illegitimacy tradition, in telling the story, they developed further the role of the Spirit with the result that Christians soon became unaware of the tinge of illegitimacy.[3]

According to Schaberg, the birth narratives of the Second Testament indicate that Mary's conceiving of Jesus is not a miraculous virginal conception, but that she was seduced or sexually assaulted during her

---

[1] Wainwright 1991, 74-75.
[2] Wainwright 1991, 174-175.
[3] Schaberg 1990, 195.

engagement.[1] This hypothesis fits into the historical setting and as a possible solution for the historical Mary, but the text itself does not point in this direction.[2]

In this narrative, a betrothed virgin is found to be pregnant in the period between her betrothal and the consummated marriage.[3] Joseph knew that the child was not his. According to Schaberg, the normal conclusions in this situation would have been adultery or rape as the causes of pregnancy. Joseph is said to be an upright man, which would mean Torah-observant. Obedience to the law forced him to plan to divorce Mary, but he wanted to do it quietly.[4] In this way, he protected Mary and himself from public shame. Joseph's choice was according to

---

[1] Schaberg's thesis about the illegitimacy is defended through the following points: 1) Matthew 1:16, where the syntax shows that Matthew did not believe that Joseph was Jesus' biological father. 2) The missing fourteenth name in the third cycle of the names. (The missing one was Jesus' biological father.) 3) Joseph believed Mary had been raped; understood on the base of Deut. 22:23–27. 4) The Holy Spirit's intervention does not exclude human paternity. 5) The lack of ancient parallels to this kind of virginal conception. 6) The interpretation of Isaiah 7:14 that 'virgin' means a woman who had no sexual relations before those from which the child is born. (Schaberg 1990, 34-77.) Schaberg arrives at the same conclusions from Luke's narrative.

[2] Against Schaberg also Schottroff 1995, 201 and Wainwright 1991, 69, n.36.

[3] Jewish matrimonial procedure consisted of two stages. First came the engagement or betrothal. The betrothal constituted a legally ratified marriage, and it initiated the girl's removal from her father's power to her husband's, giving the latter legal rights over her. She could be called his wife or become his widow. The second stage was the proper marriage, taking the bride to the groom's family home. Noteworthy here is that between these two stages, the girl was his wife. Any infringement on his marital rights could be punished as adultery. In addition, it was normally assumed that the girl was a virgin at the time of her betrothal. According to later Jewish commentary, in parts of Judea interim marital relations were not absolutely condemned. In Galilee, the wife had to be taken to her husband's home as a virgin (Brown 1977, 123-124).

[4] There are different theories concerning Joseph's uprightness. 1) He was upright, because he was merciful. 2) Joseph knew that Mary's pregnancy was the result of a divine intervention. Frightened at the presence of God Joseph drew back: he could not take as a spouse the woman whom God had chosen as his sacred vessel. 3) As in the text. For more details see Brown 1977, 126-128.

the law, but more gentle.[1] Despite the apparently overwhelming proof of legitimacy in the elaborate genealogical table, Joseph was not the biological father. The cause of pregnancy was the enigmatic Holy Spirit.

The next question is, what did Matthew mean by the words 'through the Holy Spirit'? The traditional understanding is that conception through the Holy Spirit was thought to have replaced normal human conception. This would mean that Matthew wants to emphasise that the divine birth has not originated through normal sexual intercourse. Jesus is conceived without a human father, through the power of the Holy Spirit. The lack of parallels[2], and the lack of elements that would imply anything of the kind in the immediate context, lead to an assumption that verses Matt 1:18,20 did not originally point to a virginal conception. Schaberg suggests that since nothing in the context requires us to read these verses in accordance with a virginal conception, they should be read against this view. Thus, Schaberg explains that the metaphor of divine conception is used in order to stress that God's power is the ultimate source of human life (there are three partners in every birth: God, father and mother), or in order to point out that God sometimes communicates a spiritual/psychological dimension of life to humans, over and above ordinary human existence. This demands that the Matthean phrases should not be read in a literal sense, but in a figurative or symbolic sense. It involves the creative power of God that does not replace human

---

[1] Schaberg's conclusions were that home taking would remove the suspicion of adultery in that a Torah-observant man would probably not consummate a marriage with an adulteress. But home taking would not remove the suspicion of rape. The Halakah allowed the Torah-observant man to marry a raped woman. Here, Schaberg means that Matthew shows that the angelic solution to Joseph's dilemma is a legal one. (Schaberg 1990, 58-60)

[2] There are no real parallels to this in the Hebrew or the Greek Bible. A tradition of virginal conception was evidently not known to other Second Testament writers. The earliest reference to the mother of Christ is in Paul's letter to the Galatians (4:4), in which he tells his readers that Jesus was made of woman. This reference is connected to the fact that Jesus was fully human and yet the son of God. Birth without action of a human father is known in the Hellenistic environment, where divine begetting of kings, heroes, philosophers is a common theme. These parallels, however, "involve a type of hieros gamos where a divine male, in human or other form, impregnates a woman, either through normal sexual intercourse or through some substitute form of penetration. They are not really similar to the non-sexual virginal conception..." (Brown 1977, 62)

paternity. What Matthew tells his readers is that this child's existence is due to an unpremeditated accident.[1]

It is no doubt true that the centre of this narrative is God's action,[2] but the form of the narrative should also be considered. God was also active in cases of other pregnancies in the Hebrew Scriptures, such as those of Sarah or Hanna; however, this did not transcend normal parentage. God's action could have been materialised in a more conventional narrative. *There is no historical corroboration for this event as recorded by Matthew.* For him, the law was valid, and Joseph was a law-abiding man. The narration is a Joseph-narrative, and his situation, dilemma and decision are clues to understanding the story.[3]

The hypothesis of an illegitimate pregnancy raises problems, one of which is the same as found in the theory of virginal conception. How did Matthew (or Luke) know about it? If there was knowledge about the irregularity of Mary's pregnancy – whatever the cause – why is it that only these two evangelists seem to know about it.[4]

---

[1] Schaberg 1990, 67-68. See also Fitzmyer 1973, 572 who sees the virgin birth as a 'theologoumenon'. The question is not historical or biological; Mary's virginity metaphorically affirmed Jesus' significance. Brown 1977, 527-530 leaves the question unanswered because, according to him, the rejection of Mary's biological virginity leaves room for the possibility that Jesus was illegitimate. "Undoubtedly some sophisticated Christians could live with the alternative of illegitimacy; they would see this as the ultimate stage in Jesus' emptying himself and taking on the form of a servant (Phil. 2:7), and would insist, quite rightly, that an irregular begetting involves no sin by Jesus himself. For many less sophisticated believers, illegitimacy would be an offense that would challenge the plausibility of Christian mystery."

[2] Cf. for example Aejmelaeus 1987, 469.

[3] With the hypothesis of an illegitimate pregnancy before us, it is easier to understand Matthew's problem: providing a theological sense to prevailing tradition. No matter what the cause of the illegitimacy, Jesus' origin appeared more or less tragic. It was probably not easy for Matthew to find a text that would fit the situation. Even if the word *parthenos* in LXX played any role in Matthew's choice, he was not concentrating on a virgin conceiving miraculously. Isaiah 7:14 involves an oracle to King Ahaz, and a portent referring to something that was supposed to happen shortly thereafter. The child to be born was not the Messiah, and the Hebrew word translated as *parthenos* really means a young woman. The stress is not on virginity, and certainly not on miraculous conception. (Brown 1977, 47-148). Brown himself (149) is of the opinion that the belief in the virginal conception already existed before the reflection of Isaiah 7:14 coloured the existing belief.

[4] There are some texts that are said to imply Jesus' virginal conception: Mark 6:3; John 1:13;6:42;7:42;8:41. None of these texts has anything to do with the question.

Joseph and his dilemma are in the centre. All that seems to be important for Matthew is to emphasise that *God wanted this child to be born in an irregular way, and that Joseph gives the child an identity that a mother in a patriarchal society could not.* Matthew's interest in Mary is minimal. She is present through Joseph, but we know nothing about her actions, feelings, and thoughts. She is not a protagonist in the story, no one speaks to her, she makes no decision and performs no actions.[1]

C. The Legitimate King

In my opinion, it would be more fruitful to consider the birth narrative from a less historical orientation. The whole birth narrative is enveloped in a mythological atmosphere. None of the events related in these two chapters is mentioned later on, but the expectations are answered at the end of the Gospel in the passion narrative. The irregular conception has its counterpart in the resurrection. The conception is connected to Jesus, not Mary; and the question that should be asked is, what does it express about Jesus?

Also, if we consider Mary as a character in a narrative rather than a person in a historical report, it would be easier to guess the author's intentions for including the breaks in the genealogy. Jesus is the protagonist of a narrative that is told mainly between the birth story and the passion and resurrection. Additionally, Matthew provides Jesus with a prehistory. For Matthew, Jesus is God's Son, a king. But his kingship and his *basileia* are reversed in nature. The same perplexity that belongs to his whole ministry, is also expressed in his birth narrative. God chooses the unexpected, the unrespectable, the unconventional as agents in his history – such as Tamar, Rahab, Ruth, Bathsheba – and Mary. Jesus is not born without a biological father in the narrative because sexuality is something inferior or bad, or something that needs to be excluded. For Matthew, God is Jesus' father throughout the Gospel. His origin is from God and that is also his destiny in the resurrection narrative. Matthew may connect different traditions, but it is not his intention to report historical events, but to reveal Jesus' origins in a mythological narrative.

---

[1] As Räisänen 1969, 67 says: Mary is only "the mother of the child" (cf. 2:13,14,20,21).

The contrast of the messianic kingship is made obvious. As opposed to his royal ancestors, the Messiah is born to ordinary people in very vulnerable circumstances. The faith and obedience of Abraham and Joseph are underlined. The reversal of power and glory is emphasised through the irregularity and vulnerability surrounding both Mary and the First Testament women. God's history runs through paradox and surprise, and he chooses instruments that ordinary people would not. In the form of a narrative, Matthew reveals the essence of Jesus' kingship and God's *basileia*.

In Chapter two, the birth narrative is placed within a larger context. The main characters in the narrative are the Magi who come to honour the baby Jesus, and King Herod and the chief priests who try to persecute him. The Magi are often interpreted as representing Gentiles who accept the Messiah, and Herod and the chief priests as Jews who reject him.[1] Even if the historicity of the events is unverifiable, and if we bear in mind that Matthew does not mean to write a historical report, some historical facts may still be taken at face value. Herod is not a representative of the Jews, he was a client king of the Romans, not even a Jew himself. In Matthew's narrative, he is the reigning king. In the second chapter the conflict between him and the new born Davidic king dominates. According to Horsley, people in Herod's time suffered under the repressive control of what they saw as the illegitimate 'king of the Jews', and they longed for a divinely legitimate king and liberation.[2] However, instead of focusing on Herod's time, the focus needs to be on Matthew's time, when the political atmosphere was no less tense. Matthew creates a narrative with a strong political impact, and the Magi represent a further political complication. Whoever the Magi are supposed to be – royal priestly assistants from the Persian empire or a reminiscence of the

---

[1] Brown 1977, 67-69; Hill 1972, 80; Gundry 1982,27; Schweizer 1981, 17; Luz 1989, 139; Howell 1990, 116. On the contrary Albright and Mann 1984, 16 who say that there is no indication that they were Gentiles. See also Levine 1992, 254.

[2] Horsley 1989, 39-49. Also Gundry 1982, 27 suggests that Jesus' kingship contrasts with Herod's: the legitimacy of Jesus' kingship over and against the illegitimacy of Herod's rule.

visit of Tiridates, the king of the Armenians to Rome[1] – they represent the elite of an eastern empire. The representatives of foreign rulers come to honour the new born king.

The suspicion of irregularity concerning Jesus' conception and birth are connected to his subversive kingship.[2] In Matthew's narrative, the baby king with his family and background is contrasted with the reigning king. However, Jesus is proven to be the legitimate king through the correct lineage as Herod is not. Jesus' subversive kingship is visible from the very beginning of Matthew's narrative.

4.3. The Narrative of Jesus' Ministry (3-25)

4.3.1. Peter's Mother-in-Law

A. The Context

The first incident where there is a woman who seems to respond to Jesus and the message of the *basileia,* appears as late as in Chapter 8. By then the reader has gained much information about Jesus.

The first two chapters inform us that Jesus spent his early years in Nazareth, but then a time warp occurs between the second and the third Chapters. A new scene in Chapter 3 recounts the activities of John the Baptist who eventually baptizes the grown up Jesus (3:13-16). Divine legitimation is again present – this time in the form of a dove and a voice from heaven which acknowledges Jesus as the Son of God. Right from the beginning, and now again, the reader is made conscious of Jesus'

---

[1] For more speculations see Luz 1989, 131; Brown 1977, 189-190; Horsley 1989, 53-60; Hill 1972, 80-81; Hagner 1993, 25. Brown, Luz and Hill have doubts about the historicity of the event. On the contrary, Hagner suggests that Matthew has a historical tradition behind his narrative.

[2] Blomberg 1991, 148 goes even further: "Jesus' conception and birth cast a shadow of suspicion of illegitimacy over his parentage. His claims to kingship would be viewed by the ruling politico-religious authorities as nothing but illegitimate. The truth is, in fact, exactly the opposite."

divine origin. After the baptism, Jesus victoriously subdues the Devil (4:1-11). When John the Baptist has been arrested, thus ending an epoch, Jesus starts his mission to proclaim the *basileia* (4:17).

The *basileia* wins the first followers when Jesus calls two pairs of brothers to follow him (4:18-22). These men are identified by their names, but they are not called disciples. The essential commitment of following Jesus is plain in the story as the men leave their work and their father at once because of Jesus. The motivation for their abrupt action is not given to the reader. It is not considered relevant, as the reader already knows about Jesus' origins and authority. After this, Jesus wanders everywhere in the surrounding area to preach and heal people. The people following him grow in number and are described as a large crowd (ὄχλοι πολλοί). The subject of Jesus' preaching is the *basileia;* and he makes it visible by his deeds (4:23-25).

The crowds are depicted as the motive for Jesus' long speech (Ch. 5-7) which follows. He *saw* the crowds and *called* the disciples to him.[1] However, the reader does not know through the information garnered thus far who the disciples are. It is also noted at the end of the speech that the crowd has been listening. This means either that the crowd and the disciples are the same group, or at least that the disciples at this stage are still not identified as a select group. That the disciples are especially called to the spot seems to indicate that the contents of this speech are specifically meant for them, but there is no reason to surmise that the message was not also for the crowd. This sermon encapsulates the essence of the *basileia*. Then follow the deeds of the *basileia*, as foretold in the short section before Jesus' sermon (4: 23-25). These deeds are revealed one after another, and their order forms the following structure:

Cure of a man with skin-disease 8:1-4
Cure of the centurion's servant 8: 5-13
Cure of Peter's mother-in-law 8:14-15

---

[1] Who really composed the audience of Jesus' sermon has led to different opinions which in turn imply various solutions concerning the meaning of the whole speech. In the beginning, he calls the disciples to him; this remark has led to assumptions that the teaching is for the disciples only, involving community ethics and such. In the end; however, in 7: 28 the crowd is present and is astonished at Jesus' teachings. It is also plausible to interpret the beginning in a more inclusive way, since the expression does not include the idea of dismissing the crowds. So Luz 1989, 224.

A number of cures 8:16-17
Unconditional commitment 8:18-22

The calming of the storm 8:23-27
The demoniacs of Gadara 8:28-34
Cure of a paralytic 9:1-8

The call of Matthew 9:9-13
A discussion on fasting 9:14-17

**Cure of the woman with a haemorrhage/
The ruler's daughter raised to life 9:18-26[1]**
Cure of two blind men 9:27-31
Cure of a dumb demoniac 9:32-34

Three groups of miracles, each containing three miraculous episodes, are separated from one another. Between the first two triads, there is a short announcement that Jesus also healed many other people, as well as two references to people who want to follow Jesus and are faced with the demand of unconditional commitment.[2] All the beneficiaries of a healing or a dialogue with Jesus are individuals selected from the multitude of people around him. Different degrees of connectedness illuminate variations in the manifestations of the dialogue. Each incident is different. In the second break, there is the calling of the fifth disciple, Matthew, in as stark and simple an episode as that of the first four, and a teaching about new and old wine and wineskins. All the happenings are definitely something new, and the reader is made to understand that the old will never equal the new. Following Jesus is a commitment, and this commitment will break the old traditions. The reader is made aware that the miracles are not an end in themselves, but point to a new reality.

---

[1] This episode contains two healings. It will be understood here as a unity, since the two stories are already interwoven in Mark.
[2] Wainwright 1991, 82-83 emphasises the interpretative meaning of these 'buffer pericopes' between the triads. The liberating nature of the *basileia* is connected to the break with the patriarchal household structures.

B. The Narrative

Amongst these beneficiaries are three women. From the reader's point of view, it is no surprise that people like the leper and the centurion come to ask for help, because s/he already knows about the healings Jesus has done. Both address Jesus with the word κύριε, which indicates Jesus' divine authority. However, the story of Peter's mother-in-law is different. When Jesus comes to Peter's house, the woman is lying in bed.[1] No one asks anything on her behalf. Jesus just finds her, and cures her by his touch. No faith is required beforehand either, as in the case of the servant. After that the woman gets up[2] and serves him. The manner of this serving has been dissected[3] but nothing in the story indicates that it is anything other than ordinary domestic hospitality.

As for the setting, the leper and the centurion approached Jesus outdoors, the leper on the road to Capernaum, the centurion in Capernaum right after Jesus had arrived. In contrast to these, the third healing happens in a house in Capernaum. The house belongs to Peter, a friend of Jesus, who, from the reader's point of view, is a prominent person. This healing is also different, in that the intimacy between friends may not require a request for help. The reader knows that Jesus is the Son of God with divine authority, and so it is only natural for the reader that the woman serves Jesus. The unity of these healings informs the reader that Jesus is for everyone, including a leper who is a Jew, and whom Jesus orders to go to a priest according to the Law. Jesus does not abolish the law (cf. 5:17-18). He also cures the servant of a Gentile and the relative of his friend. He breaks no boundaries, but extends them.

All three episodes reveal a response to Jesus. First, the leper and the centurion ask Jesus for help. This already indicates confidence, at least,

---

[1] Scholars have made many suggestions about her illness. Hill 1972, 160 says that in the ancient world fever was considered as a disease itself, and not merely a symptom. Davies and Allison 1991, 34 speculate that she may have suffered from malaria. Kunkel 1987, 121 suggests in his psychological approach that she was angry with Jesus who made Peter leave his work, and therefore she became ill. When Jesus came to their house, she understood that Jesus really was a Master, and got up.

[2] The verb used here can mean both rising and being raised up by another. Wainwright 1991, 85 points to the link to the story in 9:18-26 where Jesus brings a girl back to life.

[3] The verb διακονεῖν has been discussed, as to pointing to the essence of discipleship as a special kind of ministry; in which case the imperfect form implies an ongoing nature of the service. See the feminist critique later.

in Jesus' ability to heal. Jesus heals the leper by touching him, then he orders him to go to the priest and make offerings. It is reasonable to assume that the man does so, even if this is not related. The dialogue between the centurion and Jesus is longer. Jesus is willing to go with the centurion, but the man insists that he does not need to come to the place where the servant is, if he just says the word that will heal the servant. What follows is important. Jesus is astonished. The man is not a Jew but he shows more faith than the Jews. Here Jesus says that the kingdom is meant for the Jews, but they do not accept it. The statement sounds outrageous. The Jews are the υἱοὶ τῆς βασιλείας, the legal heirs, but in their stead, Gentiles will enter the *basileia*. However, the point is softened, since the reader already knows of several positive reactions by Jewish people, including the four fishermen and the leper. Jesus himself is a Jew and his ministry is accomplished mainly among Jewish followers. 'The Jews' points to an ideological antagonism. Faith is also expected from the heirs. Matthew has taken this episode from Mark (1:29-31) and abbreviated it, as he usually does with Mark's narrative material.[1] The essence of the episode does not change. Matthew has only omitted the explanatory details. In Mark, Jesus is accompanied by James and John as he enters the house of Simon and Andrew, while Matthew mentions only the house of Peter. A possible interpretation is that Jesus enters the house alone.[2] In Mark, people tell Jesus about Peter's mother-in-law, while in Matthew, the initiative is totally with Jesus. There is no dialogue at all in the whole story. No one speaks, neither Jesus nor the woman. The act of healing is also different in Matthew as compared to Mark. Matthew says that Jesus touched[3] her hand (ἥψατο τῆς χειρὸς αὐτῆς), instead of Mark's 'Jesus took hold of her hand, raising her up' (ἤγειρεν αὐτὴν κρατήσας τῆς χειρός).

---

[1] Held 1961, 159-160. Theissen 1983, 175 uses the expression 'compression' to describe all shortened reproductions. For Hill 1972, 160 this may be evidence of "a Christian 'rabbinic' mind in action, making a narrative easily remembered for the community".

[2] Theissen 1983, 177-179 states that in Matthew, the character field is generally reduced compared to Mark and Luke. By this redaction, Matthew already makes Jesus appear as the exalted Lord. That the omission of disciples shifts the focus on Jesus as the healer, see also Beare 1981, 210 and Held 1961, 160.

[3] For touching in the healing stories in general, see Theissen 1983, 62-63.

The object of the woman's serving has also been changed from Mark's αὐτοῖς to αὐτῷ.[1] Matthew's intention is to focus all attention on Jesus, who is the centre of the stories.[2]

Attention has also been drawn to the chiastic structure Matthew has created as he has rewritten the Markan story by associating three verbs with Jesus and three verbs with the woman and her healing. Jesus comes, sees and touches, the fever leaves, the woman rises and serves.[3] Another way of building the chiasm is to centre it on Jesus touching the woman's hand. Before that, Jesus sees that the woman is lying sick and in fever. After the fever left, she rose and served.[4]

In any case, the result is that Matthew's redaction has altered the story so as to focus on Jesus. The woman is remembered only because of the male relative who, next to Jesus, is the most often mentioned character in Matthew's narrative. Technically, this is more a Peter story than a woman story, but most of all, it is a Jesus story.[5]

C. Feminist Critique and Construct

Feminist critiques have justly accused this pericope of androcentrism. Jesus is the central figure who performs the miracle and who is the object of the serving. The response of the woman is service, and the narrative limits the service to Jesus only. Wainwright sees here a break in the narrative pattern because of Jesus' initiative. Normally the person, or someone on his behalf, approaches Jesus. The cause for the break or the difference is not the woman, but Peter. Peter is the cause for the story.[6] In fact, the whole setting is hierarchical. Peter is the follower of Jesus,

---

[1] Cf Luke 4:38 who also omits Andrew, James and John, but retains their telling Jesus about her, and the object of serving as plural.

[2] So also Held 1961, 159-160; Davies and Allison 1991,32; Gundry 1982, 148-149 Hagner 1993, 208 sees in the third person singular as object a christological aspect. For Schweizer 1981, 140 this "unterstreicht den Gedanken der Nachfolge. Alles Handeln und Leben soll auf Jesus allein aufgerichtet sein".For Senior 1998, 99-100 this coupled with the verb διακονεῖν implies an attitude of "reverent homage" which is more than usual hospitality.

[3] Davies and Allison 1991, 32.

[4] Hagner 1993, 209; Luz 1990, 17.

[5] Against this Nau 1992, 72, because Peter is present in name only.

[6] Wainwright 1991, 84.

and the mother is Peter's dependent, as she is living in Peter's house. Even if Peter (possibly) is not even present in this story, his name is mentioned, the woman without her own name is defined through him.

On the other hand, feminist construct has defined the woman as the central character, not Jesus. The story is about how Simon Peter's mother-in-law entered Jesus' service. The connection with the name of the town, Capernaum, makes the story serve as a reflection of the beginning of the community and therefore, the community's origin is connected with a woman.[1] We can assume that the woman was one of Jesus' followers, as she was living in a house that presumably was the centre of Jesus' activities[2], and was a relative of one of the inner circle adherents. But connecting the origin of a community with her is purely hypothetical, and not deductible from Matthew's narrative.

The woman is described externally as are the men healed before her; the single element that is crucial is the faith in Jesus. None of them has a name. In the first two incidents their faith is expressed in the form of a plea before the healing. In the woman's case, it is implied in her service afterwards. The point seems to be that it does not matter if one is a Jew, a Gentile or a woman; the criteria of the *basileia* are not dependent on ethnical or gender qualifications.[3]

A more profound question is the interpretation of the verb διακονεῖν here and in the Gospel of Matthew (and Mark) in general. In feminist approaches, there are again two opinions. It has been claimed to be a verb connected to a service that is more than concrete support, and is a fundamental part of discipleship.[4] This view has been opposed by the

---

[1] Fander 1994, 210-211. See also Wainwright 1995, 649 who sees in 'a house' a metaphor for the Matthean community and therefore 'the serving' also gets a symbolic meaning.

[2] For the archeological findings concerning Peter's house, see, e.g Davies and Allison 1991, 33.

[3] Wainwright 1991, 84 sees the first three healings as connected to three marginalised groups, namely the socially and religiously unclean, the Gentiles, and women. Here, being a woman does not here prove marginality as such; more likely Matthew may have wanted to underline the difference between the supplicants. The work of Jesus was not limited to any one group, nor was anyone left out. The role of these three supplicants as examples is seen by Held 1961, 241 and Melzer-Keller 1997, 109.

[4] Dines 1993, 438-442; Schüssler Fiorenza 1983, 320; Tolbert 1992, 267.Wainwright 1991, 86-87, 141 sees that Matthew's διακονεῖν functions on two levels: the literal level refers to the physical needs, the symbolic level to service in the new religious

view that the service Matthew has in mind here is a concrete one (based on verse 25:44). The mother-in-law served Jesus as a guest, fulfilling the traditional role of a woman.[1] A middle view would not emphasise the act of serving too much, as in this story, it indicates that the woman was healed.[2]

Matthew uses the verb διακονεῖν five times, four of which are the same as Mark's. The first one is in the account of the temptation in the wilderness where, as in Mark, 'angels came and served (διηκόνουν) him' (4:11). Angels serving could be interpreted as something out of the ordinary. On the other hand, the context could imply the service to mean concrete food and drink as Jesus had been fasting. The second occurrence is in this episode when Peter's mother-in-law served (διηκόνει) Jesus after being cured. This differs from Mark by the use of the third person singular pronoun as the object of the serving. The woman is serving Jesus, not 'them', i.e. Jesus and the disciples. The third reference which Matthew has taken from Mark involves Jesus' own words regarding Zebedee's sons and their mother who made requests on their behalf. Jesus teaches the twelve that 'among you, whoever wants to be great must be

---

community. Corley 1993, 173 points to Matt. 25:31-46 and argues that all Christian ministry (διακονία) is directed to Jesus. Also Struthers Malbon 1983, 35 sees in Mark's version a female diaconate and a house church scene. Kinukawa 1994, 103 points out that the imperfect tense for the verb in Mark renders the service as lasting, not momentary. Seim 1994,58-77 has thoroughly discussed the meaning of διακονεῖν in Luke. – Depiction of discipleship here is not only a feminist view. So also Hagner 1993, 209 who does not make any deductions regarding gender here.

[1] Dewey 1994, 126, according to whom the narrative upholds the dominant cultural values. Melzer-Keller 1997, 110-111: Her reasoning for this raises an interesting question of the possible difference between Mark and Matthew, and if it is intentional or not, as the only difference is the verse Matt 25:44. Other occurrences of the verb are the same in both Gospels. - In many non-feminist publications as well, the service is rendered as normal table service without really discussing other alternatives. So Davies and Allison 1991,35; Hill 1972, 160. Witherington III 1991, 67-68 is of the opinion that the service means normal domestic work, but he points out that according to some rabbis, women were not allowed to serve meals to men. So in this sense the woman would have been violating the conventions (in the Markan version, also the Sabbath rules). This is opposed by Corley 1993, 88 who notes that these kinds of views are from sources from the third or fourth centuries.

[2] Witherington III 1991, 66; Corley 1993, 88. Corley discusses in her book both the Markan and the Lukan version of the episode separately, but not the Matthean. Seim 1994, 62 draws the same conclusion from Luke's version of the story (4:38-39).

your servant and whoever wants to be first must be the slave of all – just as the Son of Man did not come to be served (διακονηθῆναι), but to serve (διακονῆσαι) and to give his life as a ransom for many' (20:26-28).[1] The fourth reference from Mark is in the passion narrative. There are women at the cross who had followed Jesus from Galilee and had served (διακονοῦσαι) him (27:56). The following and serving have been interpreted as references to discipleship. The verse peculiar to Matthew is verse 25:44 where the verb, in the context of the last judgement, is connected to concrete service with food and drink and clothes, and taking a person into one's house. 'Lord, when was it that we saw you hungry or thirsty, or a stranger, or naked or sick, or in prison, and did not take care of you (οὐ διακονήσαμεν σοι)?'

In Mark, the four contexts of the verb have been interpreted as referring to service that is something more than the usual domestic arrangements. Wainwright has come to the same conclusion in Matthew.[2] No doubt, Jesus sets himself as an example in serving, and the serving of the angels could be interpreted as worshipping. In my opinion, however, there is no need to think that the service of Peter's mother-in-law here means anything more than the practical concrete matters associated with the service of the women who accompanied Jesus from Galilee. *This does not exclude the idea that serving is something essential in the true following of Jesus, but the serving itself is connected to ordinary, everyday arrangements.* The word used is not definitive, but the meaning is. This is also evident in verse 25:44 in the context of the last judgement: Following Jesus means serving the poor and the helpless concretely.

One of the characteristics of the *basileia* is serving and this woman, Peter's mother-in-law, as one of Jesus' followers fulfils this trait even though the narrative is very scarce in details.

---

[1] For difficulties with this (referred to as in Mark) see the thorough discussion in Collins 1990, 248-252.
[2] On the contrary Anderson 1983, 19.

4.3.2. The Haemorrhaging Woman/The Ruler's Daughter

A. The Context

The summary that follows (8:16-17) moves the focus even closer to the healing ministry of Jesus. He drove out devils and cured people of sicknesses. All this is brought forth in the Scriptures: The new concepts that are breaking through have been foretold. The word that is used for the healing that Jesus did is θεραπεύω (8:7,16). It means 'to heal', but also 'to serve'. Social science emphasises the difference between cultures in understanding health, sickness, and healing. In the Mediterranean culture health involves a state of complete well-being rather than activity or restoration of activity. Being is more important than doing, collateral relationships are more important than individualism, and the present comes before the future. Sickness would thus be a state of being, and not an inability to function.[1] Jesus served these people by restoring their completeness of being. Social science also emphasises the effect that a disease has on others, the family and the community. From this perspective, disease can be seen as something that threatens the community's integrity, and thus the diseased person must be secluded from the social, cultural, and religious environment.[2] Therefore, healing means not only the cure of the body, but a re-inclusion in the community.

In the narrative of the Gospel, we first examine the context of the section involving miracles (Chs. 8-9). Just before the miracles, there is a lengthy, authoritative speech in the form of a monologue addressed to the crowd, the centre of which is the *basileia*. In the contrast to this, the miraculous episodes that follow are dialogues or interactions. They are stories and episodes demonstrating how the *basileia* becomes tangible. Afterwards, Jesus sends his disciples to do the same – to proclaim and to heal (10:1-15). They, in turn, make the *basileia* tangible. From the perspective of narrative, the most important aspect is the interaction among the characters. It is in this way that the reader is informed about the responses of the characters to Jesus. The women who appear in Chapters 8-9 are connected through the miracle stories.

---

[1] Pilch 1992, 26-33.
[2] Pilch 1981, 108-113.

Developing Gerd Theissen's theory[1], Antoinette Clark Wire has examined the functions of the miracle stories within an oral tradition, i.e. as individual narratives derived from oral storytelling. She has suggested that all gospel miracle stories can be divided into four categories according to the interactions that generate a miracle story: the exorcism, the exposé, the provision and the demand. According to her, miracle stories represent a breakthrough in a struggle against oppressive restrictions on human life. *In the exorcism*, the interaction is the struggle between the healer and demonic forces, and it proclaims a triumph over uncontrollable, direct evil. None of the healings of females in Matthew, nor in other synoptic gospels, belongs to this category. *The exposé story* is based on interaction or controversy between Jesus and the religious authorities; and the miracle breaks the law's restrictions. The person who is healed is usually a passive object. *In provision stories,* the context often involves the hunger and oppression that result from individuals having lost their ability to provide for themselves. The person or group does not expect or demand any miracle. *The demand stories* of the fourth group involve a demand addressed to a miracle worker. Wire underlines the active role of the recipient from the beginning in this fourth category. According to Wire, the teller of this type of narrative challenges the hearer to break out of a closed world and to demand a miracle in human life. "The teller seeks to draw the hearers into a demanding stance".[2] The idea in demand stories is that the focus is as much on the persons who are being healed as on Jesus; and thus, their point of view is also discernible. In the present Matthean context, the miracles concerning women are demand stories.[3]

The three miracles in the centre triad – the calming of the storm, the healing of the demoniacs in Gadara, and the paralytic (Mt 8:23-9:8) – all underline Jesus' authority in that he is addressed as κύριε or υἱὲ τοῦ θεοῦ. The latter words are uttered by men possessed by demons who acknowledge the authority of Jesus as the Son of God. People who witness these events become frightened of Jesus and react by asking Jesus

---

[1] Theissen 1983, 43-46.
[2] Wire 1978, 83-113.
[3] The exception is, as also Wire 1978, 100, also points out, the cure of Peter's mother-in-law. There is no demand made, and the reason for telling this story is likely to be the connection to Peter, not the healing itself.

to leave the area. The later healing of the paralytic happens inside a house where Jesus grants him the forgiveness of his sins, and refers to himself as υἱὸς τοῦ ἀνθρώπου. Here again, the people who see it are frightened; but their reaction is praise. Faced with two kinds of responses to the miracles, the reader must personally choose how to react.

The calming of the storm expresses a theme in contrast to the healings. Whereas the healed ones approached Jesus in faith and confidence, disciples are reproached for having little faith. Though they have experienced Jesus' authority, they still do not understand. Being a disciple means more than just following along in the wake of Jesus' startling actions. They must not only obey him, but also trust and believe in his ability to help.[1] This is exactly what the faith of the supplicants is about.

After his manifestation of power, Jesus calls upon Matthew, the fifth disciple, to follow him (Mt 9:9-13). Not content with astonishing the crowds, healing physically and spiritually, Jesus eats with sinners drawing condemnation from the Jewish leaders. Jesus proclaims that the *basileia* is not for healthy people, but primarily for the sick. The new wine is not meant for the old skins. The age of the new, the *basileia* has dawned.

B. The Narrative

The third triad of miracle stories (Mt 9:18-34) is linked to Jesus' teaching. The first episode actually contains two healings. The story of the healing of a woman with a haemorrhage is placed within the framework of the story of the ruler's daughter; and therefore, it is taken as one episode with two healings rather than two episodes.[2] It is reasonable to assume that the frame provides keys for understanding the story contained within. At the beginning, a ruler – a person of authority – comes to Jesus. He is merely a ruler, and he is not identified by a name. He kneels before Jesus, acknowledging Jesus' authority, not an act that accords with cultural expectations. Though a man of authority himself, he accepts the authority

---

[1] So also Edwards 1997, 30-31
[2] This structure originates from Mark, so Matthew has preserved the connection.

of an itinerant healer as greater than his own,[1] again highlighting the element of faith. Jesus is the centre. The request the ruler makes asking Jesus to bring his dead daughter back to life, is quite extraordinary. The question is not about healing; here the request exceeds any expectation associated with ordinary life. He asks Jesus to do the impossible. Jesus does not answer, but follows the ruler.

They are still on the road when a woman approaches the group from the rear[2]. She is very much the opposite of the ruler. She is out alone, without any connections to her family. She has no name; she is identified by a chronic haemorrhage, lasting twelve years. The length of the illness underlines the woman's distress and faith. She is convinced that by merely touching Jesus' garment she will be well. She makes no request, but secretly comes from behind in order to touch Jesus. When he turns and notes what happens, he simply confirms the healing. Her faith has been the indispensable element for the healing.[3]

The two stories are strongly contrasting. The ruler comes openly and states his request; the woman comes secretly from behind, and her aim is revealed only by her inner thoughts. The male represents the open, public sphere; the female the inferior status of the subordinated in the society. In the ancient patriarchal society, women belonged to men: to husband, or father. It was customary for the ruler to ask for his daughter; but the woman would have needed a man to ask for her. Jesus' response to both is the same. He addresses the woman as θύγατερ, which is an affirmative expression. It may be an even more penetrating term, since being a daughter means belonging to a family. Later, in verse 12:50, Matthew depicts Jesus defining his family as those who do the will of his heavenly Father. This redefinition of family includes this woman as a member of the *basileia*.

Then the narrative returns to the frame story about the ruler and the daughter. Jesus arrives at the house of the ruler and encounters the flute players and professional mourners. These are people who do not have faith, and they laugh at Jesus. The setting is public, but Jesus makes it

---

[1] See Dewey 1994, 126.

[2] The crowd is not present in Matthew's story, but the woman approaches Jesus, the disciples, and the ruler.

[3] Edwards 1997, 74 notices the presence of faith in the healings, but claims that it does not actually cause the healing.

private by asking people to go out of the house. He takes the girl's hand,
and the girl rises.

In neither story is anything added about what happens afterwards.
Does the woman join the itinerant group that followed Jesus? How did
the man of authority respond to Jesus? The reader has to fill these gaps
her/himself. The narrative follows Jesus. His fame is spreading far and
wide and people seek him out for help. Two blind men follow him and
shout ἐλέησον ἡμᾶς υἱὸς Δαυίδ. Jesus' authority is again on the lips of
needy people. The element of faith in the healing process is markedly
underlined by Jesus' question, as to whether they believe that he can heal
them. Their affirmative answer again contains the authoritative κύριε.
Jesus touches their eyes and says their plea is answered because they
believe. Their faith is again the cause of the healing, but once more,
nothing is said about what happens to them. Jesus warns them not to tell
anybody, but the news spreads everywhere. One more healing follows,
that of a mute man who was also possessed by a demon. The demon is
driven out, and the man starts to talk Those who brought the man to Jesus
have faith, but the mute man himself has expressed no sign of faith.
Opposite reactions are expressed by the astonishment of the crowd and
the cynicism by the Pharisees. Each, in its way, underscores the
uniqueness of Jesus' deeds. The unity of the deeds of the *basileia* is
summarized by saying that Jesus travelled extensively, taught in
synagogues, proclaimed the *basileia* and healed people.

The element of faith is central. The man of authority, and an
unknown woman, are juxtaposed in the narrative. By their need, and their
unshakable faith that contact with Jesus can fulfill this need, coupling the
requests of the two supplicants show that neither gender nor position in
the societal or religious hierarchy are relevant from the point of view of
the *basileia*. However, gender differences surface in the means the
supplicants use. A man can approach Jesus as man to man, openly,
publicly, but a woman in a patriarchal society is forced to resort to
indirect means to bring about the miracle.

Comparison to Mark again reveals Matthew's noticeable
abbreviation. All details are omitted, only the essentials are left.[1] The
ruler himself is diminished by omitting his name, which in Mark is Jairos,

---

[1] For a detailed demonstration see e.g. Hagner 1993, 246-247.

and by defining him as ἄρχων instead of Mark's ἀρχισυναγώγων.[1] An important difference is that in Matthew the girl is already dead while in Mark she is only dying when the father makes his request. In addition, the christological κύριε is missing in Matthew's account altogether. The disciples and the crowd are not present in the ruler's house in Matthew as in Mark, nor is the family mentioned. Jesus again occupies the centre of the stage. As for the story of the woman, Matthew has pruned the Markan presentation so thoroughly that only the woman's action and her thoughts have remained. These are the elements through which her faith is known.[2] And as there is no crowd present, her approach is much more apparent. What is new, is the addition of τοῦ κρασπέδου as the place where she touched.

Matthew's redaction reveals many of his intentions[3]. By changing the situation concerning the ruler's daughter (in Mark, she is merely sick; in Matthew she is already dead) Matthew shifts the emphasis to the faith of the father. As for the haemorrhaging woman, Matthew has omitted the Markan material that described the woman's despair (she had searched for help in vain and had spent all her possessions on physicians). In Matthew, the healing happens because of her faith, as she touches the fringe of Jesus' cloak; in Mark, she is healed through the δύναμις of Jesus. Matthew's story ends with Jesus' word: Your faith has healed you. Matthew seems to be constantly centring Jesus in every story. He not only has the power to heal, he is also able to raise the dead. Melzer-Keller interprets these Matthean changes as proof that Matthew places more value on the ruler and his faith, than on the woman. While in Mark, as she says, the woman was the model of faith for the ruler, here the ruler is the model of faith for the woman. The woman "wird nun mehr zu einer Bittstellerin, die auf Jesu erbarmen hofft und seiner Bestärkung bedarf".[4]

---

[1] Cf. Luke's ἄρχων τῆς συναγωγῆς. ἄρχων is a more general term for different officials. Gundry 1982, 172 reasons the change with the opinion that Matthew cannot associate this man with the synagogue anymore, because it has become 'their' synagogue, that of the Pharisees. Cf. 4:23; 9:35; 10:17; 12:9; 13:54. So also Luz 1990, 50, 52 who also says that what is meant is the leading position in general. There is no doubt, though, that the man is Jewish.

[2] So Held 1961, 169.

[3] Held 1961, 155-158.

[4] Melzer-Keller 1997, 115.

It is true that Matthew has abbreviated the story of the haemorrhaging woman and left only the essentials, but there is no need to set these two supplicants in opposition, rather, they complement each other. Matthew has wanted to emphasise their faith as essential to both the healings, and not weigh their faith against each other.

C. Feminist Critique and Construct

These miracles concerning women raise a plethora of questions. The haemorrhaging woman as ill, and the girl as dead, are often considered a source of pollution. It is interesting to note how often this particular issue is raised when discussing these women in Matthew (and Mark) both in feminist literature and in mainstream exegesis.[1] The feminist readings underline the idea of considering menstruation, relating to the story of the haemorrhaging woman.[2] a problem of pollution. The questions asked focus on whether Jesus did or did not oppose the purity legislation here, and whether it can be interpreted that Jesus solves the problem by breaking the boundaries between clean and unclean.[3] He had already done

---

[1] Hagner 1993, 248; Albright and Mann 1984, 111; Gundry 1982, 173. So also Witherington III 1991, 67, for whom the theme of the story is Jesus' concern for the women, and his willingness to violate standing rules regarding the uncleanliness of a sick person. Also Theissen 1983, 134, in any case considers the touch of a menstruating woman as harmful. Davies and Allison 1991, 128, refer to other Jewish texts which involve restrictions for menstruating women, e.g. the Mishnaic tractate Nidda which might well have been known in Matthew's environment.

[2] Wainwright 1991, 87-88, 92,94; eadem 1995, 637; Anderson 1983,11; Selvidge 1984, 619-623; Dewey 1994, 126-127; Ricci 1994, 99; Levine 1992, 256-257, on the contrary though Levine 1996, 381-386. Kinukawa 1994, 35-36, as in considering the Markan version of the story, states that "the woman is discriminated against, degraded, and dehumanized. She is a taboo to all, because of her physical otherness." (37) Wainwright 1991, 199 ponders even more between the lines: "It is clear that this debars the woman not only from participation in the religious community, but from normal human social relations and especially from sexual relations with her husband. *Her unavailability for sexual intercourse or fertility could well have produced a divorce and would certainly have prevented her from remarrying.*" (italics mine). The text gives no clue as to the identity of the woman, nor her marital arrangements.

[3] For Kinukawa 1994, 46-47 Jesus negates the purity laws by ignoring them. But it is the woman who really challenges the boundaries and helps Jesus to become "truly a saviour".

this with regard to Peter's mother-in-law. For example, Wainwright claims that this mother-in-law is a possible pollutant, since ritual uncleanness might have been connected with her menstruation.[1] She also insists that by touching the woman, Jesus breaks the boundaries defining the clean and the unclean.[2] The story about the ruler's daughter is also treated as a case of uncleanliness. Lev 15:31 teaches that a corpse is unclean. So when the father asks Jesus to touch the girl, he really asks Jesus to defile himself.[3]

Instead of the purity laws as the focus of these two stories, Levine offers other interpretations as 'healthy readings'. She compares the idea of 'following' as characterization of the discipleship[4] to the fact that here, the same verb is associated with Jesus who follows the ruler.[5] Jesus thereby sets up a model for 'following'. Levine points here to the verb ἀκολουθεῖν, which has been connected to discipleship. In this pericope, it is Jesus who 'follows' the ruler. Levine finds the ruler an exemplar of both discipleship and church leadership. The ruler is an appropriate example for members of Matthew's community to imitate. "Jesus already provides the model for the disciples in terms of healing, teaching, and suffering; he may here provide the model for following, which is something 'leaders' in the Matthean community must also do."[6] Levine also compares the ruler with the centurion in Chapter 8. Both these men have positions of authority, both of them are unable to achieve what they most want, both of them implore Jesus to help a younger and weaker person, and both of them get a positive response. Therefore, Levine argues that these two men present a proper model for authority: a leader "must be humble, must recognize the limitations of earthly authority, must make the effort to seek the sacred, must appeal on behalf of the

---

[1] Wainwright 1991, 84; eadem. 1995, 648.
[2] Wainwright 1995, 648.
[3] Wainwright 1991, 87.Wainwright also suggests that the father's request is unusual because the child is a daughter, not a son and an heir.
[4] See pages 102-103 for more details.
[5] Verse 19 as a whole is considered redactional, which makes it appear that Matthew has wanted to connect this verb to Jesus. See Davies and Allison 1991, 127.
[6] Levine 1996, 394. Gundry 1982, 173 denies any such connotations. Kingsbury 1978, 58 is of the opinion that if Matthew had used the verb consistently in a metaphorical meaning, he would not have used it here to describe Jesus following the ruler, which would make Jesus the disciple of the ruler.

others".[1] Furthermore, Levine contrasts the Gentile centurion with the Gentile Pilate and his soldiers, and the Jewish ruler with Herod the Great and Herod Antipas.[2]

The second focus in Levine's interpretation is the view that "the bodies of women serve as figurations of Jesus' own body as it hangs on the cross and rises from the tomb"[3]. Women's suffering is a model for the suffering of the Christ, and women's healings are the models for the resurrection of the Christ.[4] As Matthew altered the story so that the girl was not merely sick but dead (cf. Mark 5:23), he may have been anticipating the resurrection. The two situations differ because although the girl is brought back to life, she will die again at the end of her life. Jesus' resurrection is something quite different, as he was not brought back to his earthly life. Jesus' resurrection reveals his true identity to his followers and transcends his bodily presence first as an apparition and then as an invisible presence (cf. 28.16-20).

Nothing in the text itself gives explicit cause for speculations about purity laws and uncleanliness. Neither of the issues is mentioned.[5] All the characters involved are Jews, and no one violates Jewish practice. Jesus does not touch the bleeding woman; she touches him. Matthew does not locate the haemorrhage, and nothing in the story indicates that the bleeding is vaginal.[6] The woman could have an open sore on her leg, or breast or nose. She is ill, but not necessarily impure.[7] The text itself does not say anything about uncleanliness, neither in connection to the haemorrhage nor to the corpse. Still, some interpreters agree that the point of these narratives is that Jesus (and the Matthean community) opposed the cruel and inhuman Levitical purity legislation.[8] The problems of pollution also are the issue in pericopes about Peter's mother-in-law, the

---

[1] Levine 1996, 395.

[2] Levine 1996, 395-396.

[3] Levine 1996, 380, 397.

[4] Levine 1996, 396-397.

[5] Levine has quite vividly pointed out the weak points of this kind of thinking, which she calls 'bad exegesis'.

[6] For Davies and Allison 1991, 128 the question is *undoubtedly* of uterine haemorrhage. (italics mine), for Hagner 1993, 248 probably, but not necessarily.

[7] So also Levine 1996, 380, 394.

[8] E.g. Wainwright 1991, 200. See also Kinukawa 1994, 35-37 where she describes the humiliation that the purity laws caused women.

ruler's daughter (as a corpse), and in the later story about the Canaanite woman (due to her foreignness).

It would not seem logical to connect Matthew, who already has assured the reader that nothing in the Law will pass away (Matt 5:17-18), to an interpretation where he seems to abrogate the purity legislation. Even if we accept the social background of the purity regulations, and consider these two women as ritually unclean, the problem is not solved. The verses in Lev 15:19-33 include no prohibition for a menstruating woman to touch other people. Uncleanliness is a ritual state, not a disease. If we assume that the ancient reader in Matthew's environment was aware of the purity legislation, still another question evolve: was it followed by everyone. However, the point in the narrative is not in a controversy about Jewish tradition. Just before, in verse 8:4, Jesus had no trouble with the regulations, and he commanded the cleansed leper to follow the Law and show himself to the priest.

It would seem unreasonable to regard the purity regulations as inhuman or cruel. Questions of holiness and pollution/purity in the first century Judaism are complicated questions that have to be seen in the light of their socio-cultural background. Prohibitions were not the main issue, and many of the regulations concerning menstruation, child birth, and corpse uncleanliness, were connected with the temple and the sacrifices, thus regulating what had to be done in order to be able to enter the temple. The effect they had on ordinary life was much smaller than these interpretations have implied.[1] Matthew situates this story in Galilee, where the people were far away from the temple; and if the historical situation in Matthew's time is taken into account, there was no temple to go to.

Later theory introduces the separation of the body from the inner being of a person. Leviticus apparently considers the person an entity, thus holiness is in the person as a whole, body and inner being. Wouldn't this be what the healings really point to? Jesus heals the diseases, and frees the bodies from their ailments in order to make people whole. The body is not the issue, but the person as a whole, thus healing has a symbolic function in the narrative. Jesus treats all the people in these

---

[1] About the historical situation cf. Sanders 1985, 182-185. Uncleanliness was a ritual state which was something people were in most of the time, which was nothing to be ashamed of as such.

episodes equally respectfully, as individuals. Their own attitude is what counts. The dialogues that ensue, are initiated within the context of the supplicant. Changes resulting from their faith occur in their whole being.

In the context of the larger section of Chapters 8 and 9, there are a collection of healings, three of which happen to women. Two of these three women seem to be passive objects in the story. In the case of the ruler's daughter, the main character is the father. As for Peter's mother-in-law, the reason to repeat the story is Peter. So the only 'real' woman character left is the haemorrhaging woman. The common feature in most of the healing incidents is the supplicant's seeking Jesus' help and authority. Both this woman and men in other occasions initiate a change in their own lives.

The settings for the healings of women vary and form no pattern. Peter's mother-in-law and the ruler's daughter are healed in a house, the haemorrhaging woman outside on the road, and the Canaanite woman later approaches Jesus outside in the open, while her daughter, for whom she pleads, is probably in a house elsewhere.[1]

Levine's theory about the 'following' is connected to the proper use of authority; Jesus has given the model of proper following and proper authority himself by following the ruler. Levine's assertions about authority are reasonable, as the ruler (9: 18-26) and the centurion (8:5-13) are leaders who enter the *basileia*. The members of the *basileia* represent different ranks of the earthly hierarchy, but I see no need to go any further and assume that they are meant to be models for the leaders in Matthew's communities. The *basileia* is all-inclusive with no hierarchies, and as such, it serves as an example for the Matthean communities.

The word ἀκολούθειν is used differently in various contexts, both in Matthew and in other Gospels. The literal meaning of the word is 'following', 'going behind', but in ancient Greek it can also be understood as following in an intellectual or religious sense. In Matthew, the verb occurs 25 times[2] and it is clearly connected to following Jesus. This incident in which Matthew depicts Jesus following the ruler is the only place where it is used for Jesus.

---

[1] See also Pilch 1986, 104.

[2] Cf Mark 18 times, Luke 17 times and John 18 times. Outside the Gospels the occurrences are fewer: 4 times in Acts, once in 1 Corinthians, and 6 times in the Book of Revelation.

The verb is used when Jesus calls followers to his company, such as the two pairs of brothers (4:18-22), or Matthew (9:9). On the other hand, people who come to say that they would like to follow Jesus (the scribe in 8:19, or the rich man in 19:16-22), seem to turn away and not to become followers. In general, there is agreement among scholars that this verb is connected to the central substance of discipleship.[1] But it is used in other connections as well. On several occasions, the crowd is depicted as 'following' (4:25; 8:1; 12:15; 19:2; 20:29; 21:9) by using the same verb ἀκολούθειν. This has led to discussion as to whether the crowd are to be considered disciples.[2] I see no reason why the verb should always be interpreted in a metaphorical sense. As it also clearly has a common, everyday dimension, this is its primary sense. Matthew has used this verb to describe the responses of the disciples, but this does not necessarily mean that it is bound to the second definition everywhere in the Gospel of Matthew (or other Gospels).[3] Connecting the verb to women does not automatically make them disciples. I will come back to these questions when dealing with Peter and the disciples. It is sufficient here to conclude that not too much emphasis should be placed on individual words. 'Following' is an image clearly belonging to the *basileia*, but it is also a normal word referring to everyday life.

According to what has been stated here, there is no reason to assume anything more than the ordinary when Jesus goes with the ruler. In my opinion, what is more important is that the ruler is most likely a *Jewish* leader. Matthew has very forcefully underlined the conflict between Jesus and the Jewish leaders elsewhere in his narrative, so a strange truce seems to prevail here. Jesus heals both Jews and Gentiles; those in dialogue with the *basileia* are not categorised by ethnical boundaries.

---

[1] Held 1961, 190-192; Strecker 1971, 230-232; Hill 1972, 105, 161-162; Kingsbury 1978, 56-73; Schweizer 1981, 42-43; Thiemann 1973, 179-188; Corley 1993, 173; Wainwright 1991, 141, 296-297; eadem. 1995, 664; Schüssler Fiorenza 1983, 320.

[2] Luz 1989, 201 is of the opinion that "following on the part of the disciples does not distinguish them from the people who are sympathetic to Jesus, but the people, by following, belong together with the disciples". Kingsbury 1978, 61 opposes this view by taking the verb ἀκολούθειν as merely descriptive, having no connotations to discipleship.

[3] So also Kingsbury 1978, 58 who notes that Matthew employs the verb both in a literal and in a metaphorical sense. Anderson 1983, 19 follows Kingsbury.

Healing and suffering are not associated with women alone in the narrative. Jesus heals men and women, Jews and Gentiles. If Jesus' suffering is to be parallelled with that of the haemorrhaging woman, it should be parallelled as well with all the suffering bodies and people in the narrative, both men and women. Rather, the common denominator is a need expressed, an appeal for help, reaching out to Jesus' authority. In most cases the need is expressed in words. *Basileia* is embodied concretely in Jesus, and by turning to him, the supplicants enter into an extended reality. Ethnical considerations, or gender, or status in society do not erase any boundaries in these pericopes.[1]

4.3.3. The Canaanite Woman

A. The Context

The structure of the section is as follows:

Jesus feeds 5,000 men (14:13-21)
Jesus walks on the water with **Peter** (14:22-33)
Cures at Gennesaret (14:34-36)
    The traditions of the Pharisees (15:1-9)
    Teaching about clean and unclean (15:10-20)
    The daughter of the Canaanite woman healed (15:21-28)
Healings near the lake (15:29-31)
Jesus feeds 4,000 men (15:32-39)[2]
A sign of Jonah (16:1-4)
The yeast of the Pharisees and Sadducees (16:5-12)
Peter's profession of faith (16:13-20)

After manifesting the *basileia* through speech and deeds (chapters 6-9), Jesus sends his disciples to do the same (ch. 10). The twelve male

---

[1] So also Levine 1996, 396.
[2] Anderson has found a chiastic structure around the story of the Canaanite woman: two blind men (9:27-31), the sign of Jonah (12:38-42), the feeding of 5,000 (14:13-21), the Canaanite woman (15:21-28), the feeding of 4,000 (15:30-38), the sign of Jonah (16:1-4), two blind men (20:29-34) (Anderson 1994, 249-265 and 1983,14).

disciples are carefully identified by their names (10:2-4). Following that, the narrator starts to characterise Jesus by describing his teachings, his confrontations with the Jewish leaders, and still more healings that cause conflicts and amazement. Jesus turns away from his own relatives, since the qualifications of the *basileia* exclude biological family ties as the essence of the new family. The condition of entering into this new familial contact is doing the will of God (12:46-50). By parables, Jesus then illustrates the characteristics of the *basileia* (13).

A further contradictory element is seen when Jesus goes to his hometown and confronts rejection. His hometown people who do not understand the message (13:53-58) lack the prerequisite for miracles there. Here again, the reader is face to face with the qualification of faith, miracles need an environment of faith. Then Jesus feeds 5000 men[1] and an uncountable number of women and children with five loaves of bread and two fishes, walks on the water, and cures everyone.

The context for the next woman story is the conflict with the Pharisees over the washing of hands, followed by Jesus' teaching about purity: External purity regulations are not as important as the internal pollution that comes from the heart. The debate about dietary traditions is followed by the story of a Gentile woman.[2]

The setting of these two dialogues is different which underlines Matthew's purpose to have these pericopes linked together. The dialogue between Jesus and the woman takes place in a foreign, Gentile area, the region of Tyre and Sidon[3] where the woman, a Gentile, a Canaanite, addresses Jesus. From a Jewish point of view, she is considered ethnically, culturally, and religiously, a stranger.

The thread that runs through this section is bread.[4] Matthew skilfully uses the symbol of bread as a clue. Jesus feeds thousands of men and

---

[1] The same story is repeated in Matthew 15:32-39. Moreover, all the four evangelists include the story in their narrative, but Matthew is the only one who mentions that there were women and children present too, not only men. He too, as the three others, counts five thousand men, but he adds "not counting women and children" (14:21; 15:38).

[2] Anderson 1983, 11 suggests here an antithematical continuity.

[3] Matthew has added Sidon to the Markan "Tyre". Some commentators also see here the Matthean emphasis on the Gentile mission. As a First Testament phrase, 'Tyre and Sidon' marks the whole of the Gentile world. See e.g. Gundry 1982, 310.

[4] Wainwright 1991, 98 has pointed out that ἄρτος occurs fifteen times in the section 14:13-16:12, and in the rest of the Gospel, only six times.

uncounted numbers of women and children with bread – the story is told twice. In both of these feeding stories, men are counted, but there are women and children present too. Women have participated in the bread that was given to the crowd. Bread is also a metaphor in the dialogue between the Canaanite woman and Jesus. This positive image is set against the negative image of the yeast of the Pharisees and Sadducees.[1]

The story proceeds from the teachings of inner vs. external purity in the story of the Gentile woman, and the reader does not necessarily know what to expect. Jesus has already been presented as faithful to the Jewish tradition, even if reinterpreting it. When he sends his disciples on their mission, he warns them not to go among the Gentiles (10:5). On the other hand, Jesus has already cured a Gentile, the centurion's servant[2]. He has also encountered and cured a woman – the haemorrhaging woman – out in the open. The reader faces confusing messages. The Gentile woman contrasts and challenges the Jewish traditions which, on the other hand, are prioritised and appreciated.

B. The Narrative

The Canaanite woman is described without any relational bonds. She is given no name, nor identification through any male relative, father or husband. She is legitimated by no authority. Strangely, the one who needs healing, the daughter, who is 'tormented by a devil' is not present.[3] In the ancient world, demons or unclean spirits were considered personified forces with the power to control human behaviour which was classified as deviant in a dangerous sense, and resulted in exclusion from the community.[4] Though the story does not describe the girl nor her symptoms, the situation probably meant ostracisation for both the girl and her family. The outcome of the healing would have meant the re-inclusion of the whole family into the community.

---

[1] Senior 1998, 180 also points to the contrast between the woman and her faith, and the religious leaders in the preceding story who were considered hypocrites.

[2] Witherington III 1984, 63 and 168 n 87 considers the centurion as a God fearer.

[3] Gundry 1982, 311 is of the opinion that the woman seeks mercy for herself rather than healing for her daughter.

[4] Malina and Rohrbaugh, 1992, 79-80.

The structure of the story is a dialogue. Pairs of appeal and response follow each other:

22 ἐλέησον με, κύριε υἱὸς Δαυίδ......[1]
23 ὁ δὲ οὐκ ἀπεκρίθη αὐτῇ λόγον.......

23 ὁι μαθηταὶ .... λέγοντες· ἀπόλυσον αὐτήν......
24 ὁ δὲ ἀποκριθεὶς .....

25 ἡ δὲ ἐλθοῦσα ..... λέγουσα· κύριε, βοήθει μοι.......
26 ὁ δὲ ἀποκριθεὶς..........

27 ἡ δὲ εἶπεν· ναὶ κύριε ....
28 τότε ἀποκριθεὶς ὁ' Ἰησοῦς .....

The emphasis of the story lies in the interaction between the characters; the healing or exorcism as such is of secondary importance. The point of the story is not in the healing that is the outcome of the dialogue, but in the dialogue itself.[2] The woman addresses Jesus three times with the respectful title κύριε. The reader is not informed as to how she is aware of Jesus' ability to heal, nor how she identifies Jesus from the perspective of her own cultural and religious expectations. She does address Jesus as 'Son of David' (22b)[3], which is a Jewish title. As a

---

[1] This petition is the same as in 9:27: ἐλέησον ἡμᾶς, υἱὸς Δαυίδ by the two (Jewish) blind men. The same plea is also made in 20:30.
[2] The form critical analysis of the story has led to diverse interpretations. E.g. Bultmann 1972, 38, 63 sees this as an apophthegm but also a controversy dialogue of some sort and not a miracle story. See also Davies and Allison 1991, 541. Ringe 1985, 67 points to a problem with this view. The exchange between Jesus and the woman is a reversal to the pattern normally used in these stories. A hostile question usually comes from some bystander, and Jesus responds and has the final word. Here the situation is the opposite. It is Jesus who comes with the hostile question and is corrected. Held 1961, 155, 187-188 points to Matthew's tendency to extend the speech material, and especially sees this story as a dialogue in favour of the Gentile mission rather than a miracle story. Compared to the Markan story about the Syrophoenician woman, not only has Matthew extended the dialogue, but he has also abbreviated the outcome of the dialogue.
[3] The Markan version includes only one κύριε.

representative of a different ethnic and religious context, she acknowledges Jesus' authority using Jewish religious vocabulary. On the other hand, the title she gives Jesus, 'Son of David', has been used in the genealogy of Jesus. The title indicates to the reader that the woman understands who Jesus truly is. Jesus has entered Gentile territory[1], and is on foreign soil, the woman on her own. Still, the woman shows respect by using honorary titles from Jesus' own religion. The κύριε puts Jesus in the centre and raises the post-Easter christological thinking of the reader.[2]

This is one of the first and few times, that a woman speaks in her own voice in the Matthean narrative. In fact, she speaks three times, two

---

[1] This is what the text indicates. See also Gundry 1982, 310; Albright and Mann 1984, 187; Luz 1990, 433. Some scholars are, however, of the opinion that Jesus was still in a Jewish region. εἰς in the text would be translated 'towards'. Cf. Davies and Allison 1991, 546. Also Levine 1992, 259, in her commentary on Matthew, is of the opinion that the woman leaves her own land and meets Jesus on his ground and on his terms thus acknowledging "the priority of the Jews in the divine plan of salvation". Diverse opinions might be due to the Markan version where Jesus is going (ἀπῆλθεν εἰς) to Tyre. However, Matthew's expression, ἐξελθὼν εἰς, more clearly includes the idea of entering. Matthew also substitutes Mark's ὅρια Τύρου (towards the boundaries of Tyre?) with τὰ μέρη Τύρου. See also Wainwright 1991, 105 where she points out that from a reader's point of view, this is the second time that Jesus enters Gentile territory. The first was his escape from Herod in the infancy narrative.

[2] See Kingsbury 1975(2), for discussion about the use of the title *Kyrios* in Matthew. The title *kyrios* is found only in the mouth of disciples and believers, and thus this is one of the first and few times, that a woman speaks in her own voice in the Matthean narrative. In fact, she speaks three times, two petitions, one counter-argument to Jesus' refusal. Jesus' attitude seems oddly cold and hardhearted. First he answers nothing. Because the woman does not stop shouting, the disciples are embarrassed and ask Jesus to respond in some way. This time, Jesus answers by stating that his mission is for Israel only. It is not clear to whom Jesus' response is directed. He seems to answer the disciples, but his reply concerns the woman's plea. Considering what has been previously said in the narrative at this point the *basileia* here seems to be strangely limited, both ethnically and religiously. From a reader's point of view, Gentiles have been part of the narrative several times already: Jesus heals the centurion's servant, as well as the two Gadarenes possessed by demons. Now, a woman from a different race and culture can not be included. But the woman comes and prostrates herself before him – an act of submission (cf. the ruler in 9:18) – and once again asks for help. The word κύριε is again on her lips. The answer Jesus gives belittles the woman, counting her characterizes the acknowledgement of Jesus' divine authority. The christological overtones are also assumed in the purely conventional use of the title (255).

petitions, one counter-argument to Jesus' refusal. Jesus' attitude seems oddly cold and hardhearted.[1] First he answers nothing. Because the woman does not stop shouting, the disciples are embarrassed and ask Jesus to respond in some way. This time, Jesus answers by stating that his mission is for Israel only. It is not clear to whom Jesus' response is directed. He seems to answer the disciples[2], but his reply concerns the woman's plea[3]. Considering what has been previously said in the narrative at this point the *basileia* here seems to be strangely limited, both ethnically and religiously. From a reader's point of view, Gentiles have been part of the narrative several times already: Jesus heals the centurion's servant, as well as the two Gadarenes possessed by demons. Now, a woman from a different race and culture can not be included. But the woman comes and prostrates herself before him – an act of submission (cf. the ruler in 9:18) – and once again asks for help. The word κύριε is again on her lips. The answer Jesus gives belittles the woman, counting her among the dogs – the Jews are children entitled to table fellowship, while the Gentiles are dogs that are excluded. Jesus' answer contains an either-or aspect – take from some and give to others – again something different from what is implied in the miracle stories, which extend the boundaries to include everyone, both Jews and Gentiles. The woman does not get angry, nor does she deny Jesus' argument. Her submissive role is not even shaken. She adopts Jesus' language and uses it favourably with regard to her own status. She accepts the ethnic identification; but reminds Jesus that the 'bread of the *basileia*' belongs to 'dogs' also. The whole situation is reversed. The understanding of the *basileia* is expounded from the mouth of a Gentile woman, 'a dog' from a Jewish perspective. This degrading designation has caused embarrassment among some scholars who reduce the abuse by translating

---

[1] Wire 1978, 103 has pointed out that the difficulty is more dramatic when the healer himself becomes the obstacle.

[2] Thus Held 1961, 187 ; Witherington III, 1991, 65; Gundry 1982, 312; Filson 1967, 180.

[3] Theissen 1982, 182 does not choose between the alternatives, but acknowledges the difficulty. Jesus answers the disciples, but his answer is for the woman.

the word as 'puppies' (cf. κυνάρια).[1] This does not alter the meaning of the dialogue. The words of Jesus are a warning not to entrust the *basileia* to the Gentiles; thus the social tension remains, whether the term 'dogs' is taken to mean pets or enemies.

The story includes several contrasting aspects. First, the antagonists are a Jew and a Gentile, of different both ethnic and religious background,[2] and there seems to be no conversion involved. The woman accepts the division between Jew and Gentile.[3] There is a also the difference of man and woman – a biological difference which points to social differences. The woman sustains her submissive role the whole time, and gender roles are not violated. However, the social order remains unbalanced between the genders.[4] What then is the core meaning of this story? Is it that the dialogue between the foreign woman and Jesus makes Jesus see things differently?[5] Is he challenged by the woman's faith to transform his attitude, to think again?[6] Jesus remains the centre of the

---

[1] From a Jewish point of view, dogs and swine were unclean animals and could thus be compared with Gentiles. This view has been softened by taking this to mean house dogs. Housedogs are not despised and the comparison between children and dogs becomes more understandable. So e.g. Luz 1990, 435; Ringe 1985, 68.

[2] According to Witherington III 1984, 64 the change Matthew has made from Mark's Syrophoenician to a Canaanite, points to a religious emphasis. Mark stresses the political and national identity, whereas Matthew refers to her religious affiliation.

[3] That Matthew's point in this story is to authorise a Gentile mission to his Jewish audience (e.g. Held, 1961, 189) is a possible explanation. On the other hand, this is not the only incident where there are Gentiles present in the narrative; and also, the woman involved is not converted to anything. The narrative space is a subtle means of depicting something new, something that both Jews and Gentiles are part of. Ringe 1985, 69-70 argues that the story has not originally (Mark?) had anything to do with the idea of the Gentile mission, and it has only later been elaborated (Matthew?) to focus on questions of Jewish-Gentile relationships. The idea of Mark's story is to tell something about Jesus as the Christ, and "only consequently, something about the church".

[4] Dewey 1994, 128 sees that Matthew has changed the Markan story so much that the woman is transformed "from a model of creative intelligence interacting as an equal with a man, to that of a persistent or nagging woman – a model more traditional and perhaps less of a threat to patriarchal norms."

[5] Cady Stanton 1972(1895-1898), 121 already emphasised the woman's equality in argument and in perseverance.

[6] For Kinukawa 1994, 59 Jesus is motivated to act in a new way.

story, but for the first time in the narrative another person challenges his behaviour and his Jewishness.[1]

The differences between Matthew's Canaanite woman and the Markan story of the Syrophoenician woman, are notable. In Mark, the woman does not ask Jesus herself. Her plea isdescribed to the reader. In Mark, the disciples do not participate in the discussion, and in the main argumentation it seems that the woman wins the argument and as a consequence, Jesus changes his mind. In Matthew, this element is missing. Matthew has created a dialogue emphasising the issues peculiar to him: the exclusiveness of Jesus' mission to Israel, and the emphasis of faith as the reason for healing.[2]

C. Feminist Critique and Construct

Central questions in the feminist readings have revolved around impurity because of the woman is a foreigner and assumptions that the woman is a prostitute. These aspects underline the marginality of the woman with respect to Jesus, and as a consequence, the gap that is closed in this dialogue. Anderson has pointed out that being a *woman* and a *Gentile* underlines her marginality and the source of the faith and initiative.[3] I would not point to the marginality, but rather to the juxtaposition of the two main characters. In the context of the first century Palestinian world, they are not equals in any sense, but in the space of the narrative, a connection in terms of relational power comes into existence.

In much of the mainstream literature, this story has been interpreted as an answer to the problem of the Gentile mission in Matthew's environment, and an authorisation for such a mission.[4] The feminist

---

[1] Gnadt 1998, 496 says that "das Spannende an dieser Geschichte ist, dass Jesus hier eine Position vertritt, *die sich im Laufe der Argumentation als "kleinläubig" erweist* und überwunden wird." (italics mine) Luz 1990, 432 - citing Beare - suggests the possibility of seeing here the worst kind of chauvinism.

[2] For Melzer-Keller 1997, 146-147 this means that Matthew's emphasis here is on the question of Gentiles, not about gender. This is against Wainwright 1991, 107-108.

[3] Anderson 1983, 10-11.

[4] So Held, 1961, 188-189; Gundry 1982, 401. Hill 1972, 253 argues that the pericope was employed "for the guidance of the Matthean church in its relationship with Gentiles". The Gentiles did not have immediate entry to salvation, but exceptions could be made.

alternative – especially by Kwok from the Asian perspective – challenges this by emphasising that the dialogue is between two religious parties where no hierarchy or conversion is needed. The dialogue is even more surprising because the one participant is a woman.[1] There is no conversion, and there are no gender hierarchies; rather a dialogue exists between equals in relational power.

A provocative interpretation of women's traditions from the oral tradition and echoes of inclusive liturgies underlie the story.[2] Antoinette Clark Wire has studied the social structure of the Matthean community, and she is of the opinion that the text reflects the presuppositions of the scribes who eventually contributed to the writing of the Gospel. It has also been argued that the story manifests the tension resulting from women's participation in Matthew's community. The Gentile woman referred to as a dog contrasts women's role in the liturgical life of the church. However, Jesus' affirmation of the woman legitimises women's active role.[3]

According to Wainwright, the woman uses liturgical language in the dialogue. Her cry, familiar in the Gospel elsewhere, could have been familiar to Matthew's community, or even be a liturgical formula. ἐλέησόν με also appears on the lips of two blind men in 9:27 and in 20:30 as biblical psalm language (cf., e.g. Ps 6:3; 9:14; 26:11; 30:11). The cries of the woman reflect the prayer traditions within the Matthean community, now placed in the mouth of an outsider, they reveal the role of women in the liturgical and theological life of the community. Referring to the Gentile woman as a 'dog' therefore signifies grassroots opposition to these women's roles; but Jesus' affirmation of the woman could also be interpreted as a signal of legitimation.[4]

The question of impurity of women has been dealt with in the analysis of the story about the haemorrhaging woman, as these two stories have much in common. They have been linked because of their double marginality since both of the women are "in a male world outside the patriarchal family structure and as ritually unclean or gentile".[5] This sense

---

[1] See Kwok 1995, 71-83.
[2] Wire 1991, 121.
[3] Wainwright 1991, 240. Cf. also Schüssler Fiorenza 1992, 98-100.
[4] Wainwright 1991, 226-228.
[5] Wainwright 1991, 104. Also Anderson 1983, 11. See also Ringe 1985, 72 who depicts the Canaanite woman as "the poorest of the poor and the most despised of the

of being 'outside' is due to the narration. These women appear somewhat two-dimensional in the narrative as Matthew has not been interested in their personalities, and does not explain their backgrounds. What is common to these women is their undefined position in the course of the narrative. While the first is defined by her illness, and the other by her foreignness, their status in their respective societies is not defined. Furthermore, the 'impurity' would have assumed the guise of a problem only from the Jewish perspective. We know nothing about the social status of these women, whether they were free women or slaves, peasants or townswomen, or if they had husbands or fathers. The status of women in antiquity depended very much on the class they belonged to. The charge of prostitution against the Canaanite woman is based very much on her lack of identity and depend on her being outdoors[1] as well as the parallel with the two Canaanite prostitutes, Tamar and Rahab in Matthew's genealogy[2]. Corley also points out that "the Canaanite women have a strong connection with prostitution and sexual sin in Jewish biblical tradition."[3] As the story is stripped of unnecessary details, it is pointless to speculate if she is a prostitute, a single parent or a dutiful housewife. Matthew is not interested in her familial bonds[4], but his concern is with the new family of the *basileia*, where the woman belongs because of her faith.

However, being a Canaanite – instead of Mark's Syrophoenician – is an obsolete designation, as there were no Canaanites in Matthew's

---

outcast - a Gentile woman on her own before God and humankind."
[1] Ringe 1985, 70; Corley 1993, 166. This kind of thinking is based on the distinction between the public and the private in ancient societies. Respectable women belonged to the private sphere and those women who had freer access to 'the public' were usually prostitutes or household slaves. See e.g. Corley 1993, 15-16. Beare 1981, 341 points out that Matthew's intention was that Jesus not offends the Jewish custom by entering a house in a heathen city.
[2] Corley 1993, 166; Wainwright 1991, 105 mentions only Rahab.
[3] Corley 1993, 166. In her opinion, Matthew portrays an egalitarian community as he includes Gentile women associated with harlotry in the genealogy and in the later stories (178).
[4] So also Luz 1990, 433.

time.[1] Understood theologically as a juxtaposition, it underlines her strangeness from the Jewish point of view, and the distinction between the Jews and the Gentiles that originated in the First Testament.[2] A Canaanite could also be viewed as an enemy.[3] Thus, Matthew is depicting an encounter between persons of two different religions and cultures. Because of the gender differences, the encounter is not between equals.

In contrast to Kwok I would say that the gender hierarchy is evident in the encounter, although the woman alters the situation in her favour. The anonymity of the woman balances the situation and the outcome of the dialogue finds her equal in power with Jesus. No conversion is intended; her faith makes coexistence possible.

The issues peculiar to Matthew in this pericope are the exclusiveness of Jesus' mission to Israel, and the emphasis on faith as the reason for healing. 'Faith' is the key word here, as it was in the miracle stories before. Jesus' authority requires a counterpart in faith that brings forth the healing.[4] Here again, as in the previous miracles, the woman's need for healing sets the stage. What is different is Jesus' rudeness toward this woman. First, he does not answer at all, and when the annoyed disciples ask him to settle the matter[5], he very coldly informs her that he has been sent for Israel only. However, the woman's persistent argumentation convinces him of her faith. Matthew consistently accentuates the Jewish tradition. Nothing indicates that Jesus abrogates it or even that he changes his opinion about his mission (cf 10:5-7).[6] That a Gentile has faith implies here that faith transcends all other criteria in the *basileia,* or perhaps that the narrative about the *basileia* includes contradictory stories.

---

[1] This has caused problems for interpreters; and one way of solving them is the suggestion that Canaanite' was a Semitic way of referring to Phoenicia in Matthew's time. So Hill 1972, 253; Filson 1967, 179; Albright and Mann 1984, 187; Luz 1990, 432.

[2] See e.g. Held 1961, 188-189; Schweizer 1981, 215; Beare 1981, 341.

[3] For several other explanations see e.g. Davies and Allison 1991, 547.

[4] That faith is a typical Matthean device in the miracle stories see e.g. Held 1961, 227-228. Davies and Allison 1991, 556 says that it is the faith *along with the recognition of the divinely ordained division between Jew and Gentile* that is the reason for Jesus to give in.

[5] There are different opinions as to what the disciples actually ask him to do: to get rid of the woman, or to do as she wants.

[6] Davies and Allison 1991, 556.

The dominical authorisation of the Gentile mission as an issue of this story is in accordance with the fact that Jesus heals Gentiles and communicates with them. As the pericope of this Gentile woman follows the dispute over dietary traditions, it has led to assumptions that the uncleanliness of the Gentiles is at question here. In contrast, the healing stories involving both the centurion and the woman lack any sort of missionary aspect. It is the supplicants who seek Jesus' help. Connections with a mission are possible[1] but not necessary. Despite the disputes, Matthew is faithful to the Jewish laws and traditions, and he states clearly that the mission of Jesus is for Israel only, and that this is also the reason Jesus is sending his disciples. No doubt there were Gentiles in Matthew's community; but that was also usual in Jewish communities.[2] Gentiles, as such, were not the problem. At the same time, the woman story does not render Jews and Gentiles equals. By all accounts, the lost sheep of Israel maintain their primacy and the encounter with the woman is a mere exception.

Jesus had once before healed a Gentile, the centurion's servant at a man's request. These two conversations differ totally. The centurion speaks to Jesus man to man. He, a man with authority, approaches another man with higher authority.[3] Jesus does not react as he did to the woman by ignoring him, but follows him immediately. Both supplicants are Gentiles but the man has status in society; the woman does not. The centurion's concern centres on the act of healing, the woman's need is to achieve relatedness. In her vocabulary there is no either-or, but both-and. In this story, Jesus belongs to a patriarchal world, the world of shoulds and should nots. The woman reminds him that there is another way.[4] Faith which transcends cultural and religious boundaries does not necessarily break them, but as here, opens up a new inclusive reality.

In the larger context, there are two distinctly contradictory types in relation to responses to Jesus' authority, exemplified by Peter and this woman, those with strong faith and those with little faith. Peter fails the test on trusting Jesus' authority; and Jesus rebukes him for having little

---

[1] Another similar connection is in Acts 10: Cornelius and Peter with the latter's vision about clean and unclean.

[2] The woman knew about the Jewish traditions as is clear from the language she uses. She could as well have been considered a proselyte, or a God fearer.

[3] Malina and Rohrbaugh 1992, 70, 74-75.

[4] Kwok 1995, 74.

faith, whereas this woman's daughter is healed because of the great faith of the mother. Somewhat later, Peter is told first to profess his faith, and second, that he will be rewarded by pre-eminence in the future community. 'Faith' is presented in a twofold sense. In the first, it is the power source in all the healing episodes. People's illnesses are cured, and they are made whole through their faith. In the second, Peter's profession, faith entails acknowledging Jesus as the Son of God. This acknowledgement has already been made by all the disciples (14:33), so it is not unique in itself. But this faith means seeing in Jesus the reality that the reader has been aware of from the beginning. It amounts to recognition of Jesus' right to authority. This acknowledgement clearly belongs to the theological level of the narrative. Through Jesus' promise, the ecclesiastical structures take form, and Peter is bound to aspects of power and authority in the future community. Faith here insists accepting these structures and authoritative arrangements. In the previous healing stories, and again here, faith involves understanding Jesus' ability to heal, and his connection to the works of God. What is also significant is the juxtaposition between this faith and the faith of the disciples. Jesus has called the disciples men of 'little faith' several times (6:30; 8:26; 14:31). Their faith is limited, because in these moments, they do not trust Jesus' ability to control the situation. Through this, the meaning of faith is made clear to the reader, even though it is never explicitly defined. In the story of the Canaanite woman, Jesus himself is touched by this power of transformation. Unlike faith connected to the character of Peter, faith here does not touch upon the external structures of the community or involve theological convictions, but touches life itself.

To conclude, the Canaanite woman's words and actions underline her subordinate position to Jesus. The story itself is master-centred, and the characters form a hierarchical structure. The woman addresses Jesus with christological titles, no doubt familiar in Matthew's community, but the language and story itself render the woman subordinate. Her words do not prove that we are dealing with reminiscences of early liturgies. Psalm language could also be used otherwise in this way. Even less can be assumed of women's participation in those liturgies.

What can we then make of this story? The contradictory pairs: a Jew / a Gentile, the Jewish area / the pagan area, woman / disciples or woman / Jesus, children / dogs, represent cultural, social, gender, and religious differences. Throughout Matthew's narrative, a number of contrasts – the

Jewish leaders, the crowd, the disciples and a Gentile, disciples of little faith / a woman's great faith; the yeast of the Jewish leaders / the bread given to the crowd clash. The values of the *basileia* as presented are unexpected and subversive. The encounter of the woman and Jesus raises questions about the boundaries between 'us' and the outsiders, about oneness and exclusion. Even though Jesus does not comment on the woman's faith, and no conversion occurs in the story, it can quite fairly be interpreted as pointing towards an interfaith dialogue.[1]

The dialogue itself is subversive, as it involves a Jewish man and a Gentile woman, who, in the ancient Palestinian context, were not equals. In this story, the woman, despite her subordinate status, has relational power with Jesus. Even if no external change occurs in her status, she achieves her purpose, and as a woman, makes a connection on her own initiative. In this sense, she is very similar to the haemorrhaging woman. Both women are accepted as members of the new family; the connection they make on their own initiative confers power through the relationship they have with Jesus. The hierarchies of the world they lived in were not valid in the *basileia.*

4.3.4. The Mother of Zebedee's Sons

A. The Character

The mother of Zebedee's sons, mentioned twice (20:20; 27:55) in Matthew's narrative, is a character exhibiting continuity and some development.

When Jesus speaks about his death for the first time, the reader is prepared for the coming events (16:21). Jesus' journey is towards Jerusalem, whereon he clarifies the meaning of discipleship. One topic touched upon is the question of greatness in the *basileia*: The conclusion is that disciples must be like children if they want to enter the *basileia.* Little ones are the greatest, but in a subversive sense, they are the ones who need to be protected. Compassionate love and forgiveness, not riches or power, are the gauge of the *basileia* against which all other criteria are to be measured.

---

[1] For an Asian perspective see Kwok 1995, 81-82.

The pericopes belonging together are as follows:

A parable about the labourers in the vineyard (20:1-16)
The third prophecy of the Passion (20:17-19)
The mother of Zebedee's sons making her request
(20:20-23)
Leadership with service (20:24-28)

Preoccupations concerning reward are followed by the third
prophecy of the Passion. The reward in Jesus' life is, paradoxically,
death. After this sobering announcement, a mother appears on the scene
to request a tangible prize. This woman again has no name of her own;
she is identified through her husband and her sons by a double reference
to her male relatives. Tradition has coalesced her into one individual,
Salome. Matthew mentions her among the women under the cross as the
mother of the sons of Zebedee, while Mark identifies a woman under the
cross as Salome.[1] Because the sons belong to the inner circle, it seems
even stranger that the mother is brought into the scene. One explanation
for designating the mother as the petitioner is that the sons are presented
in a less self-serving light.[2] This is the second incident where a mother
appeals to Jesus on behalf of her offspring, the first being the Canaanite
woman. Other parallels are the ruler and his daughter (9:18-26), and the
centurion and his servant (8:5-13).

The setting of the incident is the road to Jerusalem. The presence of
the mother suggest that there are women – perhaps even families[3] – in the
group following Jesus.[4] In the feeding miracles (14:21; 15:38), it is stated

---

[1] E.g. Schweizer 1981, 259; Gundry 1982, 401.

[2] Albright and Mann 1984, 241; Gundry 1982, 401; Fenton 1978, 324; Levine 1992,
259. Senior 1998, 224 says that by having the mother make the request, Matthew
wanted to soften the discordant note of the request. Davies and Allison 1997, 86
question this kind of explanation. The boys are ashamed, and therefore put their
mother forward. Luz 1983, 101 says that here Matthew improves the image of the
disciples. Schweizer 1981, 259 sees her positively, in line with the Israelite mothers
in 1. Sam. 1 and 2. Mac 7. Another positive model in the First Testament is Bathsheba
pleading for Solomon in 1. Kings 1.

[3] Zebedeus himself was left fishing in chapter 4.

[4] Cf. also Moltmann-Wendel 1991,128. Luz 1997, 161 says that by these two incidents
where Zebedee's wife is present, Matthew wants to inform that she is a follower of
Jesus. So also Wainwright 1991, 119.

that many men shared in these meals 'not counting women and children' and that the crowds following Jesus included men, women, and children. Even the inner circle might have consisted of families, and afterwards the twelve men might have been chosen from its members as the symbolic group for the new Israel. Women in Matthew's narrative take shape only in terms of the patriarchal structures.

The sons of Zebedee are with the mother, so they cannot be unaware of her request. As a typical mother in her own cultural context, her entire concern is for her sons.[1] She kneels before Jesus, requesting privileged positions for them. Jesus' answer is in the second person plural, thus answering both the mother and the sons.[2] In replying, Jesus prints out the innate distinction between the *basileia* and the power structure of their contemporary society. Apparently the three of them have not understood. His followers must drink the same cup as he does, i.e. must imitate his life to the end. Jesus has already told them three times about his future suffering and death, but they have totally missed this connection to the essence of the *basileia*. Though all three of them answer Jesus affirmatively, under the cross (27:56), only the mother stands faithful to the promise. It could be interpreted that she has finally grasped its meaning.[3]

The other ten disciples are angry with the brothers, not with the mother. Jesus clarifies the authority ranking of the *basileia*, which is to be the reversal of earthly government. He who aspires to be the greatest, must be a servant. The first becomes the slave. Serving and even giving his life for others Jesus is the example for those who want to fully live the reality of the *basileia*.[4]

---

[1] Malina 1983, 104: A woman's most significant relationship was with her son.

[2] Many scholars are of the opinion that Jesus answers only the sons (Matthew has changed Mark's text where only the sons are present) Schweizer 1981, 259; Hill 1972,288; Filson 1967, 216; Gundry 1982, 401; Albright and Mann 1984, 242; Luz 1997, 159. That the mother is not herself seen in an unfavourable light, see Luz 1997, 161 and Levine 1992, 259.

[3] Wainwright 1991, 142. For Brown 1994, 1155 the mother's request makes the two disciples look like failures. He argues that the presence of the mother in 27:56 points to a future role for both the sons and the mother. This does not sound convincing. The mother is under the cross, the sons are not.

[4] In Collins' words "...the Son of man's διακονῆσαι leads to the opposite of all that is powerful and glorious so that he becomes the absolute standard for disciples who would belong to the kingdom." and "...it is for the purpose of setting the profane

B. Feminist Critique and Construct

Elisabeth Moltmann-Wendel has dealt with the mother of Zebedee's sons in her book *Ein eigener Mensch werden; Frauen um Jesus*[1], focusing on motherhood. She considers this woman *the* mother-image of Matthew's Gospel. As the myth of the mother of Jesus had not yet been developed Matthew brought to the scene the prototype of a Christian mother. The mother of the two sons, among the most eminent of the apostles, would be highly respected in the Jewish world.[2] Mothers lived for and in their sons and according to Moltmann-Wendel, this woman was anchored in her ancient role as a mother, since she wanted honour and glory for her sons. She did not see herself as a person in her own right. This is what Jesus wanted to return to her: her own personhood.[3]

Emily Cheney's article[4] points towards a male affirmation, as she claims that the presence of the mother in verses 20:20 and 27:56 and her later absence in verses 27:61 and 28:1, defines discipleship in Matthew. Her absence reinforces Jesus' teachings that his male disciples must renounce their former household and be loyal to the 'new family'. Biological ties do not count in the new context.[5] Cheney has no answers regarding the future of the mothers in the new family. According to her, the audience Matthew was writing to was male, and therefore not interested in the future of women.[6] In verses 28:16-20, only men are present.

---

grandeur of one way of life against the prophetic dedication of the other that Mark has brought these oddly fitting infinitives together." (Collins 1990, 252) The same applies to Matthew who has taken these verses from Mark. For Collins "serving" in the Gospels points to no special table service, liturgy or Eucharist (249-251).

[1] Moltmann-Wendel 1991, 123-133.

[2] In this light, the story about the mother-in-law of Peter is notable as he is also one of the inner circle of disciples.

[3] Moltmann-Wendel 1991, 127-130.

[4] Cheney 1997, 13-21.

[5] Cheney's idea is based on her research about travelling in ancient times. She comes to the conclusion that it was traditional that women travelled with their families and households. It is possible that the unnamed 'many women' belonged to the households of the twelve disciples. But it is also arguable that the male disciples made the break with their households, since no women are directly connected to them. (See 16-18)

[6] Cheney 1997, 20.

Moltmann-Wendel rightly points out that, in Matthew, Jesus' mother, was not 'the mother' she was in Luke, for example, or in later Christian tradition. But in Matthew, the mother of James and John, two disciples who belonged to the inner circle of the followers, was probably a highly respected person among the followers. It seems that she also had left her home and husband to join the group that was wandering about with Jesus. As for Cheney's conclusion about the non biological family, I believe she reads too much into both the absence and the change of women characters in different situations. That Matthew was writing to a male audience merely means that the events are told from the disciples' point of view. On the other hand, there are other mothers in Matthew's narrative. In the genealogy, there are four 'foremothers'; the Canaanite woman is a mother, in fact, the mother of a daughter. There are mothers under the cross: Mary, the mother of James and Joseph, who is a woman we know nothing more about. If Matthew had wanted to emphasise the non-biological relations in the discipleship, he might not have mentioned so many mothers.

The question of motherhood leads to the question of the definition of the women in Matthew in general.

The foremothers in the genealogy	mothers
Mary	a mother
Peter's mother-in-law	a mother
The haemorrhaging woman	no definition
The ruler's daughter	a daughter
The Canaanite woman	a mother
The anointing woman	no definition
The mother of Zebedee's sons	a mother
Pilate's wife	a wife
Mary of Magdala	no definition
Mary, the mother of James and Joseph	a mother

In the above, three women are not defined through any familial relationships. Besides the mothers in the genealogy, there are five mothers, one wife and one daughter (two daughters if we count the daughter of the Canaanite woman, who is not really present in the narrative). Motherhood is clearly an important relational bond in

Matthew's characterisation.[1] These mothers appear in the narrative on their own. Joseph is the only husband acting as a character, and Zebedee is not part of the narrative. The Canaanite woman is described as the mother of a daughter, not as 'a wife of a husband' or 'a mother of a son'.

On the one hand, motherhood is given a metaphorical meaning in 12:46-50, where Jesus *seems to abandon* his own mother and brothers and defines membership in the *basileia* by applying familial language. His mother and brothers and sisters are those who do the will of God. Jesus' own mother is not important, nor is the patriarchal family he belongs to. Women who belong to the new household of the *basileia* are important not primarily as 'mothers of sons', which points to the patriarchal hierarchy, but as 'sisters'. Mothers and brothers and sisters in the *basileia* do not form any hierarchical order.

On the other hand, some women described as belonging to the group of followers, are in a sense undefined, and do not belong to any patriarchal structures. Even though they are depicted as mothers, they appear in the narrative as independent individuals. They are, however, not unique. Most of the male supplicants in the healing stories are also described without any bonds, and without names. Their only mutual attribute is their need. Their need and the power-with relationship that developed between them and Jesus defines a group of people, both men and women who have 'faith', i.e. who trust in Jesus to help them. These people are not referred to by a name, as the disciples are. Furthermore, Matthew clearly makes use of these characters to describe certain characteristics of the *basileia*.

It is remarkable that in both the story of the Canaanite woman and the brief appearance of the mother of Zebedee's sons, although contextually different, involve questions of power. The Canaanite woman achieves relational power with Jesus, soon after it is reported that Jesus gives Peter the keys to the *basileia*. Hierarchical power over others is defines Peter; and relational power with Jesus defines a Gentile woman. When Zebedee's wife wants hierarchical power for her sons – perhaps higher in rank than Peter – Jesus explains that the ethos of the *basileia* is the reversal of the earthly order, just as his kingship is the reversal of

---

[1] Compared to fatherhood: of 57 occurrences in Matthew, 17 point to human fathers. The most notable fathers are Joseph, Jesus' foster father, the ruler, and Zebedee, who himself is not present (not a follower?). *The* Father in Matthew is God.

earthly kingship. The hierarchical structures seem to be in tension with the *basileia*, but Matthew does not reject them. Peter and the two sons of Zebedee are connected to the hierarchy, while the Canaanite woman is a counter figure to them, both in faith and in power.

4.4. The Passion Narrative (26-28)

4.4.1. Overview

The beginning of Jesus' ministry is related in Chapter 3, with the middle of the narrative consisting of his deeds and teachings. In Chapters 26 to 28, Jesus' life has led to passion and death. Jesus, whose origins are from God, eventually returns, through his resurrection, to where he came from.

The structure of the passion and resurrection narrative is as follows:

Instruction to the Disciples 26:1-2
    Jewish leaders plot against Jesus 26:3-5
    The Anointing at Bethany 26:6-13
        Judas betrays Jesus 26:14-16
        Preparations for the Passover 26:17-19
        Judas' betrayal foretold 26:20-25
        The institution of the Eucharist 26:26-29
        Peter's betrayal foretold 26:30-35
        Gethsemane 26:36-46
        The arrest 26:47-56
        Jesus before the Sanhedrin 26:57-68
        Peter's denials 26:69-75
        Jesus before Pilate 27:1-2
        The death of Judas 27:3-10
        Trial before Pilate 27:11-26
        Jesus is crowned with thorns 27: 27-31
        The Crucifixion 27: 32-38
        The crucified Jesus is mocked 27:39-44
        The death of Jesus 27: 45-53
    Responses to Jesus' death 27:54-66
    The empty tomb 28:1-8

Appearance to women 28:9-10
Jewish leaders' plot 28:11-15
The mission to the world 28:16-20

The bold texts of this outline point to the parts where there are women present, or mentioned, in the narrative. In Matthew's passion narrative, women frame the whole passion and become visible at the crucial turning points of the narration. In the beginning, a woman points towards Jesus' destiny; and in the moments of death and during the events connected with the resurrection, women are present. Other brief appearances of women – the female servants and Pilate's wife – serve as contrasts in the flow of the narrative.

4.4.2. The Anointing Woman

A. The Narrative

The story about the anointing woman[1] follows the conspiracy plans against Jesus. The Jewish leaders, representatives of the earthly religious authority, want Jesus put to death. After the anointing story, one of the Twelve, a disciple, betrays Jesus. Enemies come from both outside and from within. So, the story that occurs in between them, is antithetical to the actions of hatred against Jesus.[2]

Jesus is having a meal in a private house. The host is a man called Simon, who is said to be a leper, and the setting recalls the healing stories. Once again, a leper and a woman are bound together by narrative. Now, τοῦ λεπροῦ does imply that the man is still a leper. It is also possible – Jesus' fame as a healer would legitimise the assumption – that

---

[1] All four Gospels include a story of anointing, but in different forms. In Mark and in Matthew, the episode is situated in Bethany, in the house of Simon the leper, and the name of the woman is not stated. In Luke (7:36-50), a woman whose name is not stated, but who is defined as 'a sinner', anoints Jesus' feet; but not his head as in Mark and Matthew; and the place is the house of Simon the Pharisee. In John (12:1-8) the woman who anoints (Jesus' feet) is Mary, the sister of Martha and Lazarus.

[2] Cf Davies and Allison 1997, 441. Heil 1991(2), 26 also extends the antithesis to the high priest who is named Caiaphas. The priest, who is an enemy, has a name; the woman has not.

he is cured, but still had the cognomen related to the past disease. In either case, Jesus is in the house of a person who is ill, or has been healed. The situation emphasises that Jesus is again associating with social outcasts and performing the intimate companionable act[1]. The Pharisees have already reproached him for this (9:10-13).

An unidentified woman comes to Jesus. The incident happens inside the house, but it is not said if the woman belongs to Simon's household, or if she is an uninvited stranger. Still, even if the setting indicates privacy, the deed has very firm public connotations. She has a jar of expensive ointment[2] which she pours upon Jesus' head. The purpose of the anointing lies in the future, as Jesus himself explains it as a preparation for his burial. Jesus has told his followers several times about his coming suffering and death, and the reader is tempted to assume that the woman senses the implications of her deed on a deeper level of her being, even if the story itself gives no clues as to the reasons or the thoughts behind her actions.[3]

The disciples represent the contrasting element here.[4] They are not surprised by the presence of the woman, nor by the deed. It was a customary courtesy for servants to anoint guests with perfumed oil during a meal.[5] What they grumble about is the waste[6], self-righteously proclaiming that the ointment could have fetched a fancy profit[7] which could have been given to the poor. The woman is a stranger positioned against the disciples. It is her intuition against the information that the

---

[1] Davies and Allison 1997, 443.

[2] That Matthew underlines the cost of the perfume (βαρύτιμος) has been explained by the fact that Matthew was a publican. So Gundry 1982, 519-520.

[3] Senior 1998, 292 is of the opinion that the woman is fully aware of Jesus' destiny.

[4] Cf. also the role of disciples in the story of the haemorrhaging woman or the Canaanite woman, where the disciples serve as a contrast to these women characters.

[5] Malina and Rohrbaugh 1992, 135-137 who also are of the opinion that a woman's presence at a meal was anomalous. On the contrary Hill 1972, 334 says that the woman's gesture was not unusual in an eastern home.

[6] Davies and Allison 1997, 444 point to the contrast with the low price Judas accepts for his betrayal of Jesus (26:15).

[7] In Mark, the ointment was valued at "over three hundred denarii". In Matthew 20:1-16, one silver denarius was a wage paid to a man who had worked all day in the fields. For this woman, it could have meant one year's earnings. According to Schottroff 1995, 92-95, in her social historical study of early Christianity, one denarius was enough for two days' provisions.

disciples already have. From the perspective of the *basileia*, the focus is transferred to the woman who represents the interior virtue of faith while the disciples concentrate on the externals. Although almsgiving is a good thing, the woman probably gives her life savings to the confirmation of the *basileia*.

The woman has no identity, status, or background. Though she represents her gender she is very much an outsider with no voice of her own. Even when the disciples speak to her and reproach her and when her actions are the subject of the dialogue taking place between Jesus and the disciples she remains a nebulous figure. Lacking all personal features, she dwindles into a symbol of a prophetic act at a turning point of Jesus' life.

Matthew has abbreviated Mark's story (14:3-9), but the essentials remain the same.[1] In Mark, those who disapproved of the woman's deed were vaguely labelled 'some' while in Matthew they are labelled 'the disciples'. The Matthean redaction here emphasises the contrast between the woman and the disciples, who represent true-understanding and non-understanding respectively.[2] The value of the ointment has been abbreviated from Mark's three hundred denarii to πολλοῦ; and the oil that was used is not defined as Nardus, as it was in Mark. The statement in Mark, 'She has done what she could', is also left out. For Melzer-Keller the Markan story implies that the woman understood what she was doing in preparing Jesus' death, but the Matthean changes have Jesus explain the meaning of the deed. According to Melzer-Keller, Matthew reduces the importance of the woman in the story, and the anointing loses its prophetical connotations in his formulation narrowing to mean only καλὸν ἔργον.[3] The discussion of good deeds and the explanation that the anointing was for Jesus' burial appears in both Gospels, and the changes that Matthew has made do not lessen the significance of the deed, nor its

---

[1] For the details in minor changes see e.g. Davies and Allison 1997, 441-442.

[2] Anderson 1983, 17-18; Thiemann 1987, 183. Senior 1975, 32-33 interprets the Matthean redaction to portray disciples as representative Christians. The subject of the episode would then be the traditional discussion between almsgiving and good works. The original situation of the anointing pericope would then be the situation in Matthew's communities and the problem is solved here in favour of good works.

[3] Melzer-Keller 1997, 115-116. For the opinion that the Matthean redaction emphasises the anointing for the burial see also Thiemann 1987, 183; Corley 1993, 170. In Matthew, the women do not go to the tomb to anoint the body, thus substituting this as the proper burial anointing in the passion narrative. See Albright and Mann 1984, 315; Thiemann 1987, 183; Corley 1993, 170.

centrality to the story. Exceptionally, it is not the deed of Jesus that is told or remembered, but that of an unknown woman. However, the event has been taken from Mark, who had already embedded it in a patriarchal framework. The woman does not speak; the dialogue excludes her. The male representative in the story, Jesus, eventually gives a name and interpretation to the action.

B. Feminist Critique and Construct

Some feminist interpretations[1] emphasise the political aspect of the anointing which is by no means unfamiliar in mainstream biblical scholarship.[2] In ancient Israel, new kings were anointed. Samuel anointed Saul and David by pouring oil over their heads.[3] By performing the same act, the woman becomes an image of a prophet.

Another pivotal view in the feminist perspective is to see this woman as a representative of true discipleship.[4] The essence of the deed is service[5], one of the ways of defining discipleship. This woman is seen not only as an image for discipleship, but also as a model for it, in sharp contrast to the male disciples.[6]

The title of Schüssler Fiorenza's feminist reconstruction of Christian origins, *In Memory of Her*, has been taken from the Markan version of this story. In the first pages of her book, she particularly discusses the problem of naming, and concludes that the woman has virtually faded into anonymity because her name is lost to us. The stories about the faithlessness in the Peter's denial and the betrayal by Judas are

---

[1] Some of the feminist works concentrate only on Mark's story; e.g. Schüssler Fiorenza does not even mention Matthew when discussing this pericope in her book, which has been given its title from this story (In Memory of Her). So also Moltmann-Wendel.
[2] Schüssler Fiorenza 1983, xiv says that this was "a politically dangerous story". See also Wainwright 1991, 269-270; Moltmann-Wendel 1991, 101-102; Davies and Allison 1997, 445, 447-448.
[3] 1 Sam 10:1; 16:13; See also 1 Kings 1:39, 45; 19:15-16; 2 Kings 11:12; 23:30.
[4] Wainwright 1991, 136; Corley 1993, 171; Schüssler Fiorenza 1983, xiii-xiv. Also Senior 1998, 292 notes that this is an act of alert discipleship.
[5] So also Davies and Allison 1997, 448.
[6] Anderson 1983, 18. Similarly Heil 1991(2), 27, so this is not entirely a feminist view.

remembered, but the faithfulness of this disciple is forgotten because she is a woman without a name.[1]

I agree with the interpretation that the woman's act implies a prophetic commitment to Jesus. In her deed, the meaning of Jesus' kingship becomes visible, and the symbolic meaning of the gender is apparent. Contrary to Schüssler Fiorenza I would say that it is significant that the woman's anonymity directs all the attention to her action. Matthew thus introduces a female prophet who through her anointing indicates a kingship that has nothing to do with earthly ruling, but, in fact, is realized in an ignominious death. Messianic kingship and preparation for burial paradoxically become two interpretations of one reality.

The last verse (13) of the pericope corresponds to the later commission to the disciples to proclaim the Gospel to the whole world.

ὅτου ἐάν κηρυχθῇ τὸ εὐαγγέλιον τοῦτο ἐν ὅλῳ τῷ κόσμῳ (26:13)
μαθητεύσατε   πάντα τὰ ἔθνη   (28:19)

λαληθήσεται καὶ ὃ ἐποίησεν αὐτη εἰς *μνημόσυνον* αὐτῆς (26:13)
διδάσκοντες αὐτοὺς τηρεῖν τάντα ὅσα ἐνετειλάμεν ὑμιν(28:19)

Verse 26:13 uses verbs that describe proclamation and telling about things, verse 28:19 those of making disciples and teaching. The word εὐαγγέλιον is used four times in the Matthean narrative, each time in connection to the *basileia*.[2] Using proclamation language to announce the *euangelion* recalls past deeds that form the essence of the *basileia,* conversely the recollection is in the essence of the proclamation.[3] In contrast, μαθητεύω and διδάσκω (also βαπτίζω in 28:19)denote the hierarchical framework of master-disciple and, by association, the patriarchal attributes of a community. By a subtle change of expression in the last scene, the spotlight shifts from the woman to the Twelve who lay the groundwork for later hierarchical domination. What is significant is that it is not a deed of Jesus that is remembered, but that of a nameless woman, done *to Jesus – not by him.* The significant fact of this story, in

---

[1] Schüssler Fiorenza 1983, xiii.
[2] 4:23; 9:35; 24:14; 26:13.
[3] Wainwright 1991, 135 uses the verb μνημονεύω as a clue to the verse. The verb occurs in 16:9 and clearly means more than just calling to mind. The connotations of understanding and believing are present.

my opinion, is that the woman is a non-person. It is still told in memory of a female follower who is a female prophet. Like the Canaanite woman earlier, this unknown woman expresses the uniqueness of the *basileia*.

4.4.3. The Two Female Servants and Pilate's wife

A. The Narrative

In vile contrast to the sublimity and love of the anointing, a member of the inmost circle around Jesus betrays him. The reader knows that Jesus has enemies since the Jewish leaders are plotting against Jesus. But after the act of anointing, a friend also turns against Jesus. The incident of the anointing is a catalyst. The cause of the betrayal is not told; the waste of money seems more like a last straw than the cause itself.

Jesus has his last supper with the disciples. Again, the setting is that of a meal which parallels the anointing story. A female consoles Jesus for burial, but his male inner circle must be prepared by Jesus himself for his death.[1] In the narrative Jesus eats the Passover meal, symbolic of a new family, with his disciples. But strangely, this family consists only of male members. Ricci comments that historically there were both women and other disciples present, but they were not mentioned because there were males present.[2] However, whether women were historically present or not, they are excluded from the narrative.[3] While they are eating, Jesus predicts Judas' betrayal. From the reader's point of view, this means that Jesus is aware of what is happening. During the meal which was the occasion of the institution of the Eucharist, Jesus predicts first Judas', then all the apostles betrayals. Peter blusteringly protests his unswerving loyalty, though later he and the two sons of Zebedee cannot even stay awake. Three times Jesus finds them sleeping while he himself is fighting for his destiny. The message is clear: The disciples who have sworn

---

[1] So also Levine 1992, 261.
[2] Ricci 1994, 26.
[3] Schottroff 1995, 85 sees here a symbolic dispossession of women's work. Women made the bread, but both in Jewish and in Roman mealtime rituals, the paterfamilias performed the ritual and symbolic acts which included breaking the bread. In the narrative of the Passover meal, Jesus takes the role of the paterfamilias who takes the bread, blesses, breaks, and gives it. The work of women is rendered invisible.

faithfulness, can not even stay awake. Shortly they and all the rest flee
from the guards when Jesus is arrested.

Peter, however, follows at a cowardly distance (ἠκολούθει ἀπὸ
μακρόθεν), hoping to remain unidentified in the courtyard. It is through
two women, lowly serving maids, that Peter's betrayal is exposed. In front
of two servant girls, Peter denies Jesus. The contrasts are clear:

high priest	two female servants
Jesus	Peter
affirmation of messiahship	denial of knowing Jesus

Though the women are not fully developed characters, their
questions provide an essential part of the plot. The structure of the
narration places them as counterparts to the high priest. Peter stands
before them as Jesus stands before the high priest. Peter has boldly
acknowledged Jesus as the Messiah earlier; now he denies his master. The
master himself stands in front of a religious authority and affirms his
messiahship. The high priest has formal power over Jesus. Peter yields
control of himself to these women. The gender difference makes the
contrast even more dramatic. The focus, however, remains at all times on
Jesus. There can be only one hero.

Matthew has abbreviated and revised the Markan story about Peter's
denial. In Matthew two different young women ask the questions, while
in Mark there is only one. According to Matthew, when Peter denies
Jesus the second time, he takes an oath that accentuates the denial more
glaringly. Matthew plays with contrasts here. In answer to the high
priest's question Jesus declares, under oath, that he is 'the Christ, the Son
of God'; Peter, on the other hand, denies under oath even knowing Jesus.

While Jesus is questioned by Pilate, the Roman authority, the voice
of a woman is again heard. The voice of Pilate's wife is a detail peculiar
to Matthew. The woman has no name of her own; her personhood is
identified through her husband. She is not even a minor character; only
her message is delivered, a warning, resulting from a dream. Pilate
represents legal authority, as Caiaphas represents religious authority. This
is not the first message in the narrative coming through dreams. (Cf.
Joseph's instructions via dreams in the birth narrative.) The prophetic
voice and prophetic dreams are again entwined. This woman – as do the
servants – offers a powerful contrast. Jesus stands before the legal

authority, buttressed by the power structures of society, in order to be sentenced to death. A woman – she belongs to the ruling class, but holds no formal power herself – raises her voice on behalf of the accused innocent. The reader does not know if Pilate's wife knew about Jesus' reputation, but she acknowledges him and acts in a compassionate way.

B. Feminist Critique and Construct

Feminists interpret the affirmation of the three women – the servant girls and Pilate's wife – as symbolic supporters. In this way they symbolise truth, while Peter symbolises falsehood.[1] Kopas points to Peter's possibility to meet the challenge and show his readiness to follow Jesus, even to death, but Peter fails to prove even his discipleship. The female servants expose his true identity.[2]

According to McGinn, Pilate becomes a positive counter example to the male disciples, who earlier rejected the message of the anointing woman. This is because Pilate takes the message seriously and does not denigrate the message or the woman who sent it. McGinn also discusses the verb ἀποστέλλω as used for sending the message to Pilate. She asks if this might be an indirect reference to the apostolic function of Pilate's wife.[3]

I see these three women as contrasting devices in the narrative rather than characters in their own right. The high priest and Pilate are at the summit of the hierarchies, and Peter is first among the disciples. They all fail to accept the truth, or to live accordingly. The servant girls who have no status, or the wife of an authority with no formal power herself, are the screen against which the authoritative rulers are shown to be false or fallible. Jesus stands alone in the centre.

Whether Pilate takes the message from his wife seriously or not, is not clear from the narration. The counter element lies not in Pilate's understanding, but in his position. A man of power, and formal authority, he is depicted as standing above, and against, Jesus, who is a king.

---

[1] Wainwright 1991, 137; Gnadt 1998, 496.
[2] Kopas 1990, 20.
[3] McGinn 1995, 172.

4.4.4. Women at the cross and at the tomb

A. The Narrative

Jesus' Passion is framed by stories of women. A female prophet anointed Jesus for his kingship, and at the moment of his 'coronation'(his death), women are again present. "A number of women were also present, watching from a distance; they had followed Jesus from Galilee and looked after him. Among them were Mary of Magdala, and Mary the mother of James and Joseph, and the mother of the sons of Zebedee" (27:55-56). These women are depicted as ἀπὸ μακρόθεν θεωροῦσαι. Later, Mary of Magdala and the other Mary are depicted at the grave καθήμεναι ἀπέναντι τοῦ τάφου (v. 61).

Before death Jesus is tortured, humiliated, mocked by soldiers and passers-by alike. Afterwards, the narrator reports the following positive incidents:

1) The centurion, who was guarding Jesus with his men, acknowledged Jesus as the son of God. The centurion and his men are Gentiles, and are as unexpected witnesses as Pilate's wife had been.

2) The women (Mary of Magdala, Mary the mother of James and Joseph, and the mother of Zebedee's sons[1]), faithful to the end, were watching from a distance (ἀπὸ μακρόθεν). The expression is the same as when Peter followed Jesus to the high priest's house. For some interpreters this suggests fallibility[2]; stronger followers would have drawn nearer.

3) A rich man, Joseph of Arimathaea who had become Jesus' disciple, buries Jesus in his own new tomb. This is an act of a disciple. Joseph is not called μαθητής, but he is defined as ἐμαθητεύθη τῷ Ἰησοῦ. The same verb also occurs in verse 28:16 when the eleven disciples are commissioned to include all the nations within discipleship. What is noteworthy here is that Joseph is a disciple, but he is not one of

---

[1] In Mark, instead of the mother of Zebedee's sons there is Salome.
[2] For example Struthers Malbon 1983, 43. She wants to say that even if the disciples were fallible, they did not become non-followers. Malbon's article is about disciples in the Gospel of Mark where the theme of disciples differs from that in Matthew. Against the idea of fallibility see Schüssler Fiorenza 1983, 320; Kopas 1990, 21. – Witherington III 1981, 120 has an explanation that behind the phrase ἀπὸ μακρόθεν stands Ps 37:12 (LXX), and not a historical reminiscence.

the twelve. Antoinette Clark Wire draws attention to this use of the verb in lieu of the noun. The verb is used three times in Matthew, the third occasion being 13:52, where a scribe is made a disciple of the kingdom. Here Wire sees discipleship in a lesser or derived sense, as disciples of disciples.[1] This could be true in 28:19, but not necessarily in the two other verses. The scribe who is made a disciple appears in Jesus' speech in the context of the kingdom parables. Jesus asks the disciples afterwards if they understand what he has taught and they assure him that they have. Jesus then concludes by describing every scribe who has *become a disciple of the basileia*. The perspective is widened, not lessened, and is not connected to the mission of the twelve.

Joseph was a follower of Jesus, not a convert after his death. The space for discipleship is further broadened to include others besides the Twelve, or any circle close to Jesus. Joseph and the scribes belonging to the *basileia* are outside the inner circle, yet are still counted as disciples. The broadening of the discipleship extends to infinite time and space in the closing commission to include all the nations. It is plausible to read here an all-inclusive extension of the entirely male group that appears in the Gospel.

Then, there are the three different responses to Jesus' death. A Gentile confesses Jesus as the son of God; and three women witness everything. They are carefully named, and described as having been with Jesus since Galilee to emphasise their reliability. The third response is the act of a disciple. However, the reader is slightly confused about the women. They are only said to watch, nothing else. The important aspect seems to be their presence, which proves their faithfulness. Meanwhile, the twelve closest disciples have fled, but another disciple is present and doing his duty as a disciple. A possible, but not very convincing clue for interpretations is suggested in the use of the words καί αὐτός in verse 27:57. The verse has been claimed to refer back to the women in the preceding verses. Joseph *too* was a disciple, as the women were.[2]

---

[1] Wire 1991, 103. On the contrary Wilkins 1988, 161-163, who explicitly says that Matthew has not wanted to draw any distinction between the noun and the verb. "..being instructed as a disciple is a mark of a true disciple. To "be disciples" means that one who is a disciple continues to learn from Jesus about the kingdom of heaven."

[2] So Corley 1993, 173. Anderson 1983, 20 mentions this, but takes an opposing view. For her, this verse explains only why a rich man wants to bury Jesus.

Presence itself is the significant aspect, since the persons represent different relationships. The centurion belongs to the political authority. He is a member of the official power structures, who nevertheless confesses Jesus' divinity. A man of the elite, a rich man, is called a disciple.[1] It might seem problematic to include a rich man as a disciple, because the followers of Jesus had particularly been described as people on the fringe of society, not the movers and shakers. In addition, Jesus had taught about the difficulties rich people had in entering the kingdom of God (19:23-24). On the other hand, rulers had already joined those who believed in Jesus. The *basileia* is fully inclusive: leaders and servants, Jews and Gentiles, rich and poor – all can enter.

Matthew places an unexpected gathering of people under the cross. Jesus' death divides the reactions as follows:

Before death
Pilate: I am innocent of this man's blood.
People: Let his blood be on us.
Jesus is scourged.
Jesus is crowned with thorns and dressed in a scarlet cloak.
Soldiers kneel to him and hail him as a king (mockery).
They spit on him.
The passers-by mock him.
The priests and elders mock him.
The bandits who are crucified with him mock him

DEATH - THE EARTH QUAKED

After death
The centurion confesses him as son of God.
Three women are under the cross, keeping vigil.
Joseph of Arimathea buries him.

---

[1] Joseph appears in all four gospels, but his identity varies. In Luke and in Mark, he is described as a member of the council who was looking forward to the kingdom of God. In John, he is a disciple, but in secrecy. (cf. Mark 15:43; Luke 23:50-51; John 19:38).

The masses had turned against Jesus. Before his death, the narrative includes few signs of compassion (Pilate's wife and Pilate himself). The persons who have remained faithful are followers outside the inner circle. As in the miracle stories, a Jew and a Gentile equally witness Jesus' authority. Women are also present as in the miracle stories. They have no voice, they do nothing, but they cling to Jesus until the end.

On the day after the Sabbath, women are back in the narrative. Now there are two women: Mary of Magdala, and the other Mary – probably the mother of James and Joseph as before. The mother of the sons of Zebedee has disappeared. When comparing the two groups of women – under the cross and now by the tomb – it is noteworthy that two women are identified as mothers. Zebedee's sons are disciples from the inner circle, James and Joseph are lesser known followers. Still, the mothers are under the cross and at the tomb, while the sons are missing.

Something otherworldly, manifested by another earthquake and the appearance of an angel, has broken through in Jesus death and again now. The women are told about Jesus' resurrection and that they are to be means of reconciliation with the disciples. Jesus himself appears to the women and repeats the commission, to go to the disciples and tell them to go to Galilee.[1]

Considering the problem from the perspective of the *basileia*, the aspects take on a different connotation. The women's presence is coincidental with the cosmic breakthrough of the otherworldly element in Jesus' death and again when the angel descends from heaven.[2] Women witness the *basileia* that Jesus has proclaimed. Faith is a crucial factor in the *basileia* and faith is what brings the women to the cross and to the tomb.

Matthew has made some changes in the Markan material. There are only two women at the tomb (28:1), instead of Mark's three (16:1). The women come to the grave for a visit; no mention is made of their going to anoint the body. The angel's command to go and tell 'the disciples and Peter' is abbreviated to only 'the disciples'. Mark's conclusion that the women were afraid and said nothing to anyone is changed to obedience:

---

[1] If the women are to be counted as disciples, this would mean telling the news to *other* disciples. So McGinn 1995, 174.

[2] According to Davies and Allison 1997, 628, the eschatological meaning of the crucifixion becomes apparent through the "divine passives and extensive parallelism" (verses 51-53) reaching the climax in verse 54.

They run to tell the disciples. They are not only afraid as in Mark but are also full of joy.[1]

A more significant difference might be Matthew's mentioning 'many women' at the beginning of the episode (v.55), whereas Mark only lists the names of three women. Only later does he mention that there were 'many other women' (cf Mark 15:40-41).[2] In Matthew, the scene depicts many women following Jesus *from* Galilee, ἀπο τῆς Γαλιλαίας (in Mark ἐν τῇ Γαλιλαία). They were travelling with him to Jerusalem. Matthew is apparently claiming that these women were with Jesus and served him only after his leaving for Jerusalem[3], while Mark depicts women who had already followed and served Jesus in Galilee. If the hallmark of discipleship is 'following', then in Matthew the women who joined Jesus from Galilee to Jerusalem are true disciples, whereas in Mark, the sign of discipleship is 'following' during the entire time of Jesus' public life.[4] In my opinion, the preposition change is insignificant in determining who comprise the true followers.

B. Feminist Critique and Construct

In feminist literature the women at the cross are considered disciples because of the two verbs explaining their presence. They had 'followed' (ἀκολουθεῖν) and they had 'served' (διακονεῖν).[5] McGinn points to the verb θεωρέω, which is seen as implying true perception, not simply looking.[6] On the other hand, Melzer-Keller is again of the opinion that

---

[1] For further details see for example Davies and Allison 1997, 660.

[2] Also Gundry 1982, 578, Schweizer 1981, 339 and Corley 1993, 172 takes note of this. Gundry 1982, 578 also says that Matthew emphasises the women's position by using αἵτινες instead of Mark's αἱ.

[3] So Schweizer 1981, 339. Gundry 1982, 578 suggests that Matthew emphasises here the nature of the Christian ministry. Corley 1993, 172 sees no limits here to the women's time with Jesus.

[4] Explanation in terms of discipleship is given by Senior 1975, 331, Gundry 1982, 578, Wainwright 1991, 296-297.

[5] Wainwright 1991, 296; McGinn 1995, 172, 174; Corley 1993, 172. On Mark or synoptics in general also Schüssler Fiorenza 1983, 320-321; Dines 1993, 438-442; Witherington 1981, 122-123. On the contrary Anderson 1983, 19.

[6] McGinn 1995, 173. Also Wainwright 1991, 294-296 sees here an attempt to create a unique terminology "which highlights the nature of their action, but which is also in

Matthew has changed the Markan text so that the verbs originally connected to the essence of discipleship (in Mark) no longer fulfill this function (in Matthew). Her arguments concerning the verb ἀκολούθειν involve the choice of tempus. Matthew uses aorist instead of the imperfect which Mark has used to underline the continuing aspect of following. For Matthew, the verb means merely 'going behind'. The verb διακονεῖν is also used differently from Mark, where the verbs were in parallel position in the clause. In Matthew, διακονεῖν is in the form of a participle, making it appear as if the meaning of 'following' is in 'serving'.[1] Melzer-Keller is of the opinion that if Matthew had wanted to depict the women under the cross as disciples, he would have used his favourite word μαθητεύω, as he did with regard to Joseph of Arimathea in 27:57 just afterwards.[2]

In the previous sections in the narrative, three named men have been separated from the group of disciples; now, in the Passion narrative we have three named women representing the faithful followers.[3] Even more noteworthy is the fact that women have generally been nameless in the course of the narrative, but here they are carefully named – as were the disciples in Chapter 10 and the three inner circle disciples elsewhere. These named women have not been mentioned before in the narrative, and this has resulted in different interpretations. Ricci is of the opinion that because the disciples had fled and Matthew was unable to cite them as witnesses, he was forced to refer to the women who had stayed. The women had been with Jesus from the beginning, but only now, when they are the only ones present, is their presence acknowledged. The women would not have been mentioned if there had been apostles present at the cross.[4] Struthers Malbon sees the verses about women at the cross as a repeating analepsis, a retrospective section that fills in an earlier missing element. By this, she means that the reference to the women was

---

terminology acceptable to the community."
[1] Melzer-Keller 1997, 117-118.
[2] Melzer-Keller 1997, 119.Witherington III 1981, 122 on the other hand is of the opinion that Mark reserves the word μαθητής for the official witnesses or inner circle of Jesus, i.e. the Twelve.
[3] See McGinn 1995, 173.
[4] Ricci 1994, 26.

deliberately delayed until the true meaning of the discipleship could be understood by the reader.[1]

Some feminist scholars have seen the women's role here as extraordinary.[2] In my opinion, however, they only act as mediators between Jesus and the 'brothers', since the worldwide mission is entrusted to the disciples. When Jesus gives his final commission, there are only eleven men present. Even at this point, Matthew reminds that "some of them doubted". The whole setting is patriarchalised. Women are given the smallest role possible; they are needed as witnesses when there were no men available. They do not speak, they do not act.[3] *The forced affirmation of women does not change their position in the prevailing cultural context, even though the women haven proven to be completely faithful while the disciples have been shamefully unfaithful, full of doubts and failings.*

Nevertheless, this is one of the few occasions[4] in the Gospel where women have names. These women at the cross and the grave are not only named, but are also carefully identified through their sons, who are known disciples. The disciples have fled; their mothers have stayed.[5]

Kingsbury opposes using the verbs ἀκολουθεῖν and διακονεῖν as a sign of discipleship because he sees them as connected to the explanations of why women were in Jesus' company, not to describing them as disciples in the strict sense.[6] It should also be noted that even if 'following' is a verb connected to the group called 'disciples', 'serving' is something that is never mentioned as being part of their activities. Jesus himself says he serves, but the disciples are never told to serve

---

[1] Struthers Malbon 1983, 41-42. Her article is about the Markan version, but the issue itself remains the same.

[2] For example Wainwright 1991, 144 who says "contrary to the patriarchal structuring of society whereby men carry out the significant tasks, the divine message and mission is here given to women rather than men".

[3] According to McGinn, retained here is the traditional Jewish and Greco-Roman separation of spheres of male and female influence.(McGinn 1995, 175) Also Melzer-Keller 1997, 124-125 sees the role of the women only as 'tomb watchers' and messengers.

[4] Others being Mary and the foremothers in the infancy narrative, and Herodias.

[5] Heil 1991(2), 91-95 sees the mothers as substitutes for their sons and the male disciples.

[6] Kingsbury 1978, 61. So also Anderson 1983, 19.

anyone.[1] Whether these verbs describe discipleship or not depends on our understanding of the discipleship. Matthew has created a multilevel narrative where the meanings are not as simple as we would like them to be. Since the master-disciple relationship in the first century Jewish or Greco-Roman culture was androcentric, one question involves the connection between this relationship and the group of characters in Matthew's narrative. The word in the Second Testament language is mostly reserved for male persons, and in Matthew women are never called disciples.[2] Considering the patriarchal culture and the established institutions of the time, as well as the way Matthew has dealt with his characters, it is most likely that the historical disciples were male. If, on the other hand, we assume that discipleship in Matthew's ideological world is connected to faith and trust in Jesus as shown in the healing pericopes, we are dealing with another angle altogether. It would then be relevant to ask about the inclusiveness of this group of followers. Melzer-Keller has contributed valuable work by comparing the different ways Matthew and Mark deal with the verbs that are often assumed to identify a disciple. However, not too much emphasis should be placed on grammar here – nor on the vocabulary itself, as it is a way of describing the reality of the *basileia* using expressions from ordinary life. The parables and Jesus' teachings point in the same direction. Inclusiveness, as we have already seen, is not just about gender; Matthew's narration includes examples of all divisions of people: Gentiles, leaders, religious people, and outcasts. This broader way of understanding following[3] is defined by responses to Jesus in the narrative, such as faith, serving, following, understanding, and confessing.

As for the women under the cross, they are not any more or any less true followers of Jesus than are the women who have been characters in the Gospel up to this point. The women do not belong to the male group of disciples, but are as much followers in the *basileia* as the disciples are. Both Ricci's and Struthers Malbon's theories miss the point in this respect.

---

[1] Cf. also Anderson 1983, 19.

[2] Anderson 1983, 20; Kingsbury 1978, 61.

[3] Segovia 1985, 2 has defined discipleship as "the self-understanding of the early Christian believers: what such a way of life requires, implies, and entails."

While Struthers Malbon viewed the women as fallible since they stayed at a distance, Kopas argues the opposite view. For her, the women were faithful to a heroic degree.[1] This heroic faithfulness is shown in view of their taking paths disapproved for their gender in a patriarchal society, though their gender might have hindered them from going nearer. On the other hand, it might have been easier for women to be present at the crucifixion than for male supporters, since they were less dangerous. But, fallible or not, failure does not exclude anyone from the following.

All of the above leads back to the question: Are women to be counted as disciples when, in the first century patriarchal world, disciples were all male, and women are never referred to as disciples in the Gospels? I would claim that a truly comprehensive answer is that the concepts of discipleship and following should be kept separate and consider the disciples as the distinct male group they shape up to be in the narrative. The other followers are those who were healed by Jesus, served and trusted him, believed in him and confessed his authority. 'Following' in the wider sense encompasses all the followers, though in varying degrees.

4.5. Conclusion

The women in Matthew's narrative are representatives of his patriarchal environment. Gender roles are not reversed, and they remain in their conventional roles after their encounters with Jesus, in spite of the fact that they proved faithful while the disciples are doubting and cowardly. No emancipation tendencies are even hinted at in the narrative.

That some interpreters need to incorporate women as disciples is perplexing, as the term itself points to an ancient institution, and the character group called disciples fulfills the role expectations of this institution. But sometimes discipleship is understood as something broader than this character group, involving accepting and understanding the message that is intertwined with Jesus' person. This discipleship is seen as inclusive. In my opinion, this confuses the question: women do

---

[1] Kopas 1990, 21. Cf. also Schüssler Fiorenza 1983, 320 who gives a positive explanation, seeing them as Jesus' true relatives.

not belong to the group of disciples in the narrative, yet they are disciples. We cannot have it both ways.

Women and men are accepted as Jesus' followers and part of his mission with no hampering burdens of prevalent hierarchical distinctions. Jesus encounters men and women alike, Jews and Gentiles alike, rich and poor alike. Both men and women follow Jesus. Serving is proved to be the essence of the *basileia* and serving is especially connected to women. Even more conspicuous is the presence of the mothers of the disciples under the cross where the sons didn't dare to come. Mothers are faithful and courageous unlike their sons. The point Matthew makes here should not be belittled.

Women are not named as disciples in the narrative, but they fulfill an exemplary task in that they are the ones who prove to be faithful and to grasp the true meaning of the *basileia*. Some of them show such persistence and intuition which is never shown when depicting the disciples. In fact, the contrast between the women and disciples is visible on many occasions. Women serve and follow and are the first messengers of Jesus' resurrection. A modern interpretation could make these women 'new' kinds of followers; a group that includes the male disciples and the women, the Jews and the Gentiles, the leaders and the servants, the rich and the poor with Jesus as the 'magnetic' centre, not as a ruler and dominator, but as an example, a source of inspiration, and a power that makes transformation possible.

The presence of the female followers in Matthew's narrative proves that it is unjust to consider only the disciples as models for later Christian generations. In fact, it is the women who are the real examples for following and understanding.

5. Comparing the Power Structures

A helpful model for situating the different characters and character groups in the narrative map of Matthew is Michel Clévenot's illustration of concentric circles around the character of Jesus whose person creates a 'magnetic field'.[1] According to Clévenot, the text[2] itself locates the persons in these circles. Peter, James, and John are in the circle closest to Jesus. The next closest contains the Twelve, followed by the disciples, and finally the crowd. All these groups come within Jesus' influence at different levels. There are, however, certain defects in Clévenot's idea. First, it sets up a hierarchical order suggesting that those closer are also more valued. I would contend that distance and different circles are to be considered as *narrative devices* rather than indicators of authority. The diverse groups are a means to define the substance of the following. As the magnetic centre drawing each group towards its source, it reaches the named Twelve, further mentioning specific individuals among them, it does not necessarily mean these are more important than the others; rather they are individuals with unique tasks. It is as if a magnifying glass has been focused on them in order to reveal something unique about their following. This applies to Simon Peter even more than the others.

The second defect in this model is that it does not take into consideration other characters who are within Jesus' magnetic field, such as the supplicants in the healing stories, or the centurion, the women under the cross, and Joseph of Arimathea. They have been described in the narrative as emerging from the crowd, but in fact, some of them are closely examined, similar to the focus on Peter, James and John, in order to point out something unique about their way of following. Moreover, some women and men are as close to the centre as the three named disciples or the Twelve, but in a different sense. They do not fit into this image of many circles, but point to a system with only one circle; Jesus is equi-distant from all of them.

---

[1] Clévenot 1985, 86-89. The other magnetic field, the Jewish system centered on the temple, is a counter force. What is interesting in Clévenot's illustration is the presence of the crowd in both systems as the outer circle.
[2] Clévenot studies Mark's text, but the model is also applicable to Matthew.

In what follows, I shall discuss all the groups of characters in Clévenot's model, i.e. the disciples, the Twelve, Peter as the only disciple with a continuous story line of his own and the crowd – in the context of Jesus' magnetic field. I shall compare these characters and groups and their power structures with those of the women characters and analyse the different modes of following.

5.1. Peter and the Twelve

Start grandly – end up miserably. This is Simon Peter's course of life in Matthew's narrative. Oddly enough, he is the only disciple who has a story line of his own in this Gospel. His sad fading out of the narrative – the last fact told about him is that he wept bitterly – has its compensation in a unique blessing and authority in the community after the death of Jesus. He is no doubt *the disciple*. In his failure, he is still lifted above the others. In the previous chapter I have followed women's encounters with Jesus, emphasising the interaction that profiles the characters. The consequent dialogue or conflict indicates the response to their encounter. Jesus is the centre against whom every character or character group is projected. It seems that the three closest disciples are tightly bound to the hierarchical structures of the patriarchy while women represent a looser communication model connected to relationships grounded on faith. Since later interpretations have placed Simon Peter first among the disciples and a model for both discipleship and leadership, it would be fruitful to compare Peter and the women. Peter is one of the Twelve, so the role of this group will be considered in the narrative as well.

Simon Peter is a round character with strengths and weaknesses. He assumes the role of spokesman for others, but he is more than that. He is the only face to emerge from among the disciples; he heads the list and stands 'first' among the brothers, thus representing a normative authority, a leader. The disciples in Matthew have been considered representatives of the members of the Matthean community[1], and accordingly, Peter is seen as an example of what it is to be a disciple.[2]

---

[1] For example Luz 1983, 98-127. Kingsbury 1975(1), 31-37 sees the time of Jesus and the time of the church overlapping in Matthew.

[2] Kingsbury 1979, 72. Peter stands out as an example and as a sharp warning to post-Easter Christians. Cf. also Kunkel 1987, 23.

That the Matthean community bears a Jewish-Christian label more than the other Gospels is almost unanimously accepted.[1] Because some interpreters accept Peter as a representative of Jewish Christianity, his portrayal is entwined with an understanding of Matthew's community. Matthew stands at the epicentre of the controversy between Jewish and Gentile Christianity in the community. Contradicting views over Peter, his character, his significance, have been interpreted as reflecting this conflict, especially the condemning criticism (Pauline opponents?) as well as the views of the tradents.[2]

Michael Goulder's theory of two missions illustrates what might have been going on in the Matthean community. Goulder's main point is that, from the beginning, there were two missions, one centred in Jerusalem and led by Peter; the other led by Paul. He sees Matthew, though conservative, 'liberal' Petrine, conservative, while Mark is the radical Pauline, whose material is subtly changed by Matthew to accord more favourably with the Petrine mission.[3] This theory is vivid and exciting, but the portrayal of Peter causes problems. Even if the critical passages are mostly taken from Mark, Matthew's description is still not favourable. Matthew may be Petrine in questions about the Law and Jewish practice, but his attitude towards Peter himself is, at least, ambivalent.

Insightful treatises on Peter in Matthew's Gospel offer a variety of profiles. Peter has been considered a representative of a typical individual Christian[4] or 'the first among the equals' among the disciples and in Matthew's community.[5] The ambiguity of Peter's role projected by Matthew, has been explained by Matthew's need to neutralise Peter's traditional prominence, and to equate him with the other disciples, in order to present Jesus at the centre of the narrative.[6]

On the narrative level, it is interesting to note that most of the Petrine material in Matthew is situated within and in proximity to the

---

[1] For example Brown et al 1973, 75. See above 3.2.
[2] Segal 1991, 3-37.
[3] Goulder 1994.
[4] Strecker 1971, 198-206.Wilkins 1988, 172 connects Peter and the disciples as a group: "If the church as a whole can learn from the example of the disciples, the individual believer and leader in Mattthew's church is able to learn from the example of Peter."
[5] Kingsbury 1979.
[6] Nau 1992, 37, 143. He notes, however, that usually (95%) Peter stands alone in Matthew, while the other disciples act *en masse* (74). See also Syreeni 1999, 148-152.

discourse on the community.[1] On the one hand, ecclesiastical concerns are integral to the character of Peter (Chapter 18). On the other hand, Peter is inserted into the underline point of Matthew's Gospel in the discourse on the parables of the kingdom (Chapter 13). All the significant Petrine material occurs after this and before the community discourse (Chapter 18). The connections can be drawn two ways.[2] The questions of authority (Chapter 10) and community (Chapter 18) are both connected to Peter.

Most of the material on Peter is taken from Mark, and therefore represents a generally Markan view of Peter. However, Matthew omits some references to Peter. One is the pericope about the ruler's daughter. In Mark (and in Luke), Jesus allows only Peter, James, and John to follow him inside the house; in Matthew the story is shorter and there is no explanation regarding the people present inside the house. In the episode about the withered fig tree, Peter is presented as a spokesman in Mark (11:21), while in Matthew, it is the disciples who wonder about the withering (Matt 21:20). In Mark 13:3, the four first-called fishermen are with Jesus, and ask him about the signs. In Matthew's version those who ask are 'disciples' (24:3). The most interesting omission – if it is an omission – occurs in the resurrection scene when women are sent to the disciples with the news. In Mark, they are to go and tell Jesus' disciples *and Peter* about the good news (Mark 16:7). In Matthew, Peter disappears from the narrative after the denial and the repentance, and he is not mentioned again even though his presence among the eleven can be assumed at the end. The omissions are not very significant as such, but they point to a tendency to reduce the references to individual disciples (in order to reduce the references to Peter(?)), and a preference to understand the disciples as a unity.

Nevertheless, there are three Matthean passages about Peter that have no parallels in the other Gospels; they present a significant contribution to the Matthean characterisation of Peter. These passages are

* Peter's walking on the water (14:28-31)
* Jesus' blessing after Peter's profession of faith (16:16b-19)
* the temple tax pericope (17:24-27)

---

[1] See also Brown et al 1973, 79, 105-106.

[2] According to Goulder 1994, 42-43 the kingdom of heaven is already present for Matthew (though for Paul it is something in the future), and the *ekklesia* somewhat overlapping with the kingdom.

I shall consider Peter's character from three angles. First as a member of the Twelve (and the group of disciples in general), and second, his relationship to Jesus, third, the connection of the theme 'forgiveness' with Peter, and fourth, Peter's remorse after he has denied Jesus.

5.1.1. One of the Twelve

A. The Calling

Simon Peter enters the scene just after Jesus has revealed his message. Although Jesus has not yet started his ministry, *the calling of the two pairs of brothers (4:18-22)* ensures that there will be reliable witnesses of everything that happens in the narrative. It is by no means an accident that of the four called by Jesus, three will belong to the inner circle: Peter, James, and John. Andrew, the fourth, disappears from the narrative after this pericope. His name is mentioned when Matthew lists the twelve in Chapter 10, but otherwise he is not present. It is noteworthy that Matthew does not tell about the calling of all the twelve disciples. The calling of a fifth disciple, Matthew, is related very briefly in Chapter 9 and that is all. In Chapter 10, all five names appear in Matthew's list. They are among the official circle of disciples, the Twelve. When their calling was first disclosed, however, they were not explicitly named disciples. The actual word μαθητής occurs for the first time in the beginning of Chapter 5. For the reader, the disciples could as easily be the four fishermen as the crowd (4:25), since the latter is also depicted as following. The exact word ἀκολουθέω is, however, used as the result of the calling (verses 20 and 22).

The calling is strategically placed just before the description of Jesus' public ministry. This is meant to authenticate the story for the reader; these men were with Jesus right from the beginning. The location of the calling, after the first proclamation of Jesus' message, also underlines the meaning of the message. The coming of the *basileia* means radical obedience. But to whom or to what is not yet clear.

In this pericope of calling, though Matthew has taken over the Markan material (Mark 1:16-20), the redactional changes he has made are insignificant.[1] What can be significant is the presentation of Simon as τὸν

---

[1] Matthew addds δύο ἀδελφούς to verses 18 and 21. In verse 22 Mark's εὐθύς which is changed to εὐθέως is moved from its place before ἐκάλεσεν to before the participle

λεγόμενον Πέτρον. The same description occurs in verse 10:2 in the list of the Twelve. In Matthew, Simon is known from the beginning as Peter, while in Mark, it is Jesus who changes Simon to Peter (Mark 3:16).[1] The difference is in Mark's using the name as a proper name, while Matthew remembers Peter as a cognomen, and uses the form Simon Peter.[2] Only twice does Matthew merely use 'Simon' (16:17 and 17:25). The purpose of the name Peter first becomes explicit in verse 16:18.[3] Before that, it seems like a cognomen – probably in order to differentiate him from the other Simons.[4]

The setting of this calling scene is the Sea of Galilee, linking the scene to the preceding passage. The setting is not without significance. As an area, Galilee is considered less Jewish than Judaea; Matthew calls it the district of pagans (Γαλιλαία τῶν ἐθνῶν 4:15). As the centre of the Jewish world was Jerusalem, Matthew might have wanted to emphasise the difference. Galilee is far away from the centre, even if it is undeniably Jewish territory. The four men are fishermen[5] working in an everyday situation. Matthew has omitted the reference to Zebedee's day workers mentioned in Mark. The reversal found in Matthew's narrative emerges again as the setting where Jesus starts his practice is 'the Galilee of the

---

ἀφέντες. This causes verbatim agreement with verse 20. Matthew also abbreviates the ending of the final verse of the pericope. He omits the reference to Zebedee being in the boat with his hired servants and changes the words concerning the response of the men to ἠκολούθησαν αὐτῷ. This also creates verbatim agreement with verse 20. All this seems to be deliberately created parallelism between the two callings. – Held 1961, 220 and Trilling 1977, 538 consider these alterations more than just stylistic, they are catechetical.

[1] In Mark, Peter is called Simon until he is named Peter in verse 3:16. After that he is consequently called Peter.

[2] Just for comparison, Luke describes him as Simon whom he named Peter (6:14), and in Acts, he has dropped the Simon when repeating the name list (Acts 1:13).

[3] See page 156-157.

[4] Also Davies and Allison 1991, 33. For Syreeni 1999,121, the name 'Peter' is his ordinary name (τὸν λεγόμενον), which later (16:18) is interpreted by Jesus.

[5] Schottroff 1995, 84 has drawn attention to the invisible work of Galilean women. She points out that the women who followed Jesus from the beginning in Galilee (Mark 15:40; Matt 27:55), came from the same milieu of small fishing communities at the northern end of the Sea of Galilee as these four men. Schottroff assumes that they were probably as much engaged in fishing as the men were, but this work is not mentioned. Women are not defined in terms of their work.

Gentiles', not Jerusalem.[1] In Galilee, his followers are fishermen, not scribes or learned men.[2]

The men themselves in this story are faceless. Their affirmative reaction to Jesus is not explained. The reader has no information about their previous knowledge of Jesus nor about their reasons for reacting so radically. The only feature mentioned about them is their work. Their economic situation, education, or religious attitudes are not referred to. But even their work is described differently. Simon Peter and Andrew are casting their nets, while James and John are mending their nets.[3] Jesus sees these men working but they do not see him. Jesus seizes the initiative and chooses his companions. The whole situation underlines the essence of following, and the response to Jesus' call is to leave everything – family, possessions, work – on the spot.[4]

That Simon Peter is mentioned first is sometimes seen as pointing to his primacy in the early church. The text itself does not necessarily support this kind of thinking.[5] The fact that Simon Peter and Andrew are mentioned first, and Simon Peter is before Andrew, does not yet underline his primacy. Simon Peter is introduced along with three other men. His

---

[1] Clévenot 1985, 85 in his materialist reading of the Gospel of Mark, has pointed out how everything is centred or magnetised by Judaea, Jerusalem and the temple. When the practice of Jesus approaches the centre, Jerusalem, "the compass needle jumps around, the codes clash, the old tissue is torn and there is confrontation".

[2] Grant 1994, 55-57 argues that the traditional thinking that Peter (or the other apostles) was humble and poor is mistaken. Fishing was a flourishing activity in Bethsaida, and the town was one of the most important trade routes of the Near East. Peter was most probably in a good economic situation. According to Mark, Zebedee and his sons had additional laborers in their fishing business; information that Matthew omits. For Grant, these men were rather looking for exciting new ways of life instead of "backbreaking hard work and harsh competitiveness." Grant also points out that in order to carry out his mission, Peter must have been at least bilingual, if not orally trilingual, so he was not uneducated. For Peter's linguistic abilities and his education see also Thiede 1986, 20-22.

[3] Fenton 1978, 73-74 interprets these activities as foreshadowing different allocation of work. Simon Peter and Andrew are fishing, so their work foreshadows their future work as fishers of men. As for James and John, the word for mending (καρταρτίζειν) is associated with perfecting the church, which is part of the ministry. For Fenton this means that casting a net into the sea may prefigure the evangelistic aspect of the ministry to those who are outside the church, while mending their nets prefigures the pastoral ministry to those within. Cf. also Hill 1972, 106.

[4] Cf. Matt 8:21-22: Jesus' answer to the disciple: "Follow me, and leave the dead to bury their own dead."

[5] So also Nau 1992, 71.

presence among the first four who are called emphasises his authority and authenticity, but not more than that of the other three.

If we consider the association of each of these four men and Jesus, each is in the same relational position. Jesus calls them, and he makes such a strong impression on them that they follow. Compared to the women in the healing stories – the haemorrhaging woman and the Canaanite woman – the difference lies first in the manner of the encounter and second, in the initiative. Men are called to follow, women are healed. Women, aware of Jesus and his powers, actively approach to ask his help. These men, ignorant of Jesus, are approached and told to follow. In either case, Jesus is the cause of the action.

B. The Missionary Discourse

Questions relating to Peter's 'firstness' among the Twelve also appear in *the missionary discourse* (Ch 10). In the beginning of the discourse, the twelve disciples are named, and the focus in the narrative shifts for a time away from the mission of Jesus to the small group chosen from his disciples. In the beginning of this section, Jesus summons the Twelve, and it is noteworthy that this is not for the purpose of selection.[1] For Matthew, they already are a defined group, and now they receive their mission.

There are two points of interest in this passage. First, the list of the names[2], and second, the authority given to the Twelve. The naming of the Twelve comes rather late in Matthew's narrative[3] perhaps leaving the readers puzzled about earlier references to the disciples.[4] Five of the Twelve are introduced in verses 4:18-22 and 9:9, but other names emerge without any other reference elsewhere. The author continues, however, to use the phrase 'disciples' after the listing. Does it mean that 'the disciples' from this point on are meant to be understood as 'the Twelve', or does this defined and named group fill some symbolic function in the narrative?

---

[1] Otherwise Mark 3:13-15; Luke 6:13.

[2] The list of names have been given four times in the Second Testament, and they do not agree in details. Cf. Mark 3:16-19; Luke 6:14-16; Acts 1:13.

[3] The passage about sending the Twelve is a combination of two Markan pericopes, 6:7-11 which is the story of sending and 3:16-19 where Mark lists the names.

[4] Syreeni 1999, 122 says here: "The mention of a great mass of followers effectively creates the impression that other disciples were called, too."

The word ἀπόστολος is used only once in Matthew (10:1), in
reference to the listed names.[1] The authority given to the Twelve parallels
the mission of Jesus, and concerns healing and exorcism.[2] Questions of
leadership are not present.[3] The word πρῶτος at the beginning of the list
has led many to take it as a reference to Peter's firstness and his
leadership among the disciples.[4] Although it may be unnecessary to pay
particular attention to the beginning of the list,[5] this usage could easily
refer to Peter's primacy in order of calling, and not in any primacy of
authority.[6] It is also notable that the names are listed in pairs in Matthew,
and thus, Simon Peter is coupled with Andrew. The 'firstness' of calling
might just as well be interpreted as referring to this pair of brothers.[7] My
conclusion is that it is better not to read too much into this one word.
Peter is one of the two men who were called first. Any emphasis on his
firstness in authority would need information about the tradition of the
later events in his life.

Nau interprets this 'being first' in the light of another saying in
Matthew 19:30, where Jesus' words to Peter and the disciples include a

---

[1] Luz 1983, 109 suggests: "The members of the community could identify with the
μαθήται, but not with the ἀπόστολοι who had become by that time figures of the
past." The word ἀπόστολος also occurs only once in Mark (6:39).

[2] The pericope itself is unclear as to whether the Twelve are really sent or just the
object of instructions. In Mark and in Luke, the absence of the sent disciples is noted
explicitly, in Matthew no such statement is made. The main point relates to the
instructions. Luz 1983, 100 states that Jesus' instructions will be fulfilled only in the
post-Easter period.

[3] Against this Syreeni 1999, 124 who points to leadership in connection with verse
9:36. There Jesus notes that the crowd is like sheep without a shepherd. As I see it, the
shepherd does not necessarily point to leadership, the next verse already changes the
image to agriculture and talks about labourers who should bring in the harvest. Also,
if we connect verses 9:36-37 to Jesus' instructions to the Twelve, no positions of
authority or leadership are given to the disciples. The disciples are to proclaim the
message, to heal sick, and to exorcise – all these point to serving, not leading.

[4] Davies and Allison 1991, 154; Hagner 1993, 265-266; Fenton 1978, 151; Thiede
1986, 27-28; Trilling 1959, 133.

[5] So also Schweizer 1981, 153.

[6] This also supported by Kingsbury 1979, 70-71. Nau 1992, 75 uses the phrase 'pride
of place'. It should be remembered, though, that the text itself gives no clue regarding
authority. That kind of question presupposes a later interpretation of Peter's role in
early Christianity. Syreeni 1999, 125 sees Peter's firstness as a symbol of honour and
authority.

[7] Augustine Stock has also considered Matthew's presentation of Peter in terms of
irony and he emphasises the wordplay Πέτρος, πρῶτος. The πρῶτος indicates to
him importance, weight, and rank (Stock 1987, 67).

warning: "But many that are first will be last, and the last first." In 20:27 Jesus says to the disciples: "Whoever would be first among you must be your slave." The parable of the labourers in the vineyard ends with the statement, "So the last will be first, the first last." Nau suggests that in the light of these statements, Matthew's portrayal of Peter can be read as 'a good beginning – and a poor ending'. "He who was once 'first' in terms of his call, ends up last, nameless and out of sight in the post-Passion accounts."[1] Nau's point is plausible. In Matthew, priority and pre-eminence do not belong to the values of the *basileia*. Peter's initial high visibility ends up poorly in Matthew's narrative.

Peter, James, and John form the inner circle of Twelve (cf also 17:1; 26:37), while the other nine men remain unknown except for their names: Philip, Bartholomew, and Thomas, as well as James, the son of Alphaeus, and Thaddeus occur only in the list in Chapter 10. Matthew, the tax collector, is mentioned in the list and also in the story about his calling (9:9), which is very brief. Another Simon is described as ὁ Καναναῖος (derived from Aramaic *qan'an* meaning zealot). Matthew would have known this as a term for a revolutionary, but at the least, it refers to nationalism and hatred of Rome. This Simon is mentioned nowhere else in Matthew's Gospel. Judas Iscariot, on the other hand, is referred to more often (26:14, 25,47; 27:3), but always – apart from this list – in the passion narrative. Matthew already describes him with the attribute "who was also his betrayer" when including Judas in the list in Chapter 10. A pivotal point is the precise identification of these twelve men. They are a striking combination of fishermen, tax collector, zealot, and traitor.[2]

---

[1] Nau 1992, 75-76.

[2] The historicity of 'the Twelve' has been defended by the fact that Judas has been said to be chosen by Jesus himself. The community would not have invented something so offensive. (Cf. Davies and Allison 1991, 151-152) Nineham 1992, 15 has argued, when commenting on Mark, that the fact that the Twelve did not have an important role in the early Church makes it less likely that the appointment of the Twelve would have been invented. Sanders 1985, 101-102 argues that the phrase 'the Twelve' is used symbolically, pointing to the restoration of Israel. The group itself was not limited to twelve men. That the Twelve is a symbolic number is also compatible with the fact that the lists existing in the Second Testament are not in agreement. It is plausible that Jesus had a closer circle of disciples among the followers, but their function and number are defined only after Jesus' death and resurrection.

C. Visible Hierachy

On the other hand, some visible hierarchy is connected to Peter's character when viewed from another angle. In the pericope concerning *the healing of Peter's mother-in-law* (8:14-15)[1], Simon Peter is only indirectly present. The healing happens in his house, and the woman concerned is legally related to him. The retelling of the incident is most probably due to this personal connection to Peter. It also seems that Simon Peter's house was a centre of activities. Jesus might have used it as a base for his teaching journeys (cf. Matt 4:13; 9:28-31; 17:25-27).

The structures within the context of this story are worth looking into a little more closely. The element of subordination is present in the first three episodes of the miracle section. Jesus cures the leper and orders him to go to the priest. The verification of the healing is left to the legal authority. The centurion who pleads for his servant is a Gentile, and the relationship is one of subordination: a master and a servant. The hierarchical construct is made even more complex as Jesus is described as an authority and the centurion as a supplicant.

Matthew inserted the story of Peter's mother-in-law after these incidents, and explicit mention is made of the relationship between the woman and Peter: once again a relationship of subordination, but because of gender. The patriarchal structure is revealed through Peter and the woman. It is not his wife or his own mother, but a more distant member of the household, whose head, no doubt, is Peter himself. The emphasis is shifted to Peter. He is the reason for retelling the story, and the significance of the healing is that it happens to a member of his household.[2] There is no criticism of the structures of subordination, they are described and accepted as they exist. Even the reason for the woman's healing reeks patriarchy, if it was done in order to make her able to serve the men who otherwise would be without food. It is also significant to note that the woman was Peter's mother-in-law, which implies that at least one of the Twelve was married (Peter's wife is mentioned in 1 Cor 9:5), and that the abandonment of family ties is not to be taken literally. The mention of the house points out that not all possessions and stability in life were abandoned.

---

[1] See also page 83-90.
[2] So also Syreeni 1999, 123.

Thus, Peter's primacy and authority as a hierarchical status is at least implied here. It should be noted that hierarchy as such is not necessarily negative in Matthew. The directive functions in society are inevitable, but they should never lead to inequality among the followers. Modern business practice makes a distinction between management and leadership, ie. between directing things and leading people. The relationship between the leading positions among the followers and the equality among the followers in *basileia* can be understood in a similar way. This distinction can also create different shades of meaning in terms of Peter's assumed firstness. His later authoritative status in the church does not place him above other followers, but rather in charge of things.

D. The Twelve and Israel's Restoration

According to Matthew, the Twelve are sent to 'the lost sheep of the House of Israel' (10:6), and the number twelve points to the twelve tribes of Israel (cf. also 19:28). The disciples as a group of Twelve symbolise the new Israel. Other incidents specifically involving the defined Twelve are in verse 11:1, where the episode of instructions ends, and verse 20:17, where Jesus predicts his passion exclusively to the Twelve. In the Passion narrative, the Twelve are referred to three times; twice when defining Judas as one of the Twelve, and the third time when underlining that only they are present at the Passover meal.

The tradition concerning the Twelve dates back to time before Matthew, who for his part used Mark as the source.[1] The earliest text that refers to the Twelve is 1 Cor 15:5, where Paul quotes a tradition, according to which the Resurrected appeared to Cephas and then to the Twelve. The Twelve seems here to be a symbolic entity; for example, it does not say 'Cephas and the eleven'. In verse 19:28 the narrative refers to the coming glory, when the followers of Jesus will sit on twelve thrones and rule the twelve tribes of Israel, thus promising the twelve men a role in Israel in an eschatological future. The background for the

---

[1] Matthew uses the expression οἱ δώδεκα 8 times (cf. Mark 11 times). Matthew has altered the Markan οἱ δώδεκα to οἱ μαθηταί twice (13:10//Mark 4:10; 18:1// Mark 9:35). Matthew has also completed the title οἱ δώδεκα with μαθηταί (10:1; 20:17; 26:20). He has never done it the other way round, though. Luz 1983, 99 concludes that Matthew has taken the identification between the twelve and the disciples from Mark; and accepts it as it is. Wilkins 1988, 133 also considers the use of the longer form to point to identification between those two.

number twelve relates to the restoration of Israel, which was a common expectation in Second Temple Judaism. The symbolic function is to imply the eschatological restitution of the whole of Israel. However, the mission of the Twelve is not only restricted to Israel, but also restricted in content. They are given *authority* over unclean spirits with the *power* to drive them out. The questions of leadership are not connected to them or their mission (10:8).

In the eschatological future, however, the Twelve are promised a special reward. After the pericope about the rich man (19:16-22) and the warnings against wealth (19:23-30) Peter asks Jesus: "Look, we have left everything and followed you. What are we to have then?" Jesus' answer is surprising. The Twelve are promised a glorious destiny. In the eschatological future they will sit on twelve thrones to judge the twelve tribes of Israel.[1] But the promise continues: "And everyone who has left houses, brothers, sisters, father, mother, children or land for the sake of my name will receive a hundred times as much, and also inherit eternal life." The latter part of the promise is for everybody who gives up what s/he loves.

The promises point to separate directions, the first being a Jewish vision of the restoration of the whole of Israel (the implication of the twelve thrones and twelve tribes), the latter a vision of the reward from the perspective of the *basileia*. This seeming contradiction finds an interesting parallel in Chapter 20, where the mother of Zebedee's sons asks Jesus to give her sons privileged positions in the future kingdom. These sons are James and John, the two inner circle disciples besides Peter. Jesus, however, does not agree to promise this, and he reminds them of the fate of a disciple. Then he teaches all twelve what leadership means: He who wants to be great must become a servant and he who wants to be first must become a slave. This is the reversal of any hierarchical order and domination. Leadership and authority in the community are – as it is described in Chapter 18 – 'brotherly', being in relation with each other more than exercising authority over others. More explicitly, in 23:8-12 Jesus teaches both the disciples and the crowds that there is only one teacher; all the others are brothers. Serving others is the heart of his message.

---

[1] This is Matthew's text. The Markan version does not include eschatological rewards. Beasley-Murray 1987, 275-276 sees the disciples sitting as assessors in the court when Israel is judged. The thrones are – Beasley-Murray refers to Dan 7:9 – strictly designated to the court scene.

On the narrative level, there is no definitive separation between the Twelve and the disciples.[1] The Twelve seem, however, to be more a group connected to the historical past because they are identified with names and they have a special mission. The disciples are a more flexible and variable group. Peter belongs to both groups and therefore can be considered a representative of the Jewish Christian practice as well as a model disciple in general. Matthew is clearly in trouble trying to combine the hopes of the Jewish restoration with the *basileia* vision.

From a feminist perspective the idea of a historical institution of the apostles as the chosen and commissioned twelve men to be the apostolic leaders in the early Church has led to the exclusion of women from leadership functions in the church in general.[2] Schüssler Fiorenza has dealt with this problem and challenged maleness as integral to the function of this group.[3] It is also worth while to question the exemplary status of this group in modern churches. Is the ancient master-disciple model a present-day norm for the Christian church, and if it is, is it also a sanctification of the social structures of the ancient Jewish society? I prefer to consider the institution of the Twelve as a symbolic entity connected to Israel rather than the founding of a historical group of twelve leaders. Their role is then not decisive when discussing leadership functions in later Christian churches.

The Twelve are sent on their mission twice in Matthew's narrative: first to Israel in Chapter 10, then to all the nations in the last verses of the narrative. The ones sent in the second missioning are also explicitly the Eleven, not 'the disciples', which seems to point to a more limited group

---

[1] On the contrary Luz 1983, 99, who sees that Matthew accepts the already Markan identification between the disciples and the Twelve. Strecker 1971, 191-198 goes further as he sees that Matthew even tries to make this identification complete. On the other hand, Matthew uses the expression οἱ δώδεκα less (8) than Mark (11). He sometimes replaces οἱ δώδεκα with οἱ μαθηταί (13:10; 18:1). That he sometimes completes the expression οἱ δώδεκα with μαθηταί proves according to Wilkins 1988, 133 that Matthew assumes an identification of the Twelve with the disciples. Syreeni 1999, 124 discusses the possibility of dividing the representational functions of the Twelve and the disciples. He concludes by noting that a clear-cut division is impossible.

[2] Congregation for the Doctrine of the Faith: Declaration Inter Insigniores on the Question of the Admission of Women to the Ministerial Priesthood (15 October 1976); Mulieris Dignitatem: Apostolic letter of the Supreme Pontiff John Paul II on the Dignity & Vocation of Women on the occasion of the Marian Year (1988); Ordinatio Sacerdotalis: Apostolic Letter of His Holiness Pope John Paul II on reserving priestly ordination to men alone (1994).

[3] Schüssler Fiorenza 1983. See also eadem 1993, 104-116.

of followers. The Twelve are entrusted with a mission and promised special rewards, but these are not in line with the promises of the *basileia*.

E. Peter's Profession of Faith

Thus, up till now, Peter's primacy among the Twelve is not at all clear. Let us move on then to the pericope that has been traditionally used to 'anoint' Peter as the head of the Church to see if the claims for his primacy of authority are better justified. This episode consists of two parts that need to be read in tandem. First, Peter's profession of faith and then his rejection as a stumbling block (16:13-23).[1]

The episode, as a whole, is mostly Markan material (Mark 8:27-33) with a few inserted verses (17-19) from Matthew's own sources.[2] Jesus asks his disciples' opinions about who he really is and Simon Peter acts once again as a spokesman.[3] The emphasis of the Matthean narrative, however, shifts from Jesus to Peter in verses 17-19. Peter is no longer representative of all; he alone is said to be blessed, and he alone is named as the rock upon which the community will be built.[4] Jesus' answer, μακάριος ἐι, Σίμων Βαριωνᾶ, is incontestably in the singular.[5] On the

---

[1] Following the Kingsbury model, which consists of three parts (1:1-4:16; 4:17-16:20; 16:21-28:20), it is worth noticing that the combination originating from Mark here falls into different parts of the threefold structure. This seems to speak against Kingsbury's solution.

[2] The redactional changes Matthew has made to the Markan parallel are not significant. Jesus' question has been changed (Jesus calls himself Son of man). The answer to the questions includes the names of prophets and Matthew adds Jeremiah to the list. In Mark 8:29, the name is in the form 'Peter', in Matthew 'Simon Peter'. The prohibition has been changed.

[3] For Peter's role as a spokesman in Matthew see also 15:15; 18:21; 19:23.

[4] On the contrary Wilkins 1988, 193 who emphasises the pronoun *this*, referring to Peter as he is at that moment: a courageous confessor, a spokesman for the disciples, a recipient of a revelation. It is upon *this Peter* that Jesus builds his church. On the other hand, he says that Peter is never placed above the other disciples ,who are also part of the foundation. It is hard to follow Wilkins' reasoning here. If he sees Peter as a spokesman for the others, a leader among them, if he thinks that Jesus used Peter to build the church and he was the tool Jesus used to lay the foundation work (193-194), it is not logical to assume that Peter was not 'above and apart' from the others. If he has leadership, he is 'above'. The difficulty seems to be that Peter is clearly representative of something more than the other disciples. If we had only this text, Peter's representational leadership would be obvious. The text itself is clear. More confusing is the meaning of this leadership in its wider context.

[5] The name 'son of Jonah' has caused some difficulty. In the fourth Gospel the name

other hand, the mysteries of the *basileia* are entrusted to all the disciples (13:11) and the disciples have already confessed what Peter says here (cf. 14:33). From this perspective, Peter is not so unique, even though he is singled out here.

Simon is a very common name in the Second Testament and almost every Simon has a cognomen or an attribute of some kind.[1] As for Simon Peter's Πέτρος, it is a plausible assumption that it has been later understood as a proper name.[2] Originally, the Greek word could have been a cognomen given as a reference to a person's outer appearance or character. In secular Greek, πέτρα means a large and solid rock, which can symbolise firmness, immovability, hardness and lack of feeling. Πέτρος is used more for isolated rocks or small stones. The two forms are often used interchangeably, with no apparent difference.[3] Πέτρος as a cognomen for a man is in the masculine form. Verse 18 itself is dubious. Simon is given a new name, which he has really had in the narrative the whole time.[4] The wordplay πέτρος/ πέτρα has caused debate and the πέτρα on which the community will be built has been interpreted in different ways:[5] Peter's faith or confession, Peter's preaching office, the truth revealed to Peter, the twelve apostles, Jesus, or God himself.

All these alternatives are ambiguous and do not necessarily fit into the narrative itself, where it clearly refers to Peter.[6] The number of interpretations show the difficulty of interpreting this blessing. How is it possible for Peter to be the foundation of the church, since a few verses further on, in the next episode, Jesus calls Peter a Satan. The πέτρα could point to the confession as such, to mean that Peter acknowledges 'the

---

is Σίμων Ἰωάννου (John 21:15) For possible explanations see, for example, Davies and Allison 1991, 622.

[1] For example in Matthew see 10:4; 13:55; 26:6; 27:32.

[2] The name itself has already been known by Paul. He uses the Aramaic form *Kefas* (1 Cor 1:12; 3:22; 9:5; 15:5; Gal 1:18; 2:9, 11,14). The linguistic origins have been thoroughly discussed in Wilkins 1988, 190-191.

[3] Cullmann 1973, 95.

[4] Thiede 1986,38 explains this problem by saying that in this scene the name is not given, but explained to Simon. He points to Isaiah 51:1-2, which could give clues for Peter's understanding of his name, especially if he knew about the rabbinical explanation of the passage, where God sees in Abraham a rock on which he can build and found the world. (See also Thiede 1986, 219 n. 54)

[5] For alternatives see Davies and Allison 1991, 627f.

[6] This has also been the interpretation of many of the early church fathers, of the contemporary Roman Catholic Church and of several scholars, among others Brown et al 1973, 92-93.

things of God', but in the next minute he is a Satan, a stumbling block for Jesus (16:23), because he thinks in a human way.[1] Matthew has indisputably inserted the Petrine material in the earlier Markan combination of two episodes concerning Peter. This indicates that he wanted the blessing to be read in the light of the rebuke.[2]

The word ἐκκλησία occurs only twice in the canonical Gospels, here and in Matt 18:18. Originally, the word referred to an assembly of citizens. Later it signified the church. If the Matthean community had already parted from Judaism,[3] it is natural that the new group tried to differentiate themselves from the mother-synagogue and thus the ἐκκλησία would challenge the synagogue.

As already mentioned, the word πέτρος can have two connotations. Literally it means an isolated rock or a small stone, a pebble. It is also reasonable to assume that the masculine cognomen could be associated with the feminine word πέτρα, in which case the definition is widened to include a large and solid rock. In Matthew's narrative, Jesus says that he wants to build the future community on the rock of Peter and his confession of faith, and so utilises the imagery of his name. It would be natural to assume that this indicates something favourable. On the other hand, if we consider the next episode where Jesus rebukes Peter as Satan, the ambiguity of the blessing in Matthew is apparent. The communities addressed by Matthew are already aware of the influence of Peter, but resistance to it exists also. Matthew presents him in a mainly unfavourable light; this blessing is the only incident where Peter is depicted favourably. Matthew does not highlight his eminence, and the description hardly suggests a bedrock on whom to build. In fact, Matthew's overall portrait of Peter proves that he might more fittingly be

---

[1] Brown et al 1973, 93.

[2] Also Nau 1992, 112-114 reads these pericopes together and sees the latter as a direct counterbalance to the former. He also points out – referring to Burton Scott Easton in the 1920's – the isolation of the verses 16:17-19 in the other material on Peter in Matthew or even the conflict that prevails between these verses and the rest of the material. Another explanation emphasises Peter as a symbol of forgiveness. His pre-eminence makes his misunderstanding universal. If he did not grasp the truth, the truth was hidden from all. Peter's fall from the heights shows that he is not an idealized figure. (Davies and Allison 1991, 665-666.)

[3] This alternative is favoured for example by Stanton 1993, 124-131. See also 3.2.

likened to the 'loose sand' of verses 7:24-27.[1] On the other hand, the multiple range of meanings could also be considered as the background of the blessing. Peter, who is known to be the leader of the new movement, is blessed by Jesus himself, not as a full-time rock, but also as a part-time pebble, as the narrative proves.

The ἐκκλησία is to be built (the future tense οἰκοδομήσω) on one rock. This episode relates that Peter is being given a unique task in the future community. The wordplay may be taken as ironic or toned down to a gentle sense of humour. The already existing cognomen may have prompted this wordplay because Peter's task and his prominent status among the disciples has been acknowledged and it clearly points to Peter's life after the death of Jesus. If Matthew's aim had been to present Peter as the foundation of the church it probably would have been more evident throughout his Gospel. No such evidence is present elsewhere.[2]

This does not mean that Peter's firstness and authority in Matthew's time in respect to the ἐκκλησία is any less valued. In the narrative, he is the sole recipient of the blessing .However, the blessing is not about having power in the early communities (or later for that matter). He is given the keys to the *basileia*[3], which has been interpreted as opening for entry. An interpretation could be to identify the keys with entry. Having keys to the *basileia* would mean that Peter will open the door to the *basileia*, he will enter through it and perhaps the door then will remain open, so no one else will need the keys. Thus, this would point to a unique task, not to the power to control others. On the other hand, if we interpret the keys as a power-over position in the *basileia,* this would be

---

[1] Stock 1987, 66 argues in his article that Matthew's presentation of Peter is ironic. The words in verse 18 mean the opposite of what they seem to say in an extreme form of irony. Also Anderson 1994, 91-92 points to the irony of the name 'Rock'. 'The Rock' rebukes Jesus, thinking the things of men (16:33) and denies him (26:69-75).

[2] Caragounis 1990, 118-119 has argued in his book about Peter that Matthew's theology about the rock on which Jesus will build his church contains Peter's confession that Jesus is the Messiah. His further suggestion is that the expression συ εἰ Πέτρος functions as the equivalent of an oath formula in order to underline the solemnity of the utterance. "As truly as you are Peter, on this rock (of what you have just said) I will build my church."

[3] According to Strack-Billerbeck 1922, 736-739 the authority of the keys belongs to the rabbinic concepts pointing towards community discipline and the power to interpret the law. See also Goulder 1974, 390. The meaning of the keys has been interpreted in different ways. Brown et al 1973, 96, 100-101 refers to a generic power given to Peter. Kingsbury 1979, 76 to the power to open and shut the doors of the kingdom.

in contradiction with the images that describe its values.[1] Matthew may be repeating an older tradition here, but his redaction, the context where he presents these words waters down their meaning. Here, if anywhere, the critique against the growing hierarchy and accompanying values is visible. Furthermore, the words "whatever you bind on earth will be bound in heaven; whatever you loose on earth will be loosed in heaven" are repeated later in the narrative (18:18) to all the disciples. Here the connection between the keys and the bindings and loosings is relevant. If they refer to the same thing, then the keys are entrusted to all the disciples.[2] Peter is celebrated for his uniqueness, but soon after, he is relegated again to the rank and file of the group.[3] It is possible to see this fact in terms of a criticism of incipient establishment of a hierarchy in the Christian communities.

Furthermore, if Peter's blessing is taken in the light of the rebuke that follows, the ἐκκλησία might not be considered in an entirely promising light. There may have been tension between the emerging

---

[1] On the contrary for example Beasley-Murray 1987, 184-185 who sees that the community and the kingdom can be equated.

[2] Brown et al 1973, 97-101; Trilling 1971, 115-118. One way of looking at the problem is to see that Peter himself is dead when the Gospel was written. In the narrative he represents interpretation of the law and this power after him is common to the whole community. See also Schweizer 1981, 223. Bornkamm 1983, 94-95 interprets the situation in the light of the strained encounter between Hellenistic and Jewish Christian traditions. There is no indication that historically Peter ever had the role which is ascribed to him in 16:17-19. The founding of the church on Peter is interpreted as Peter being the guarantor and authorized interpreter of Jesus' teachings. Another perspective comes from the history of the early church. In Wilkins' words: "Peter was the special medium through whom the proclamation of the gospel was first made, which opened the kingdom to all peoples." This also explains why Peter alone is given the keys. Once the doors are opened, the keys are no longer needed. Keys would mean opening the *basileia* to Jews and non-Jews alike. Binding and loosing belong to the proclamation of the gospel and therefore these are entrusted to all disciples (Wilkins 1988, 195, 197). This is an interesting thought, but distant from the content of the text.

[3] Schweizer 1974, 153 says: "Das zeigt, dass Petrus weithin *exemplarisch für alle Jünger* das sagt und das zu hören bekommt, was jeder Jünger sagen und hören könnte." (Italics from Schweizer) Also Wilkins 1988, 189, 198 sees Peter here as a spokesman for the disciples and thus also the blessing and revelation are directed to the group as well. For Wilkins, Peter is individually singled out for the act of confession, but "his leadership role is from *within* the circle of disciples." (Italics from Wilkins) Here again the difficulty of these verses confronts us. How can one combine Matthew's clear tendency to put Peter on the same level as the others and at the same time recognize his unique position among the other disciples. If he is the leader he is above the others. It seems that the problem originates with Matthew.

church in Matthew's time and the values of the *basileia,* and in that case Matthew's message would be that Peter, the pebble, and his ἐκκλησία match each other. This would be in line with the other pericopes about Peter.

5.1.2. Peter, the Twelve, and Jesus

The Twelve clearly represent a privileged, closer circle of followers in the narrative. Besides their inclusion in Chapter 10 and being sent on their mission, they appear when Jesus takes them aside (20:17) to reveal his own future to them. The Twelve are promised a special eschatological reward (19:28). They are also, in the end, the ones who are given the task of the worldwide mission (28.16-20). They are characters who have their own special task among the followers.

A. Peter Walks on the Water

Taking into account the relationship Peter and the Twelve have to Jesus, I shall take a closer look first at the pericope where *Peter tries to walk on the water* (14:22-23). This episode was originally taken from Mark, but Matthew has added the material about Peter and changed the conclusion (cf. Mark 6:45-52).[1] The material peculiar to Matthew, Peter's walking on the water and failing, presents him as a disciple with an experience reserved for him only.[2] Peter fails to walk on the water and is rebuked by Jesus as ὀλιγόπιστος; he does not trust Jesus' ability to control the situation.[3] He could be contrasted with the Canaanite woman who, unlike Peter, had faith. The conclusion is Matthean[4]: The others in the boat confess their faith and worship Jesus saying: "Truly you are the Son of God." The attention is focused on the contrast between Peter and the other disciples. A possible explanation is that all the disciples – except

---

[1] On the additional material including phrases typical to Matthew see Held 1961, 193-195.
[2] Thiede 1986, 29 has tried to find an explanation of why this episode in Mark (and in the other Gospels) is connected to Peter himself. Peter's portrayal in Mark is meant to give a balanced amount of information rather than depicting the strengths and weaknesses of his faith.
[3] Cf. Nau 1992, 102-103.
[4] In Mark the disciples are left completely dumbfounded.

Peter – recognise Jesus as the Son of God. Somewhat later in the narrative, Peter seems merely to repeat what the other disciples have already said in verse 14:33 (cf. 16:16). He is not presented in a favourable light. He is too arrogant in his faith, fails and is rebuked by Jesus. Some interpreters want to see in him a typical disciple[1], eager in love and insufficient in faith, 'a disciple on the way of discipleship'.[2] On the other hand, he alone is not accused of being ὀλιγόπιστος, as the disciples are all rebuked as such elsewhere (8:26; 16:8).

Despite the addition of the Petrine material to the Markan story, the episode remains very much centred around Jesus, the 'Lord'. While Peter is not all bad, the whole episode emphasises Peter's failure and his dependence on the risen Lord.[3] All the disciples in the boat worship Jesus, which diminishes the uniqueness of Peter's later profession diminishing it to a repetition.[4]

B. The Transfiguration

Another episode in which Jesus is clearly in the centre, accompanied by Peter, James, and John, is the transfiguration scene (17:1-8). Matthew following Mark (Mark 9:2-8) here[5], makes only one significant change, the way Peter addresses Jesus. In Mark, Peter addresses Jesus as 'rabbi',

---

[1] Schweizer 1981, 211. See also Anderson 1994, 93-97. For Wilkins 1988, 181-182 Peter is an example both in a positive and in a negative sense. He advances from the group of disciples and his walk is a real attempt at faith. But he fails in his faith by looking away from Jesus. His faith and failure result in worship of Jesus by all of the disciples. For different alternatives of interpretation see further Brown et al 1973, 81-83.

[2] Held 1961, 195.

[3] The episode in John 21:7-8 forms a partial parallel. The recognition and the 'Lord' are characteristic of resurrection scenes. It has been considered possible that these two scenes have the same underlying tradition. Cf. Brown et al 1973, 81; Schweizer 1981, 209. On the contrary Thiede 1986, 29-30 who considers 'the Lord' as a conventional courtesy, 'Sir'.

[4] Wilkins 1988, 182-183 emphasises Peter's role by noting that the disciples as a group do not recognise the significance of Jesus until Peter leads the way through his example of faith. In 8:23-27 the disciples only 'marvelled'. Despite Peter's role here, the other disciples are seen in a more positive light than Peter. He fails, they worship.

[5] The changes he makes are mostly insignificant. Matthew uses the same word as Mark in verse 2 μετεμορφώθη, but adds to it "his face shone as the light". The heavenly voice says in Mark, "This is my beloved Son". In Matthew, it is "This is my beloved Son, with whom I am well pleased." The latter part originates from Isa 42:1 where it refers to the suffering servant. For Matthew's verses 6-7 there is no parallel in Mark.

but Matthew changes it to Κύριε. Peter addresses Jesus as 'Lord' elsewhere in Matthew as well (14:28,30; 16:22; 18:21). In verse 4, Peter speaks in the singular while Mark uses the plural. In Matthew, he is not a spokesman for others; he speaks only for himself.[1]

Here Peter is with James and John, the two other inner circle disciples. Jesus' rebuke of him in the previous chapter has not endangered the relationship. He is again 'the rock' who is privileged with a private epiphany. Two First Testament figures, Moses and Elijah, appear to Jesus and the three disciples.[2] The presence of Moses and Elijah is a puzzle in itself as these two figures do not appear in the First Testament together and it seems to mislead Peter as well. He expresses his wish to make shelters for the three, but says nothing about shelters to the three disciples. This offer to make the shelters seems more like a gesture of respect towards Jesus and the First Testament figures than a wish to stay on the mountain. The mistake Peter makes is of course ranking Jesus with Moses and Elijah. This time he is not rebuked, but a bright light symbolising the presence of God[3] covers them (Jesus, Moses and Elijah?)[4] with a shadow and a voice from the clouds speaking the same words as in the baptismal scene. It is the voice of supreme authority and fear is the emotion that overcomes the disciples. Jesus is the 'Lord' whose status is affirmed by God himself.

Both these scenes are clearly kyriocentric. Jesus is the Lord and Peter, James, and John acknowledge their submission.

5.1.3. Peter and Forgiveness

The third major perspective in Matthew's Peter stories is the strand of forgiveness. The episode to be considered is about the temple tax paid by

---

[1] Nau 1992, 79-80 points here to the Matthean redaction where Peter is always seen in relation to Jesus. Christology is the theme here.

[2] The background to this scene may well have been Ex 24:16, where Moses spends six days on the mountain with Joshua and the Lord calls to him from a cloud on the seventh. In Ex 34:29 Moses descends from the mountain and his face shines. Traditionally, Moses has been seen representing the law and Elijah the prophets. Moses is the representative of the first covenant and therefore could be taken as a predecessor of Jesus. Elijah can be interpreted as pointing to John the Baptist. (See for example Thiede 1986, 47.)

[3] Cf. Ex 40:34; 24:16

[4] All the synoptic gospels agree that the disciples, including Peter, were not within the cloud, but outside of it. See Thiede 1986, 49-50.

Jesus and Peter. It has no parallels in the other Gospels and the whole incident is somewhat puzzling as the question of the temple tax (τὰ δίδραχμα) has no link to Matthew's community, where the purely Jewish tax, which was no longer even valid, was hardly a problem.[1] Even if the tax referred to the Fischus Iudaicus, a purely pagan tax paid to the temple of Jupiter after AD 70, it would not make any sense in this context.[2] The context surrounding this pericope does not help unlock its meaning either, as it seems more or less an isolated incident.[3]

In this story, the collectors of the didrachma approach Peter and ask: "Does your teacher not pay the tax?" and Peter answers promptly: "Yes." This is the only time Peter speaks for Jesus in the Gospels. But when he enters the house Jesus asks him, addressing him as 'Simon', not Peter: "From whom do earthly kings collect toll, from their sons or from others?" Simon answers: "From others." Jesus points out then that the sons are free. But in order not to give offense, Simon is to go fishing and the mouth of the fish will contain a stater to give to the tax collectors for Jesus and himself.[4]

The fact that Peter was involved in the conversation and favours paying the tax could be taken as reflecting Jewish Christian interests in the narrative. This might imply that Jewish Christians paid the tax before AD 70 and that this episode derives from that period. It might also refer to the attitude of Jesus himself about the temple tax. All this would, of course, be irrelevant to Matthew's own communities. The point in Matthew's narrative is something other than a mere reporting of a past episode that is no longer relevant.

Peter exercises authority that Jesus accepts. He is the one who is asked the question and he answers. What this answer meant for the Matthean communities is not clear. The fact that Jesus backs up Peter's attitude has been interpreted as backing up Peter's authority in general

---

[1] Before AD 70 the didrachma was to be paid by every male from age twenty. Women, slaves, Samaritans, and Gentiles were excluded. Cf. Ex 30:11-16. For more details see, for example, Garland 1996. See also Schweizer 1981, 231-233.

[2] Thoroughly argued in Garland 1996, 78-85. Also Brown et al 1973, 103; Thiede 1986, 56.

[3] Brown et al 1973, 101 have suggested the redaction is due to the location of the incident. Capernaum was the town where Jesus paid his taxes.

[4] For Nau 1992, 57 this means that Peter is more closely identified with Jesus than the other disciples.

and in this way emphasising Peter's leading position.[1] This *theological* explanation assumes more than the narrative itself suggests.

Again Peter acts as a spokesperson. The tax collectors do not approach Jesus directly. Instead of interpreting the episode as an isolated unit, the clue to understanding lies in its context. Jesus is paying the tax 'in order not to cause offense'. Thus the pericope prepares the way for Chapter 18 where the focus is on 'the little ones' and limitless forgiveness.[2] The historical tax is not the issue here. As Peter acts as spokesperson both here and in Chapter 18, his first lesson is 'not to cause offense' and later, the lesson is to give up one's own rights for others: unlimited forgiveness.

The Petrine material is very compact in this narrative section; it is restricted on the one hand to the kingdom discourse and on the other hand to the community discourse. Peter tries to walk on water. He starts eagerly, but fails. He acts as a spokesman in a discussion on purity. He professes his faith and is given a unique blessing, but immediately afterwards he proves that he still does not understand and is rebuked severely. When Jesus is transfigured, he again misses the point. And in the episode concerning the temple tax, he is given a lecture on 'not causing offense'. In Chapter 18 Peter asks Jesus: "Lord, how often must I forgive my brother if he wrongs me? As often as seven times?" Noteworthy here again is the 'Lord' from Peter's mouth. Jesus' answer implies limitless forgiveness.[3] Matthew's narrative explains this in the form of a story, the king forgives his debtor, but the debtor learns nothing. The point is the result of forgiving. The change is what counts.

5.1.4. Peter's Remorse

In my opinion, Matthew has used the Petrine passages in order to criticise Peter's possibly too prominent position in some of the Christian communities. The hierarchical order becomes clear: Jesus is the ultimate

---

[1] For example, Brown et al 1973, 104. For Nau 1992, 106 this is together with 16:17-19, the tradition that gives a more positive picture of Peter.

[2] Garland 1996, 90-91; Nau 1992, 117-118. Also Davies and Allison 1991, 748-749.

[3] According to Nau 1992, 119-120 verses 18:21-22 are "the whole story of Peter in Matthew in a nutshell: good beginning – poor ending, the first becoming last, and a rock dysfunctioning as a stumbling block. Peter is the epitome of unfulfilled promises.

authority, Peter only a man, like others, with strengths and weaknesses,[1] who is very dependent on Jesus. He is no doubt a leading figure in Matthew's narrative world, but the interpretation that Matthew gives is ambiguous. Matthew clearly presents him, at times, as a rock and, at other times, a pebble.

This tension continues to the end. Peter's role in the Gospel ends abruptly in the Passion narrative. After the last supper – where only the Twelve are present – Jesus and the disciples go to the Mount of Olives. Jesus predicts that all the disciples will fall away from him. Peter's response is a firm protest: "Even if all fall away from you, I will never fall away." Jesus answers to him: "In truth I tell you, this very night, before the cock crows, you will have disowned me three times." But still Peter insists: "Even if I have to die with you, I will never disown you." Disowning, denying is in fact more or less the same as deserting or falling away.[2] When Jesus then prays in Gethsemane, the three disciples Peter, James, and John fall asleep. The contrast to the bold promises of all three is clear. James and John have already assured Jesus that they can drink the cup that he is to drink (20:22) and Peter has declared that he will never fall away even if he has to die. Jesus' words to Peter echo a mild irony: "So you had not the strength to stay awake with me for one hour." Matthew has changed the singular in Mark to plural, so the reproach does not concern Peter alone. When Jesus is arrested, all the disciples desert him and run away. However, as Jesus is brought to the house of Caiaphas the high priest,[3] Peter follows him at a distance to the high priest's palace. Three times he is asked if he has been a follower of Jesus and three times he denies that he has. The cock crows and Peter remembers what Jesus said. Peter feels remorse: he goes out and weeps bitterly. But this does not imply that he would have turned and admitted openly to being a follower of Jesus. After the resurrection, the eleven disciples set out for Galilee and it is legitimate to assume that Peter is among them. However, he is never mentioned again in Matthew's narrative.[4]

---

[1] Garland 1996, 97-98 states that Peter is a unique leader of the whole church, but he must be "entirely dependent on the instruction and guidance of Jesus." See also Syreeni 1999, 152, and Nau 1992, 134.

[2] Nau 1992, 84-85 underlines the verb σκανδαλίζω which Matthew uses 19 times (Mark 8 times). For Nau this proves that the 'falling away' was for Matthew a serious problem. Note especially 16:23 of Peter.

[3] The name of the high priest does not appear in Mark (or Luke).

[4] Contrary to this, Peter is depicted as receiving an individual appearance of the Lord in Luke 24:34 and 1 Cor 15:5.

A striking parallel to Peter's remorse is Judas' fate, which is peculiar to Matthew (27:3-10).[1] His remorse[2] compels him to return the money to the priests and elders and commit suicide. Parallel with this, Peter's weeping 'outside alone' does not imply his way back into the narrative.[3] In the end, the focus is shifted from Peter to the group of disciples as a whole.[4]

The intimate circle of three, Peter, James, and John, show their weakness by sleep and denial; Judas betrays Jesus and the rest of the Twelve abandon him. This group of followers is not depicted as heroic figures in the Passion narrative. Furthermore, they are explicitly excluded as witnesses. However, other followers are brought centre stage. The circle of three named disciples is replaced by three named women[5] who keep watch of Jesus' death from a distance and are privileged to witness the resurrection.

5.1.5. Comparing the Power Structures

Simon Peter's profile in Matthew is, as stated earlier, ambiguous. The author has blurred the picture of the firm and reliable 'rock' on whom the community will be built. It is probable that Peter was looked upon as an authority in the Matthean environment, at least by some. The criticism of the opponents is heard in the negative evaluations. This controversy in the Matthean communities might have centred on Peter's person or widened to encompass the whole question of Jewish heritage. One explanation offered for the retention of the negative material is the prevailing tension

---

[1] Another kind of death is described in Acts 1:18-19. Papias mentions still another variant. As all these exclude one another, I shall concentrate only on Matthew's version.

[2] Van Unnik 1974, 47 points to the different verb used here. It is μεταμεληθείς, not μετανοεῖν and can only be translated 'he changed his mind', not repented.

[3] On the contrary van Unnik 1974, 57 who rejects firmly any parallelism between Peter and Judas. According to him, the offences of Peter and Judas were totally different kinds. Judas was a curse according to the law and by hanging himself he tried to remove this curse.

[4] Cf. Wilkins 1988, 214.

[5] The parallelism between the group of three disciples and the group of three women is noticed by Ricci 1994, 127.129 who follows here Hengel (Martin Hengel, "Maria Magdalena und Frauen als Zeugen" in *Abraham unser Vater. Festschrift* O. Michel AGSU 5 [1963] 243-256).

between the Jewish Christians and the Gentile Christians. The Jewish mission brought Jewish converts who venerated the apostles more than the Gentile Christians did. If Matthew sympathised with the latter's views, it is possible that he generally depicted the disciples and Peter as failing and lacking understanding. He could not deny their achievements totally because they were attested by other traditions, but he could present them in an unfavourable light.[1] Matthew is certainly not an admirer of Peter, but he still inserts material about Peter that is peculiar to him and retains the image of Peter's primacy (even if the substance of this primacy is debatable). Whatever the reason for this contradictory and mainly critical approach to Peter may be, the narrative displays Jesus as the 'Lord' and the supreme authority under whom Peter, as well as everyone else, is ranked. The narrative does not contain moral criticism. It is not so much a question of playing down Peter's influence, but rather of emphasising Jesus' authority over everything and everybody. Peter's story line is very much dependent on and coexistent with Jesus. Peter calls Jesus 'Lord' (Κύριε) several times.

Peter is encompassed in the realm of hierarchical power, and most of the Petrine material concentrates on the ecclesiastical part of the narrative. His presence appears significant in the discussions on community affairs, the hierarchy, community discipline, forgiveness. Nevertheless, authority belongs to Jesus alone. The subversive message about Jesus and his *basileia* is combined with the reality of Matthew's communities with their developing, dominantly patriarchal ideology of obvious hierarchical structures and the irreplaceable influence of Peter and the Twelve disciples. Peter's figure in the narrative remains contradictory. On the one hand, he incorporates the values of the growing hierarchy, as Simon 'the Rock'. On the other hand, we have the human image of a disciple who is, at times, 'a Pebble': a faithful, but weak member of the *basileia*. Gradually through time, Simon 'the Rock' became more dominant, but in Matthew, Peter as 'the Pebble' is the prime focus.

In scrutinizing the power tapestry amongst the characters in the narrative, the women, the twelve men, and Jesus, both power-over and power-with relationships are evident. Jesus alone is in the centre, the supreme authority in the *basileia*. Although all the characters mentioned

---

[1] So Grant 1994, 62-63.

above hold equal positions in their relationship to Jesus, the women and the men recognise hierarchical levels amongst themselves.

5.2. The Disciples[1]

As a group, the disciples have been mentioned several times in connection with the women, the Twelve, and Peter. It is clear that Peter and the Twelve are part of this larger group, but who else belongs to this group is an open question.[2]

The relationship between the group of disciples and the Twelve calls for further reflection. The disciples are arguably not always interchangeable with the Twelve. As pointed out above, the historical mission of Israel constitutes the role of the Twelve when they are sent as a group to continue the mission of Jesus himself. In contrast, the disciples are an unidentified, nebulous and varying gathering which clustered around Jesus. Sometimes the group is small, as e.g, it accompanies Jesus in a boat (8:23-27)[3]; sometimes the disciples are mixed with the crowd, blurring the exact limits.[4] This might have been Matthew's purpose. The complete mingling of the crowd, the chosen Twelve and the disciples is reached in Matthew's closing scene. The same eleven who had already been sent to Israel, are entrusted with a mission to all nations.[5] However, they are no longer the Twelve, but 'disciples'. This mission achieves the final mingling when old and new disciples become indistinguishable.

---

[1] The major publications on the disciples in Matthew are Barth 1961, Strecker 1971, idem 1983, Schweizer 1974, Luz 1983, Edwards 1985 and 1997, Wilkins 1988. Among other works that take up the issue of disciples in Matthew are Kingsbury 1988(1), 129-145, Byrskog 1994, 221-236.

[2] Sometimes Matthew equates 'the disciples' with 'the Twelve' (10:1), but he also knows the disciples as a wider group (8:21; 27:57). According to Wilkins 1988, 167 Matthew "refers to the Twelve when he refers to the μαθηταί, but he does not mean to imply that Jesus has no other disciples."

[3] Against this, for example, Gundry 1982, 153 who supposes that the crowd takes other boats to follow. For Gundry the crowd consists of disciples.

[4] For example 5:1 compared with 7.28; 12:15, 46-50, 13:2-3; 23:1.

[5] For Kingsbury 1988(1), 130 this means that the disciples finally grasp the evaluative point of view of discipleship. But nothing is expressed here of understanding, rather we have a scene of a new beginning in history.

The relationship of a master and his disciples is familiar in both the Hellenistic society and the Jewish environment.[1] Discipleship abounds in Matthew's contemporary world; John the Baptist has disciples (9:14; 11:2-3), as have the Pharisees (22:16)[2], so being a disciple is not a unique relationship connected to Jesus alone. Strangely, the concept of discipleship is not explicitly defined or even expressed in Matthew, but it is clearly a dominant feature in Matthew. From the calling of the four fishermen to the arrest of Jesus (after which the disciples flee, to return in the end for their mission) the disciples are present in the narrative most of the time.[3] Their role is not very significant despite their strong

---

[1] See Weder 1992, 209: In the world where the Second Testament came into existence, 'disciple' was a technical term for the pupil of a philosopher or a teacher. The term and the social institution it is connected with were known both in early Judaism and in Hellenistic society at large. The teacher-student relationships of the Jewish scribes and, later, the rabbinic schools are also comparable institutions. The Jewish institution of discipleship resembles in many ways the form of discipleship in early Christianity Wilkins 1988 has studied both of these backgrounds. He has come to the conclusion that in Hellenism at the time of Jesus and the early church the emphasis of the "discipleship" was not in being a pupil, rather in adherence. So μαθητής is the one who adhered to his master and the type of adherence was determined by the master himself. (41-42). So also Saldarini 1994, 95-96. As for the Jewish context, Wilkins rejects the formal relationships and sees the disciples as a means of communicating the revelation to Israel (91). According to Wilkins "μαθητής was able to become a specialized term for Jesus' followers because common usage was general enough to hold the specialized connotations the Christian community appended to it." (125) For Weder 1992, 209 there are considerable differences between the Jewish context and Jesus' disciples, especially concerning the substance of teaching and the person of the teacher, as the rabbinic scholar is bound to the Law, but Jesus' disciples are connected to the person of Jesus in a particular way. Saldarini points out that the master-disciple relationship cannot derive from Second Temple Judaism, which is the cultural context of Jesus' ministry. Matthew is using early Christian traditions and a Greek model (95-96). Also Weder considers the early Christian form of discipleship as being closer to the Hellenistic teacher-disciple relationship (209). Byrskog 1994, 236 on the contrary argues for the continuity between the concerns of the Jewish culture and the transmission of the Matthean community as related phenomena.

[2] This is conspicuously Matthean. In Mark they are 'some' of the Pharisees (Mark 12:13)

[3] Edwards 1997, 17 has used graphics to demonstrate this and the responses of the disciples. On the word level, Matthew uses the noun μαθητής which surpasses Mark (46) and Luke (37) and he usually uses it as a plural, only three times in a singular form (10:24, 25, 42). The word is not used in the Second Testament outside the Gospels and the Acts. Other words connected to μαθητής are the verbs μανθάνω and μαθητεύω. The latter occurs only in Matthew. As for μανθάνω it occurs three times in Matthew (in Mark once and not at all in Luke), two of the uses in the context of

presence in the narrative. They are with Jesus[1], and fulfil the task of following[2], but they seem more like an amorphous audience than a group of distinct individuals.

I shall consider the role of this character group in the Gospel from three angles. First, their relationship with Jesus, second, their role as a contradictory element in the narrative, and third, the relationship of discipleship with a more inclusive following as depicted above.

5.2.1. Disciples and Jesus

It has already become evident that Simon Peter has been depicted with the purpose of emphasising the central authority of Jesus. Jesus the centre, the authority whose Father is God and whose eminent position cannot be shaken. On several occasions, Simon Peter acts as a spokesman for the others, which seems to indicate his middle position between the other disciples and Jesus. On the other hand, the disciples appear as a unified group without any individual member standing out.

One of the roles that the disciples as a group fulfil is that of pupil.[3] Jesus is the teacher, and the disciples are taught by their master. They are depicted as the primary audience for the Sermon on the Mount (5:1)[4]; the Twelve disciples are the sole audience for the missionary speech in 10:5-42, and in 23:1-12 they are part of the crowd. A supplementary role in the narrative is to ask questions in order to further the teaching (for example 13:10-17;13:36). Similar occasions where Jesus instructs his disciples are in 17:10-13; 17:22-23; 18:1; 19:23-26; 20:24-28; 21:18-22; 24:1-3. No doubt, discipleship in Matthew closely resembles the ancient master-disciple institution, in which Jesus is the centre around which the

---

non-believers (9:13; 11:29) and the third (24:32) of disciples. All three are in the aorist imperative, pointing to a demand to learn. But this learning does not necessarily tell anything about discipleship. Contrary to Edwards, Wilkins 1988, 160, 162 sees learning at least as part of discipleship and the imperative form as demanding commitment.

[1] Kingsbury 1988(1), 131 has argued for the importance of the expression. 'Being with Jesus' underlines the close association the disciples have with Jesus. Jesus is only 'with' his own.

[2] Another expression connoting the discipleship. See above page 102-103.

[3] For Byrskog 1994, 221-236 this is the major role of the disciples.

[4] The disciples are not the only audience, as the crowds are present too. I shall come back to the question of the crowds later.

disciples gather. It is quite extraordinary to note that in Matthew the disciples never use the word 'teacher' for Jesus. The disciples address Jesus as Κύριε (8:21, 25; 14:28, 30; 16:22; 17:4; 18:21; 26:22).[1] Only outsiders call him teacher (8:19; 9:11; 12:38; 17:24), and in that context pose questions to him, giving rise to different types of parables, teachings, and even reproaches. These characters number among them, the disciples of John the Baptist (9:14; 11:2), as well as his antagonists, the Pharisees and the scribes (9:3; 12:2, 38; 15:1-2; 16:1; 19:3; 21:23; 22:15-23, 35). Thus questioning seems to provide a context for Jesus' words rather than emphasising discipleship. Jesus is the centre to which everything is drawn.[2]

Another major element in the relationship between Jesus and the disciples, which has been discussed at length in Matthean literature, is their capability, or lack there of, to understand.[3] Matthew has clearly changed Mark's tendency to describe the disciples as non-understanding.[4] On three occasions, an explicit statement proves that the disciples understand (16:2; 17:13; 13:52). It is clear that Matthew's overall portrait of the disciples is more positive than Mark's, but he does depict them as uncomprehending as well (8:25; 16:8; 17:20; 26:8,56). As Luz points out, the disciples' grasp of the message is dependent on Jesus' teaching and explanation (Matt 13:10-17, 13:51). According to Luz, their understanding is not meant to idealise the disciples, but to show that they are capable of proclaiming and teaching (28:20) to all the nations, for the very reason that they understand.[5] Kingsbury concurs that it is in Matthew's interest to depict the disciples as enlightened followers of

---

[1] See also Held 1961, 191; Bornkamm 1961, 51; Luz 1990,24.

[2] See also Wilkins 1988, 164-165.

[3] Barth 1961, 99-104 has studied the term συνιέναι in detail and even if he notes that there are other expressions for understanding, understanding is usually accompanied by this term. So also Byrskog 1994, 228-229. Luz 1983, 102-103 agrees with Barth except on one point, namely that understanding is given to disciples, but the people are hardened. According to Luz, the disciples receive more special instructions in Matthew than in any other Gospel illustrating that the disciples often fail to understand, but that they come to understand through Jesus' explanation.

[4] See Barth 1961, 99-104.

[5] Luz 1983, 103. For Luz understanding means: "mit dem Kopf begreifen, was die Gottesreichparabeln mit dem Leben zu tun haben. So gehört das Verstehen zum Fruchtbringen." (1990, 363). See also Strecker 1971, 228-229. Wilkins 1988, 165-166 says that Matthew's point is to emphasise that Jesus instructs them in the way of discipleship. Jesus is "the effective Teacher of his disciples".

Jesus.[1] It is true that the disciples (and the Church) are depicted as capable of understanding Jesus' message, but in their relationship to Jesus they are divided: They grasp at least some of his message, but their faith could remain weak.[2] Conversely, for women (such as the Canaanite woman or the anointing woman) faith and understanding overlap[3]. In contrast to Kingsbury I find that in both of these pericopes the disciples are explicitly cited as those who do not understand the significance of the situation.[4] Jesus teaches the disciples and they receive the teaching, but this understanding does not guarantee faith.[5] Understanding the teaching of Jesus does not necessarily lead to faith nor does faith need as its basis the understanding of Jesus' teachings.

Matthew seems to have a problem with this character group. He wants to present them in a favourable light as understanding recipients of Jesus' teachings, but they doubt and fail in their faith, which, in turn, implies that they have not grasped the essence of Jesus' message. Furthermore, the responses of the disciples to Jesus' deeds and teachings are not always told (cf. 16:24-28); sometimes it is merely observed that they were astonished (19:23). Another telling incident is that of the mother of Zebedee's sons requesting for special favours. The petition is clearly misplaced, manifesting an almost total lack of appreciation of the reality of Jesus, his message and his mission. This is all the more surprising because the sons were presumably the instigators of the petition. Tellingly, it is the mother whom Matthew has ask the wrong question.

Other revealing episodes disclose the nature of relationship and following, the advance of two potential disciples (8:18-22), and immediately thereafter, the stilling of the storm (8:23-27).[6] In the latter

---

[1] Kingsbury 1969, 126.
[2] See 6:30; 8:26; 14:31; 16:8; 17:20.
[3] For Luz 1983, 103 this difference is due to the fact that faith is directed to the person of Jesus and understanding is related to his teaching. So, understanding would not point to Jesus' identity. For him, understanding separates the disciples from the crowd who does not understand. "Das Verstehen" is part of the existence of a disciple. (Luz 1990, 361). Also Gundry 1982, 280 sees understanding as the mark of true disciples.
[4] Barth 1961, 105 is of the opinion that it would be artificial to separate faith and understanding in the storyline of the disciples, and that understanding is not the presupposition of faith.
[5] Barth 1961, 105 is of the opinion that it would be artificial to separate faith and understanding in the storyline of the disciples, and that understanding is not the presupposition of faith.
[6] Held 1961, 189-192 claims that Matthew has connected these stories in order to make

case, while the disciples are present during most of the narrative, this is one of the few times they participate as characters. Usually they are just reported as present, or their questions exist to move the narrative forward, or their reaction is expressed. Curiously, the disciples, as a group, remain in the background for the most part.

Verses 8:18-22 are not taken from Mark, but from the Q-material and closely parallel Luke (9:57-62). What is noteworthy in Luke is that three persons have a dialogue with Jesus while Matthew is content with only two.[1] First there is a scribe who approaches Jesus and says: Διδάσκαλε, ἀκολουθήσω σοι ὅπου ἐὰν ἀπέρχῃ. He uses the honorific 'teacher', which is not used by the disciples any where in the narrative, thus denoting he is not a disciple[2], rather an aspirant for discipleship. This is not Matthew's aim, but the dialogue indirectly implies different categories of following. The aspirant clearly has faith in Jesus and he wants to join the itinerant group more permanently.[3] Jesus' answer has caused problems for interpreters. On the one hand, it has been seen as pointing to Jesus' poverty and homelessness[4]; on the other hand to rejection by people.[5] What Jesus promises to the aspirant is the expectation of the same fate as a disciple. The dialogue does not include any response from the scribe as to whether he was willing to accept this kind of poverty and insecurity or turned away.

Another person approaches Jesus in the same manner, and this time he is identified as a disciple. This is apparent in that his addressing Jesus

---

the stilling of the storm a story of following rather than just another story of Jesus miracles. So also Bornkamm 1961, 51-53 who says that the story is a kerygma and a paradigm of the danger and glory of following.

[1] Gundry 1982, 154 makes a note of the third one and explains the omission by saying: "Matthew has his wheat and his tare, his true disciple and the false. The third dialogue therefore vanishes." Hagner 1993, 213 claims that the third dialogue in Luke comes from his other sources rather than being omitted by Matthew from the Q-source.

[2] So also Kingsbury, 1988(2), 48-49 and Hagner 1993, 216. On the contrary Gundry 1982, 151 who carefully lists several points in favour of the discipleship. None of these points is completely convincing and there is no reason to suppose the scribe to be a disciple. The point of the dialogue does not alter either way. Held 1961, 191 leaves the question open.

[3] For Gundry 1982, 152 this positive response is the proof of his being a true disciple. For Gundry the question here is not being a disciple, but if one is a true or a false disciple.

[4] Luz 1990, 24 says that "die Armut Jesu ist buchstäblich zu verstehen."

[5] Gundry 1982, 152.

as 'Lord'.[1] He is apparently already among Jesus' permanent followers, but he wants to take leave to bury his father, a grave filial duty in Jewish culture. Jesus' answer: "Leave the dead bury their dead", is cryptic. The offence of these words is often moderated by explaining that the father in question is not yet dead, but the disciple does not want to leave his father until he is dead.[2] This makes Jesus' answer less offensive.[3] There is, however, no reason to soften Jesus' words in this way. What Matthew indicates here is that the obligation of a disciple to Jesus is more important than family obligations or bonds with the past.[4] Here again, the response of the disciple is not recorded. Neither response is recorded leaving the reader uncertain of the overcome. But the point in these dialogues is Jesus' message, not the men's response.[5]

Both of these dialogues, as well as the episode about the rich man (19:16-26), point to the radical nature of following Jesus. In the reality of the *basileia* there are no divided loyalties.[6] In these teachings Jesus expresses a more profound relationship among the citizens of his *basileia* than that of the usual master-student. Attraction to Jesus' teachings or the desire to be with him is not to be identified with following. Thus, the most we can deduce is that some of the disciples are followers, some are not.[7]

The two first dialogues are followed by the story about the stilling of the storm. The disciples are in a boat with Jesus. Jesus is asleep and as the storm breaks out the frightened disciples wake him up and ask him to save them. When they beg for safety, they use the title κύριε, the term

---

[1] On the contrary Gundry 1982, 153.

[2] For example Filson 1967, 114 or Beare 1981, 214. See also Goulder 1974, 323.

[3] The obligation of the burial of one's parents was very important in ancient Judaism. Strack-Billerbeck 1922, 487-489.

[4] So Kingsbury 1988(2), 56, Luz 1990, 27. So also Gundry 1982, 152 who hereby sees this second person as a false disciple as his response shows his unwillingness to obey immediately and fully.

[5] Barton 1994, 145 sees also no reason to contrast these two men nor to evaluate them as Kingsbury and Gundry do.

[6] Luz 1990, 25-27 sees in Jesus' words "ein Oxymoron", the meaning of which was to shock and alienate, not to express some general truth. Jesus is performing a prophetical act.

[7] Kingsbury 1988(2), 45-59 points to the fact that the true disciple-master relationship is consistently begun on Jesus' initiative. It is Jesus who calls his disciples. See also Hagner 1993, 216. In my opinion, this is not at all clear especially in the light of these dialogues. Being a follower is not to be equated with being a disciple.

used by a disciple.[1] Jesus rebukes them as 'men of little faith'[2], less offensive than Jesus' question in Mark: "Do you not have faith?" Compared with the previous dialogues about the following, the disciples are less understanding. The emphasis in the text is on 'faith', but this faith seems to be something else in reality than in the healing stories. As they turn to Jesus for help, the disciples are rebuked for their weak faith. Strong faith would have been utter, unquestioning trust in Jesus' power.[3]

Considering the power-relationships between the disciples themselves and between Jesus and the disciples, Jesus is clearly the only authority. He summons, commands, teaches. He always takes the initiative and the disciples follow and obey. Jesus makes things happen; the disciples lack all independence in the narrative. Paradoxically, the seemingly hierarchical role of Jesus is turned upside-down in the light of his teachings about who is the greatest. He himself has come to serve, not to be served; therefore his authority is seen in what he does for others and how he influences them than in his position (20:24-28). The model Jesus gives to his disciples involves self-denial, service, suffering, even death (cf. 10:34-39; 16: 24-25; 19:29; 20:26-27), in stark contrast to the power aspirations of society.

Matthew contains parallel expressions that easily equate with the word 'disciples'; namely, in 12:49-50 Jesus points to his disciples and defines them as his family. "Here are my mother and my brothers. Anyone who does the will of my Father in heaven is my brother and sister and mother." Jesus uses the word ἀδελφός at least 11 times when referring to his disciples.[4] This does not mean, however, that Matthew's Jesus would consider kinship relationships as a model community. On several

---

[1] This is a Matthean redaction. In Mark there is διδάσκαλε.
[2] For Beare 1981, 215 it is important that the disciples have some faith, even if it is weaker than it should be.
[3] Luz 1990, 29 interprets the faith/little faith issue otherwise: the little faith meant that the disciples had forgotten the power of Jesus. "Die Stärke des Glaubens besteht in nichts anderem als dass er sich dem Herrn zuwendet und von ihm gehalten wird. Richtig verstehen kann sie nur wer selbst "im Schiff" ist." The disciples did turn to Jesus and were still rebuked for little faith.
[4] 5:22-24; 5:47; 7:3-5; 10:21; 12:46-50; 18:15; 18:21; 18:35;23:8; 25:40; 28:10. This is clearly a language belonging to the community. Notably, 'sisters' in a similar meaning are mentioned only twice (12:50; 19:29), both times in connection to 'brothers'. For Barton 1994, 129 the description of the men in the call story of the two pairs of brothers has significance also with respect to Matthew's ecclesiology. This is perhaps over doing the meaning of the word ἀδελφός here. It does point to biological brotherhood and these is no indication of a double meaning here.

occasions (see for example 8:21-22; 10:35) he subordinates family ties and obligations to the following, and to the *basileia*.[1] Commitment to the *basileia* outranks commitment to the family. Using kinship language[2] supposes close and egalitarian relationships, even more so when the father is omitted from the picture. In the ancient world the father has power over the other members of the family, so the omission of this figure points to the subversive character of the *basileia*. The father in Matthew is, of course, God. Jesus also calls his followers 'brothers' in 23: 8-11, where the audience consists of both disciples and the crowd, Jesus warns them not to call anyone 'rabbi' because they are all brothers. No one is to be called father either because there is only one Father in heaven. This egalitarianism is taken even further in verses 11-12, where being brothers means serving each other. Another parallel to 'disciples' is οἱ μικροί[3], which points to the subversive order of authority in a similar manner, the little ones are the first.

Still another image used to describe the relationship between the disciples and Jesus is that of 'being with him'. The disciples are 'with Jesus' through most of the narrative. The importance of this image is emphasised through the name 'Immanuel' in the beginning of the narrative and the promise Jesus makes in the last scene to be 'with them' always. This 'being with' points to the close association of Jesus with his disciples before the resurrection and, after that, with his church.[4]

The model of authority and leadership that Jesus teaches to his disciples is consensual and egalitarian. This ideal anticipates the same revolutionary upheaval as Jesus' own mission.[5] But, Matthew clearly shows that the disciples do not imitate this model. The disciples do not seem to really understand this reversal of hierarchy. If the disciples are meant to represent Matthew's communities/the church[6] or church

---

[1] Barton 1994 has shown this in his study about the discipleship and family ties in Mark and Matthew. See especially pages 218-219.

[2] Jesus is the Son of the heavenly Father (3:17), disciples are 'brothers' among themselves (23:8).

[3] 10:42; 18:16, 10, 14

[4] Kingsbury 1988(1), 131 has especially emphasised this dimension of the narrative.

[5] Stanton 1996, 144-148 claims that the ministry of Jesus is a model for his followers. As Matthew emphasises Jesus' meekness, humility, and compassion, these qualities are also transferred to his followers. Stanton states in the end: "Since the reader readily identifies with the disciples, the pattern of their ministry is clearly intended to be a model for later readers of the Gospel." (148)

[6] Luz 1983, 98-127. For Wilkins 1988, 169, 171-172 the disciples are 'examples' for Matthew's church. The positive examples show the fate of true disciples, the negative

leaders[1], is Matthew really telling his church that it is they who misunderstand the real essence of the *basileia*? It is possible to describe this through the narrative in a subtle way. Unfortunately, this subtlety has been sadly misunderstood in the later development of the Christian church.

5.2.2. Disciples as a narrative device of contrast

A very significant element in the disciple characters is their role as a contrast, against which the important aspects of the *basileia* are highlighted. The first contrast is between the disciples and Jesus, the master.[2] The disciples are a necessary foil who, though with Jesus the whole time, and who have privileges to inside information, in the end flee. They stand unmasked having, after all, not assimilated his teaching. Calling them disciples stands, in fact, in contrast to what they prove to be. Against their weakness and failure to understand, Jesus stands out as the master who controls the situation. He does not in fact *need* the disciples; they are more like a device used to highlight Jesus' teaching. The narration needs these characters, but only in a supportive role.

In the analysis of women stories, that of the Canaanite woman provides another contrast scene. The disciples serve in the role of a signpost to the woman's faith. Embarrassed, they ask Jesus to silence her, since the woman challenges Jesus' faith like no other person in the narrative. The disciples, though holding a privileged position, never challenge him in the narrative. The relationship between the disciples and Jesus does not seem reciprocal, as that between the woman and Jesus. In the anointing scene as well, the disciples in their reproach of the woman

---

examples show what can happen to disobedient disciples.

[1] Minear 1974, 31-33.

[2] Kingsbury 1988(1), 129-130 points to a conflict between Jesus and the disciples, because the disciples fail to accomplish Jesus' evaluative point of view. Through this conflict Jesus instructs the disciples. Even if this points to the same idea as the contradictory element in the narrative, I see the word 'conflict' as too strong. This even more so because the conflict between the Jewish leaders and Jesus sets them on different sides, but the disciples are definitively on the same side of this conflict as Jesus. Conflict seems to imply at least some measure of hostility, which is not the case between the disciples and Jesus. Also Wilkins 1988, 172 sees Jesus as the supreme Lord and Teacher in Matthew.

are found wanting in their inability to grasp and imitate the patently unquestioning faith of the woman.[1]

Still another contrast appears between the disciples and Pilate (and his wife). Pilate seems to sympathise with Jesus and despite his role, is shown to be more on Jesus' side. His own disciples run away, ironically leaving supporting voices from only a Roman authority and his wife.

5.2.3. Discipleship or Following

The term 'discipleship' in the ecclesiastical language of our time derives from the character group in the Gospels. They are considered the chosen, privileged persons, respected by later adherents of Christianity The apostles, the Twelve, are considered as predecessors to bishops and their gender has been interpreted as an essential part of their calling.

On the narrative level, it seems that the name has led many interpreters astray. The disciples – both in Matthew's narrative and in the other Gospels – are often seen as representing the faithful, believers in respective communities or Christians in general.[2] The disciples are Jesus' followers, but the followers are not necessarily to be equated with the disciples. The narratives deal with several other characters who fulfil the function of following, believing, understanding; some even more so than the disciples. Not withstanding, the disciples, as characters representing the true, chosen followers, have been used to justify the priority of the male sex in various representative functions throughout the history of the church.

The disciples, including the Twelve and Peter, are a character group in the narrative whose role is to tell something about Jesus and his

---

[1] In Mark, only 'some' were complaining. It seems that Matthew wanted to insert 'disciples' as the complaining party. For an explanation see, for example, Hill 1972, 333. The same happens in 26:56, where Matthew says that οἱ μαθηταὶ πάντες ἀφέντες αὐτὸν ἔφυγον. In Mark there was only πάντες. Here also, Matthew may have explicitly wanted to make the disciples appear to be in direct contradiction to Jesus himself. See also Gundry 1982, 540; Senior 1975, 155; Wilkins 1988, 132.

[2] Luz 1983, 98-127; Kingsbury 1975(1), 31-37; Segovia 1985, 2; Hagner 1993, xlii. On the contrary Strecker 1971, 194 and idem 1983, 67-84 who sees the disciples in Matthew as historical figures in an unrepeatable past. Howell 1990, 15-18 abandons both of these views and instead of history or theology offers a literary interpretation: For him discipleship is acceptance of the value system embodied in Jesus' life rather than membership in any kind of character group.

basileia. Other characters – women and men – show another facet of following, no less valuable. Some scholars consider Matthew's women to be better examples of true disciples than the group of disciples. Joseph of Arimathea, a rich man in carrying out another action of a follower, is called disciple, though he was not among the disciples in the itinerant group with Jesus.

The confusion surrounding discipleship resulted in its vague definition leading to inequitable situation. Discipleship is all-gender inclusive when advantageous to be so, but in some key areas, the gender of a limited group of early followers determines the gender of ministry in the Christian life. The narrative itself does not legitimise leadership roles for disciples, who, quite the opposite, are taught that to be first means to serve others. The disciples formed only part of the larger group of followers, and their mission was not to govern others.

The images of following are shown minor and subversive. The disciples are described as failing, doubting and non-understanding. The underlying, subversive message exclaims that all followers are bona fide insiders, each in a way that proves relational power to be valid in the *basileia*. Women and men from the margins are healed and empowered to reach full membership in it. The disciples – including the Twelve and Peter – were taught by word, example and personal experience that the *basileia* is not about governing others.

5.3. The Crowd

The role of the crowd in Matthew is much more significant than in Mark. An outstanding trait is that the crowd often expresses a positive response to Jesus.[1] Can the crowd also be accepted as followers in Matthew's narrative? What is their claim?

P.S. Minear has treated the problem in an article and come to the conclusion that the crowd usually represented Matthew's contemporary laymen while the disciples reminded the reader of the vocation of contemporary leaders.[2] Warren Carter, on the other hand, sees the crowd

---

[1] Gundry 1982, 172-173 argues that Matthew identifies μαθηταί with ὄχλοι. This is opposed by Wilkins 1988, 138, 143. Both groups are clearly separate, fulfilling different functions in Matthew's narrative.

[2] Minear 1974, 41. Beare 1981, 122. So also Gundry 1982, 139, 290 for whom the crowds are "the foretaste of the disciples who will come from all nations". For Luz

as recipients of Jesus' ministry, a ministry that was to be continued by the disciples. He says:"At times crowds exhibit some perception that God is at work in a special way in Jesus, yet they lack both the faith and understanding manifested by the disciples and the hostility displayed by the Jewish leaders".[1] Kingsbury points to a contrast between the crowds and the Jewish leaders on the one hand, and the crowds and the disciples on the other[2], while for Luz the crowds are potential disciples.[3] For Wilkins the crowd is a neutral group, from which emerge both Jesus' disciples and his opponents.[4] All these interpretations demonstrate that the role of the crowds in the narrative is far from unambiguous.

In the course of the narrative the crowd is sometimes present when Jesus teaches[5] (5:1; 7:28; 12:46); they follow Jesus (4:25; 8:1; 12:15; 14:13; 19:2; 20:29); they show amazement and/or praise God for Jesus' deeds (9:8; 9:33; 12:23; 21:8-9; 22:33). They are also the object of Jesus' ministry, as he teaches them (11:7; 13:34; 15:10), heals them (14:14; 15:30-31; 19:2), and performs miracles for their benefit (14:13-21; 15:32-39). The only scene where the crowd clearly stands on the opposite side[6] is the Passion, where Judas has ὄχλος with him and where the priests and elders stir up the crowd to ask Pilate to set Barabbas free and have Jesus put to death. If we use Clévenot's terms, the crowd stands inside Jesus' magnetic field most of the time and only in the end do they shift to the Jewish leaders' magnetic field. In this sense we can conclude that the crowd fulfills different functions as a character group in the narrative.

1989, 206 the crowds and the disciples are not two circles that are completely distinguished. Matthew indicates rather that discipleship will expand in the church. See also Luz 1989, 224.

[1] Carter 1993, 64. Stanton 1996, 153-154 agrees with Carter on this point. The crowds do not foreshadow the later distinction between ordained and lay ministries.

[2] Kingsbury 1988(1), 23-24.

[3] Luz 1989, 456.

[4] Wilkins 1988, 170-171.

[5] Byrskog 1994, 226 argues that even if the crowd is present during the Sermon on the Mount, Jesus does not inform them about the demands of discipleship. It must be said, first, that the Sermon is not said to be a teaching of discipleship and second, nowhere is it expressed that discipleship, or rather following Jesus, is limited to the disciples only. Nor is it contended that the crowds would not understand Jesus' teaching.

[6] Carter 1993, 58, however, points to events after Jesus' birth and actions against John the Baptist and argues that "while the crowds are not linked with any of these events, their places of origin are, nevertheless, associated with negative as well as with positive responses to God's actions."

Some of them are potential followers and some of them potential members of the *basileia*.

Some of the interpretations (Minear, Gundry, among others) assume that the disciples represent the community leaders in Matthew's communities. As we have already concluded that the disciples/the Twelve as a group fulfil diverse functions in the narrative, this presumption is incompatible with the facts.[1] Furthermore, the disciples and the crowd are present at the same time on several occasions, especially during Jesus' teaching. This is true at the Sermon on the Mount, where the crowd functions as the object of Jesus' ministry (4:25). They *followed* Jesus just as the disciples followed Jesus and there is no reason to assume that this following is any less committed in nature than that of the disciples.[2] The verb used is exactly the same ἀκολουθεῖν[3]. In verse 5:1 the crowds and the disciples appear together. As the narrative continues with Jesus going up to the mountain alone and summoning the disciples to him, it seems to effect a separation of the two groups. But the crowds are not dismissed at any point and in the end they are reported to be amazed at Jesus' teaching. Thus, there is no reason to assume their absence.[4] This, of course, does not mean that the disciples and the crowds are identified, but their presence is acknowledged. The response of the crowd is mentioned in 7:28; a response from the disciples is absent.

For Carter, the main difference between the disciples and the crowd is the faith element. Even if the disciples are rebuked for being men of little faith, they still have some while the crowds have none.[5] He ignores the individuals that emerge from the crowd, namely the supplicants for healing, who show deeper faith than the disciples (Chapters 8 and 9). No reason is advanced for excluding these individuals from the crowd as a character group although the scene offers proof of the overlapping of the different follower groups in the narrative. Faith, the exemplary attribute, is evidenced by individual followers among the crowd while the disciples

---

[1] So also Wilkins 1988, 171 who sees the crowd as the object of Jesus' ministry and later on Jesus ministers through the disciples.

[2] Kingsbury 1978, 56-73 sees the following here indicating physical movement, not the response of a disciple as previously in 4:18-22. Kingsbury also argues for a literal sense of following in 8:1,10; 12:15; 14:13-14; 19:2; 20:29; 21:9. (61)

[3] For a discussion about the verb see pages 102-103.

[4] For discussion about the audience of the Sermon see among others Luz 1989, 224, Davies and Allison 1988, 425, Gundry 1982, 66, Minear 1974, 32-33.

[5] Carter 1993, 59

evidence little faith. This puny faith is also attributed to Peter, whom some have wanted to hold up as leader and exemplar of the disciples.

Carter also points out that even though not called by Jesus, the crowds follow, while the four fishermen and Matthew had to be called by him before following. If, therefore, being called is the characteristic of a disciple[1], then the disciples are the only followers in the narrative. This must be ruled out, however, because other characters also follow and serve Jesus in a profound way, not just in a literal sense, out of curiosity or mob psychology.

Another contrast is drawn between the crowds and the disciples. The disciples are described several times as understanding, while the crowd seems more astonished than comprehending of Jesus' actions.[2] Indeed the crowd sometimes seem to be outsiders (cf 13:11-15). Yet, followers do emerge from the crowd as examples, and nothing indicates that they are the only ones. The crowd is obviously more than just a neutral group and the relation between the disciples and the crowd is far from clear-cut.

In summary, although the disciples and the crowd are two different groups, the crowd, in my opinion, should not be disposed of too hastily as outsiders, as uncomprehending 'non-disciples'. It would be too narrow a view to consign the crowd to mere objects of Jesus' ministry, which is to be continued by the disciples alone. They are subjects for ministry, but not exclusively that. Part of the crowd responds positively to Jesus' teaching and action; many follow him just as the disciples do, some showing even greater faith than the disciples. The latter form merely one group within the *basileia*; there are other followers, too.

5.4. Citizens of the *basileia*

The problem in many interpretations concerning the disciples and the crowd is that these groups are seen as distinct representatives of Matthew's communities, such as leaders and laymen, community members and subjects of missionary work. I see both of these groups as much more amorphous. The disciples do not prove themselves leaders at all, and incidents indicative of leadership in the narrative are more critical than supportive of any such functions. The basic idea Matthew displays in his narrative is a revolutionary order. Those who want to be first must

---

[1] Carter 1993, 58.
[2] Carter 1993, 62 suggests the crowds function as a contrast to the disciples.

be servants. All his representations depict the insiders of the *basileia* as marginal people, little ones, children, servants.

The disciples are not model characters; they represent little faith as much as understanding. Those who explicitly represent faith in the narrative are outside the group of disciples. The crowd following Jesus displays different kinds of responses; in the end, hostile ones. This apparent incongruity seems to indicate that these groups of characters – the disciples and the Twelve, the crowd and the women – are followers representing different aspects of the *basileia*. Clevenot's concentric circles also point in this direction, but I would rather see these groups as partly overlapping, partly independent in their characteristics as followers. Most of the disciples in the narrative – especially those who are depicted as a group in Jesus' company – are part of the crowd that walks with Jesus. Other disciples, who do not seem to belong to these groups, such as Joseph of Arimathea, emerge in the course of events. The supplicants in the healing stories, among them women, are part of the crowd, but individual women characters also appear, such as Peter's mother-in-law or the anointing woman. The disciples were male, but it is legitimate to question the role of the women who are named in the Passion narrative and are described as serving and following Jesus. What has been proven is the existence of different groups among the followers of Jesus. Each of them represent different aspects of following and in this respect are recognizable models for later Christian followers. All of these groups are independent of one another, but equal in their relationship to Jesus, who alone stands in the centre.

Using a modern concept, I claim that all of them share equal citizenship in God's present *basileia*. This citizenship means a commitment to the radical values that are carried out for the poor and helpless. These deeds eventually are the final test to the eternal life which is the future *basileia*.

6. Conclusion

The aim of this thesis was to sketch an alternative perspective for the idea of following in Matthew's narrative. The disciples as a character group have, for too long, enjoyed the prime status as followers in the Christian society. One reason for this has partly been due to the lack of names for the others. These other character groups can become more visible by changing names and definitions. Thus, especially women, who represent following in all respects in Matthew, will be admitted. One means of doing this has been the feminist emphasis on the idea of relational power instead of domination and control. This feminist power-with is to a great extent compatible with Matthew's concept of *basileia.*

The *basileia* does not have the same values and regulations as Matthew's community, but despite the tension, the two are not contradictory either. The disciples (the Twelve included) belong to Matthew's concrete world and their authoritative status and question of power and hierarchy filter through the narrative. As many scholars tend to equate the disciples with Matthew's communities, Matthew's critical attitude towards the disciples is also a critique on the power relationships in these communities. The women characters, on the other hand, are identified with the values of the *basileia.*

Feminist perspectives in the concrete exegesis of the Gospel of Matthew seem to be divided into two major camps. The first tends to emphasise women's marginality in Matthew's patriarchal narrative. Women characters are described by attributes, supposed, not apparent, in the narrative. Matthew's tendency to abbreviate Mark's material and present his material in compact form, leaves the reader uninformed about the details and background of the characters. This has led to a tendency to imagine the women characters to be even more oppressed and devalued than is deducible from the text itself – and has resulted in the need to emphasise, for example, prostitution and pollution. This is connected to the need to empower women. By widening the gap and emphasising the marginality of women, this camp makes the affirmation of women even more revolutionary.

The other perspective weighs in on the women traditions in Matthew's community. They are considered traceable through the women stories in Matthew. In this view the basic problem is the notion of equality. Basing their presuppositions that a tradition of actual equality between genders will be found in and extricated from the deeper layers of the narrative, the proponents of this theory saw equality as a part of Jesus' ministry and these traditions reflected in Matthew's narrative. Egalitarianism, as seen in Matthew, however, needs to be carefully defined and differentiated from the modern understanding of the concept. Questions of complementarity, mutuality and reciprocity must be taken into consideration more explicitly as the question of egalitarianism or equality always concerns power relationships. The kind of equality and relationship sought (equality in position, equality in power, equality in dignity, equality in rights, equality in title, etc) must also be clarified.

The women in Matthew belong to the patriarchal environment of Matthew's time. In the narratives where they appear, gender roles are not transgressed and the women do not transcend their conventional social status in their encounter with Jesus. But this does not mean that nothing happens in these encounters. The new element is the initiative and challenge some of these women represent in their relationship with Jesus. Their faith initiates a change in their lives fueled by the power of Jesus who makes transformation possible. The change concerns the *basileia,* where the little ones, the powerless, the weak are transformed into true citizens. This change does not necessarily affect the hierarchical structures of Matthew's time, but it nevertheless challenges the structures of any era in church history.

My aim in this work was to search for clues to define the inclusive following in Matthew's narrative. A plausible answer exists in the story of the *basileia,* which is the larger context of Matthew's narrative. Jesus is the centre, the authority, the king in this kingdom and the citizens of his kingdom consist of various groups of followers, all appearing in the narrative. My starting point was the model from Michel Clévenot's reading of Mark's gospel. In this model, the characters and character groups in Jesus' magnetic field are placed in concentric circles around the centre, Jesus. These circles are the crowd, the disciples, the Twelve and finally those closest to Jesus: Peter, James, and John. I found this model too restricted, however, in that it excludes many of the characters in Jesus' field of influence. They can, of course, be counted in the last circle of the crowd, but this does not do justice to their uniqueness as followers. Among these characters are all the supplicants in the healing stories, both men and women, the anointing woman, as well as the women under the cross and at the tomb. The model, therefore, needs to be modified. Firstly, I see all the circles as partly overlapping and none of them in a privileged position in regard to Jesus. All of these circles represent different aspects of following Jesus, and together they comprise the citizens of the *basileia,* the central reality of Matthew's narrative. This overlapping means that the crowd following Jesus also includes disciples (the Twelve) and women, but there are also disciples and women outside this crowd. The Twelve and the disciples are not identical, even if the Twelve are part of the character group of disciples. In Matthew, the disciples are a more open group, and their identity is perhaps intentionally vague.

Next, we can summarise the characteristics of these different groups based on their description as followers. The Twelve, and some specific individuals among them, represent *the continuity* of the message. They are carefully identified by their names and their presence at the Last Supper and when they are sent to all nations to win over new disciples is precisely recorded. After being instructed, they understand enough of Jesus' teachings to be sent to continue his work and to expand his kingdom to all nations. In their mission they form no hierarchy, their lot in life is serving, suffering, helping, healing, proclaiming and teaching. Their trustworthiness is attested by Jesus' confidence in them, shown when they are sent, not once, but twice, to Israel and then to all nations. In Matthew, distinguishing between the Twelve and the disciples as a whole is an ever-present problem. I see a solution in the missioning. Only the Twelve are sent.

Among them, Peter's role in the narrative is unique, but Matthew's clear intention is to place him among the other Twelve. It is clear that although Peter, James and John may have experienced something unique with Jesus, this does not give them a privileged position over the others.

The disciples, a larger group who walk with Jesus, are also taught by him, experience his presence and influence, but are not sent to gather new members. Their representative role is to be present, to ask, to be amazed, to understand something, but they lose their grip in crucial moments. These disciples include those who perhaps are not strong enough to follow, but who are nevertheless disciples, such as the one in the dialogue in 8:23, or Joseph of Arimathaea. The disciples have no leadership functions.

The supplicants in the narrative who look for Jesus and his help – among them women – represent the aspect of faith among the followers. They experience deeper understanding, and absolute trust that the disciples were incapable of reaching. This deeper level is another way of experiencing the essence of the *basileia*. The women take the initiative in seeking help from Jesus. Their faith makes transformation possible, as it did for the woman present the crucial moments of Jesus' life: the anointing woman at the beginning of his Passion as well as the other named women under the cross and at the tomb. The fact that the women are named emphasises, as it does with Peter, James, and John, the unique experience of certain individuals, this time women. Their fulfilling the role of witnesses in the moments of Jesus' death and resurrection does not, however, elevate them above others. They are also the first messengers in the narrative, even if the baton is then passed on to the Twelve. Named women are also present in the beginning of the narrative, when Jesus' continuity to Israel's history and his otherworldly origin are expressed. Jesus's genealogy is connected with women with a vulnerable history and despite his royal ancestry, the reversal of power and glory is revealed through the irregularity and vulnerability of both Mary and the First Testament women. The Gospel as a whole, like the Passion narrative, is framed by the presence of women.

The role of women under the cross and at the tomb is to witness the most important moments in Jesus' history. The mission to teach is entrusted to men while the task of transmitting personal experience is given to women. Written in a patriarchal milieu, this may be a way of expressing women's potentiality for evangelism: to transmit the faith to individuals and coming generations. A different task, but no less valuable.

The crowd demonstrates the widespread attraction of Jesus' words and deeds. It is clearly diverse: some follow Jesus, others do not. Because certain individuals emerge, the crowd is also shown as a group of individuals rather than a faceless mob. The role of the crowd is to represent different reactions, mainly positive, but in the end, hostile.

In terms of power, the disciples are men from a patriarchal order who need to be taught that the kingdom is not about control and domination, but of serving, suffering and healing. Women and men from the margins of the society would hardly need this lesson. Different groups of people enter the *basileia* from different backgrounds, needing different lessons for transformation. The powerless people in the patriarchal society need empowerment and encouragement while the teachers, leaders, and masters in the society need to learn the new relational power models prevailing in the *basileia*. Matthew uses the different character groups to convey this message. The citizenship of the *basileia* includes both disciples and other followers, both Jews and Gentiles, both leaders and the servants, both rich and poor, and of course, both women and men.

All this is in accord with feminist power being relational, creative and non-professional as Jesus is the source of transformation in the *basileia*. Being a citizen in the *basileia* does not mean position in the hierarchy, but a process of inner transformation. Contrary to feminist critique, however, is the power-over present in the characters of Peter, James, and John. This control is questioned and rejected in some episodes where Jesus teaches the Twelve or the disciples. Nevertheless, the hierarchical structures do emerge in the eschatological promises made to the disciples and carry over into the future *basileia*.

In the end, Matthew was mired in the customs and mores of the contemporary society. In a modern context, a problem remains: Although Matthew designates the Twelve 'judges over Israel', this mantle of hierarchical power does not exempt them from all scrutiny as in the other eschatological scene everybody is weighed according to his/her deeds. The received tradition is not completely redacted in Matthew to fit the new visions. Taking the text at face value, without reference to the historical Matthew or the *basileia* content against hierarchy, it argues for an eschatological *basileia* in which residual elements of hierarchy remains. This assertion in turn claims that the afterlife is not a state of static perfection. Instead, changes and development occur because the final goal (not yet reached) is an existence of equality.

Just as Matthew gave the old traditions a new meaning by his redaction, we can continue the same line by revisioning Matthew's narrative. The narrative as a text incorporates the potential for that despite its roots in a patriarchal society.

A critique from the feminist point of view pinpoints the social structures of ancient society. Women are less visible, often nameless and driven into the background while men conquer the stage. This is exactly what happens in Matthew's narrative. Women are present at the crucial history-marking, future-moulding moments of Jesus' history, but when the narrative points to beyond its own time, it is men who take charge. Men are sent on the worldwide mission to teach and to preach. The symbolic group of the Twelve consists only of men while women are denied the position due a follower. Discipleship turns out to be a male endeavour, in accordance with the patriarchal society of the time. A modern reader can justifiably pose the questions, "Are these ancient social structures still valid?", "Do they justify the patriarchal order in the churches?"

From a feminist point of view the answer is negative. Matthew's narrative demonstrates that despite the patriarchal society women are as much a part of early Christianity as men, and therefore a new way of understanding the following is warranted. Women are part of Jesus' history in an irrevocable manner, not only of his birth and prehistory but also of his life, death and Resurrection. Women are also the harbingers of the new era. In their vast capacity for faith they challenge traditional conventions and create new life within the patriarchal boundaries of the narrative.

What can be said about the feminist approach and its usefulness as research tool after this limited investigation of Matthew? I have concluded that it is important to highlight women characters and references to women in the biblical texts in order to make visible the presence of women in the recounting of the Christian (and Jewish) heritage. Women's contribution must be hailed because it has been ignored for so long. Other characters who have been given a minor role, such as the male supplicants in the healing stories, must be specified. We have read the Gospels at the slant of descendants of the disciples too long. History has been shaped too often by and after male heroes.

This study has concentrated only on characters and character groups (though not all of them). It can be unequivocally stated that the Gospel includes abundant material indicating egalitarianism, at least as an accepted value of the *basileia*. This must be left for future studies. Here I only wish to point out that the essence of the *basileia*, as it appears both in the stories of these characters and elsewhere, is subversive and relational and from any feminist point of view a valuable tool for revising the narrative.

Creating consciousness of the inclusive role both men and women had in early Christianity also means promoting an acceptance of the inclusive role of both men and women in the churches today. Conscientization, a transformation process that affects behaviour and lifestyle, leads to a whole new way of viewing all relationships, not only between men and women, but also between races and classes. Accepting the different roles of people in the formation of early Christianity can also lead to an acceptance of diversity and pluralism as inclusive in modern Christianity. The pericope of the Canaanite woman points even further. The encounter between Jesus and a representative of a different religion and culture shows that authentic faith demands no conversion from one religion to another.

It is equally important to question the hierarchical models in the texts and envision strategies for anti-hierarchical models. The *basileia* ideology provides tools for an alternative reading. It is of course only one application of many possible, suitable for new insights into Matthew.

In regard to feminist interpretations, I find the desire to prove that women's equality existed in the ancient world in order to grant them equality now unsatisfactory and unproven. Injustice in the first century – by modern standards – does not legitimate injustice in our age. The main question does not have to be whether women were disciples, priests or leaders in early Christianity. Rather, we need to inquire into the expectations and values of relationships in the new movement in its early years. The stage and actors have changed since then, but the play goes on.

Bibliography

Abrams, Meyer Howard
1971   A Glossary of Literary Terms. Third ed. New York: Holt,
                Rinehart and Winston.
Aejmelaeus, Lars
1987   "Joulun satu ja sanoma Uuden testamentin tekstien kriittisen
                tutkimuksen valossa." – TA 92, 463-470.
Albright, W.F. and Mann, C.S.
1984   Matthew. Introduction, translation, and notes. AB 26. Garden
                City: Doubleday.
Anderson, Janice Capel
1983   "Matthew: Gender and Reading" – Semeia 28, 3-27.
1987   "Mary's Difference. Gender and Patriarchy in the Birth
                Narratives." – JR 67, 183-202.
1994   Matthew's Narrative Web. Over, and Over, and Over Again.
                JSNTSup 91. Sheffield: Sheffield Academic Press.
Arendt, Hannah
1958   The Human Condition. Chicago: The University of Chicago
                Press.
Bacon, Benjamin W.
1930   Studies in Matthew. London: Constable&Co.
Baker-Fletcher, Karen
1994   "Anna Julia Cooper and Sojourner Truth. Two Nineteenth
                century Black Feminist Interpreters of Scripture." – Searching
                the Scriptures I: A Feminist Introduction. Ed. by E. Schüssler
                Fiorenza. 41-51. London: SCM Press.
Bal, Mieke
1985   Narratology. Introduction to the theory of narrative. Toronto:
                University of Toronto Press.
Barth, Gerhard
1961   "Das Gesetzesverständnis des Evangelisten Matthäus." –
                Günther Bornkamm, Gerhard Barth, Heinz Joachim Held:
                Überlieferung und Auslegung im Matthäusevangelium. 2.
                durchgesehene Auflage. WMANT 1. Neukirchen:
                Neukirchener Verlag. 54-154.
Bartky, Sandra Lee
1975   "Toward a Phenomenology of Feminist Consciousness." –
                Social Theory and Practise: an international and
                interdisciplinary journal of social philosophy, vol. 3:4.
Barton, Stephen C
1994   Discipleship and family ties in Mark and Matthew. Cambridge:
                Cambridge University Press.
Bass, Dorothy C.
1982   "Women's Studies and Biblical Studies. A Historical
                Perspective." – JSOT 22, 6-12.

Bauer, D.R.
1988   The Structure of Matthew's Gospel. A Study in Literary
                       Design. JSNTSup 31. Sheffield: Sheffield Academic Press.
Beare, Francis Wright
1981   The Gospel according to Matthew. A Commentary. Oxford:
                       Blackwell.
Beasley-Murray, G.R.
1987   Jesus and the Kingdom of God. Reprinted. Grand Rapids,
                       Mich: Eerdman's.
de Beauvoir, Simone
1988   The Second Sex. (Le Deuxieme Sexe, first published 1949).
                       London: Pan Books Ltd.
Berlin, Adele
1983   Poetics and Interpretation of Biblical Narrative. Bible and
                       Literature 9. Sheffield: Almond.
The Bible and Culture Collective
1995   The Postmodern Bible. New Haven: Yale University Press.
Blomberg, Graig L.
1991   "The Liberation of Illegitimacy. Women and Rulers in
                       Matthew 1-2." – BTB 21, 145-150.
Bornkamm, Günther
1961   "Die Sturmstillung im Matthäusevangelium." – Günther
                       Bornkamm, Gerhard Barth, Heinz Joachim Held: Überlieferung
                       und Auslegung im Matthäusevangelium. 2. durchgesehene
                       Auflage. WMANT 1. Neukirchen: Neukirchener Verlag. 48-53.
1983   "The Authority to "Bind" and "Loose" in the Church in
                       Matthew's Gospel: The Problem of Sources in Matthew's
                       Gospel." – The Interpretation of Matthew. IRT 3. Ed. by G.N.
                       Stanton. 85-97. Philadelphia and London: Fortress Press and
                       SPCK.
Boss, Sarah Jane
1996   "Dualism." – An A to Z of Feminist Theology. Ed. by Lisa
                       Isherwood and Dorothea McEwan. 41-42. Sheffield: Sheffield
                       Academic Press.
Bredin, Mark R.J.
1996   "Gentiles and the Davidic Tradition in Matthew." – A Feminist
                       Companion to the Hebrew Bible in the New Testament. Ed. by
                       Athalya Brenner. 95-111. Sheffield: Sheffield Academic Press.
Brooten, Bernadette
1980   "Feminist Perspectives on New Testament Exegesis." –
                       Conflicting Ways of Interpreting the Bible. Concilium 138, 57-
                       61.
Brown, Raymond
1977   The Birth of the Messiah. A Commentary on the Infancy
                       Narratives in Matthew and Luke. New York: Image Books.
1982   "Rachab in Matthew 1,5 probably is Rahab of Jericho." –
                       Biblica 62, 79-80.

1994   The Death of the Messiah. From Gethsemane to the Grave. New York: Doubleday.

Brown, Raymond; Donfried, Karl and Reumann, John (eds.)
1973   Peter in the New Testament. A Collaborative Assessment by Protestant and Roman Catholic Scholars. Minneapolis, MN: Augsburg Publishing House.

Brown, Raymond; Donfried, Karl; Fitzmyer, Joseph and Reumann, John (eds.)
1978   Mary in the New Testament. A Collaborative Assessment by Protestant and Roman Catholic Scholars. Philadelphia, PA: Fortress Press.

Brown, Raymond and Meier, John
1983   Antioch and Rome. New Testament Cradles of Catholic Christianity. New York/Ramsey NJ: Paulist Press.

Brown Zikmund, Barbara
1985   "Feminist Consciousness in Historical Perspective." – Feminist Interpretation of the Bible. Ed. by Letty M. Russell. 21-29. Oxford: Blackwell.

Bultmann, Rudolf
1972   The History of the Synoptic Tradition. Revised edition. Oxford Blackwell.

Byrskog, Samuel
1994   Jesus the Only Teacher. Didactic Authority and Transmission in Ancient Israel, Ancient Judaism and the Matthean Community. Coniectanea Biblica NT series 24. Stockholm: Almqvist & Wiksell International.

Cady Stanton, Elisabeth
1972 (1895-1898)   The Woman's Bible. Repr. Edition. New York: Arno Press. (First edition: New York: European Publishing Company 1895/1898)
1971 (1898)   Eighty Years and More. Reminiscences 1815-1897. Reprinted. New York. (First edition 1898).

Caragounis, Chrys C.
1990   Peter and the Rock. BZNW 58. Berlin: de Gruyter.

Carter, Warren
1993   "The Crowds in Matthew's Gospel." – CBQ 55, 54-67.
1994   Households and Discipleship. A Study of Matthew 19-20. Sheffield: Sheffield Academic Press.

Chatman, Seymour
1978   Story and Discourse. Narrative Structure in Fiction and Film. Ithaca and London: Cornell University Press.

Cheney, Emily
1997   "The Mother of the Sons of Zebedee (Matthew 27.56)." – JSNT 68, 13-27.

Clévenot, Michel
1985   Materialist Approaches to the Bible. Maryknoll, NY: Orbis Books.

Corley, Kathleen E.
1993   Private Women, Public Meals. Social Conflict in the Synoptic
                   Tradition. Peabody, MA: Hendrickson Publishers.
Collins, John N.
1990   Diakonia. Re-interpreting the Ancient Sources. Oxford: Oxford
                   University Press.
Cullmann, Oscar
1973   "πέτρα" – TDNT vol VI, 95-99.
Culpepper, Alan
1983   The Anatomy of the Fourth Gospel. A Study in Literary
                   Design. Philadelphia: Fortress Press.
Daly, Mary
1973   Beyond God the Father. Toward a Philosophy of Women's
                   Liberation. Boston: Beacon Press.
1979   Gyn/Ecology. The Metaethics of Radical Feminism. Boston:
                   Beacon Press.
Davies, W.D. and Allison, Dale C.
1988   A Critical and Exegetical Commentary on the Gospel
                   according to Saint Matthew, Volume I. Introduction and
                   Commentary on Matthew I-VII. ICC. Edinburgh: T&T Clark.
1991   A Critical and Exegetical Commentary on the Gospel
                   according to Saint Matthew, Volume II. Commentary on
                   Matthew VIII-XVIII. ICC. Edinburgh: T&T Clark.
1997   A Critical and Exegetical Commentary on the Gospel
                   according to Saint Matthew, Volume III. Commentary on
                   Matthew XIX-XXVIII. ICC Edinburgh: T&T Clark.
Dewey, Joanna
1994   "Jesus' Healings of Women. Clues for Historical
                   Reconstruction."– BTB 24, 122-131.
Dines, Jenny
1993   "Not to be served, but to serve: women as disciples in Mark's
                   Gospel." – The Month, 438-442.
Dunderberg, Ismo
2002   "The Beloved Disciple in John: Ideal Figure in an Early
                   Christian Controversy" – Fair Play: Diversity and Conflicts in
                   Early Christianity. Essays in Honour of Heikki Räisänen. Ed.
                   by Ismo Dunderberg, Christopher Tuckett and Kari Syreeni.
                   243-269. Leiden, Boston Köln:Brill.
Edwards, Richard A.
1985   "Uncertain Faith. Matthew's Portrait of the Disciples."
                   Discipleship in the New Testament. Ed. by Fernando F.
                   Segovia. 47-61. Philadelphia: Fortress Press.
1997   Matthew's Narrative Portrait of Disciples. How the Text-
                   Connoted Reader is Informed. Harrisburg, PA: Trinity Press
                   International.

Fander, Monika
1994   "Historical-Critical methods." – Searching the Scriptures I: A
            Feminist Introduction. Ed. by E. Schüssler Fiorenza. 205-224.
            London: SCM Press.

Fatum, Lone
1992   "Women, Symbolic Universe and Structures of Silence:
            Challenges and Possibilities in Androcentric Texts." – Kan Vi
            tro på Gud Fader. Ed.by Hanna Stenström. 263-286. Uppsala:
            Svenska kyrkans forskningsråd.

Fenton, J.C.
1978   The Gospel of Matthew. Reprinted. Harmondsworth: Penguin
            Books.

Fetterley, Judith
1978   The Resisting reader. A feminist approach to American fiction.
            Bloomington: Indianan University press.

Filson, Floyd V.
1967   A Commentary on the Gospel according to St. Matthew.
            BNTC. 2nd. Ed. London: Adam&Charles Book.

Fitzmyer, Joseph A.
1973   "The Virginal Conception of Jesus in the New Testament." –
            JTS 34, 541-575.

Fredriksen, Paula
1988   From Jesus to Christ: The origins of the new Testament images
            of Jesus. New Haven: Yale University Press.

Freed, Edwin D.
1987   "The Women in Matthew's Genealogy." – JSNT 29, 3-19.

Forster, E.M.
1963   Aspects of the Novel. Reprinted. First published in 1927.
            Harmondsworth: The Penguin Books.

Garland, David E.
1996   "The Temple Tax in Matthew 17:24-25 and the Principle of not
            Causing Offense." – Treasures New and Old. Recent
            Contributions to Matthean Studies. Ed. by David R. Bauer and
            Mark Allan Powell. 69-98. Georgia: Scholars Press.

Genette, Gerard
1980   Narrative Discourse. Oxford: Blackwell

Gnadt, Martina S.
1998   "Das Evangelium nach Matthäus. Judenchristliche Gemeinden
            im Widerstand gegen die Pax Romana." – Kompendium
            Feministische Bibelauslegung. Hrsg. Von Luise Schottroff und
            Marie-Theres Wacker. 483-498. Gütersloh: Kaiser.

Gössmann, Elisabeth
1994   "History of Biblical Interpretation by European Women." –
            Searching the Scriptures I. A Feminist Introduction. 27-40.
            London: SCM Press.

Goulder, Michael
1974   Midrash and Lection in Matthew. London: SPCK.

1994	A Tale of Two Missions. London: SCM Press.

Graham, Elaine
1995   "Gender." – An A to Z of Feminist Theology. Ed. by Lisa Isherwood and Dorothea McEwan. 78-80. Sheffield: Sheffield Academic Press.

Grant, Michael
1994   Saint Peter. London: Weidenfeld and Nicholson.

Gundry, Robert Horton
1982   Matthew. A Commentary on his literary and theological art. Grand rapids, Mi: Eerdman's cop.

Gunew, Sneja (ed.)
1990   Feminist Knowledge. Critique and Construct. London and New York: Routledge.

Haapa, Esko
1969   Matteuksen evankeliumi. SUTS 2. ed. Helsinki: Kirjapaja.

Hagner, Donald A.
1993   Matthew 1-13. WBC. Dallas: TX Books.

Hampson, Daphne
1990   Theology and Feminism. Oxford: Basil Blackwell.

Hanson, A.T.
1978   "Rahab the Harlot in early Christian Tradition." – JSNT 1, 53-60.

Harding, Sandra
1986   The Science Question in Feminism. Milton Keynes: Open University Press..

Heil, J.P.
1991(1)   "The narrative Role of the Women in Matthew's Genealogy." – Bib 72, 538-545.

1991(2)   The Death and Resurrection of Jesus. A narrative-Critical Reading of Matthew 26-28. Minneapolis: Fortress Press.

Held, Heinz Joachim
1961   "Matthäus als Interpret der Wundergeschichten." – Günther Bornkamm, Gerhard Barth, Heinz Joachim Held: Überlieferung und Auslegung im Matthäusevangelium. 2. durchgesehene Auflage. WMANT 1. Neukirchen: Neukirchener Verlag. 155-287.

Heyward, Carter
1982   The Redemption of God. A Theology of Mutual Relation. Labham, MD: University Press of America.

1984   Our Passion for Justice. Images of Power, Sexuality, and Liberation. Cleveland, Ohio: The Pilgrim Press.

1989   Touching our Strength. The Erotic as power and the Love of God. San Francisco: Harper.

1996   "Empowerment." – An A to Z of Feminist Theology. Ed. by Lisa Isherwood and Dorothea McEwan. 52-53. Sheffield: Sheffield Academic Press.

Hill, David
1972   The Gospel of Matthew. NBC Commentary. London:
                             Oliphants.
Horsley, Richard
1989   The Liberation of Christmas. The Infancy Narratives in Social
                             Context. New York: Crossroads.
Howell, David B.
1990   Matthew's Inclusive Story. A Study in the Narrative Rhetoric
                             of the First Gospel. Sheffield: Sheffield Academic Press.
Illich, Ivan
1983   Gender. London: Marion Boyars.
Isasi-Diaz, Ada Maria
1994   "La Palabra de Dios en Nosotros – The Word of God in Us." –
                             Searching the Scriptures I. A Feminist Introduction. Ed.by E.
                             Schüssler Fiorenza. 86-97. London: SCM Press.
Isherwood, Lisa and McEwan, Dorothea
1993   Introducing Feminist Theology. Sheffield: Sheffield Academic
                             Press.
Jantzen, Grace M.
1990   "Who Needs Feminism?" – Theology 93, 339-343.
Johnson, Marshall D.
1988   The Purpose of the Biblical Genealogies with special reference
                             to the Setting of the Genealogies of Jesus. MSSNTS 8. 2. ed.
                             Cambridge: Cambridge University Press.
Kingsbury, Jack Dean
1969   The Parables of Matthew 13. A Study in Redaction Criticism.
                             London: SPCK.
1975(1)   Matthew: Structure, Christology, Kingdom. Philadelphia and
                             London: Fortress Press and SPCK.
1975(2)   "The Title Kyrios in Matthew's Gospel." – JBL 94, 246-255.
1978   "The verb Akolouthein ("to follow") as an Index of Matthew's
                             view of his community." – JBL 97, 56-73.
1979   "The Figure of Peter in Matthew's Gospel as a Theological
                             Problem." – JBL 98, 67-83.
1988(1)   Matthew as Story. Second edition. Philadelphia: Fortress Press.
1988(2)   "On Following Jesus: The 'Eager' Scribe and the 'Reluctant'
                             Disciple (Matthew 8.18-22)" – NTS 34, 45-59.
Kinukawa, Hisako
1994   Women and Jesus in Mark. A Japanese Feminist perspective.
                             Maryknoll: Orbis Books.
Kopas, Jane
1990   "Jesus and Women in Matthew." – Ttod 47, 13-21.
Kramarae, Cheris and Treichler, Paula A.
1985   A Feminist Dictionary. London: Pandora Press.
Kunkel, Fritz
1987   Creation Continues. A Psychological Interpretation of the
                             Gospel of Matthew. First edition 1946. New York/Mahvah:
                             Paulist Press.

Kwok Pui-Lan
1995 Discovering the Bible in the Non-Biblical World. The Bible and Liberation series. Maryknoll, NY: Orbis Books.

Lappalainen, Päivi
1990 "Isän ääni. Kirjallisuushistoriamme ja patriarkaalinen ideologia." – Marginaalista muutokseen. Ed. by Pirjo Ahokas and lea Rojola. 71-93. Turku: Turun Yliopiston offsetpaino.

Lehtiö, Pirkko
1999 "Ei enää vaikenemista, ei enää salaisuuksia. Kristillinen usko ja elämä Aasian naisten näkökulmasta." – TA 104, 72-80.

Lerner, Gerda
1986 The Creation of Patriarchy. Women and history, vol 1. New York, NY: Oxford University Press.

Levine, Amy-Jill
1992 "Matthew" – Women's Bible Commentary. Ed. by Carol A. Newsom and Sharon H. Ringe. 252-262. London:SPCK.

1996 "Discharging Responsibility. Matthean Jesus, Biblical Law, and Hemorrhaging Woman." – Treasures New and Old. Recent Contributions to Matthean Studies. Ed. by David R. Bauer and Mark Allan Powell. 379-397. Atlanta, Georgia: Scholars Press.

Luomanen, Petri
1998 Entering the Kingdom of Heaven. A Study on the Structure of Matthew's View of Salvation. WUN T 2; 101. Tübingen: Mohr Siebeck.

Luz, Ulrich
1983 "The Disciples in the Gospel according to Matthew." The Interpretation of Matthew. Ed. by G.N. Stanton. IRT 3. 98-128. Philadelphia and London: Fortress Press and SPCK.

1989 Matthew 1-7. A Commentary. Minneapolis, MN: Augsburg.

1990 Das Evangelium nach Matthäus. 2. Teilband Mt 8-17. EKKNT. Zürich: Benziger Verlag.

1997 Das Evangelium nach Matthäus. 3. Teilband Mt 18-25. EKKNT. Zürich: Benziger Verlag.

Malina, Bruce J.
1983 The New Testament World. Insights from cultural anthropology. London: SCM Press.

Malina, Bruce and Rohrbaugh, Richard L.
1992 Social Science Commentary on the Synoptic Gospels. Minneapolis: Fortress Press.

Marjanen, Antti
1995 The Woman Jesus Loved. Mary Magdalene in the Nag Hammadi Library and Related Documents.

1997 "Jeesuksen naisoppilaat." – Nasaretilaisen historia. Toim. Risto Uro ja Outi Lehtipuu. Helsinki: Kirjapaja.

1998 "Women Disciples in the Gospel of Thomas." – Thomas at the Crossroads. Essays on the Gospel of Thomas. Ed. by Risto Uro. Edinburgh: T&T Clark.

Mattila, Talvikki
1999   "Naming the Nameless: Gender and Discipleship in Matthew's
               Passion Narrative." – Characterization in the Gospels.
               Reconceiving Narrative Criticism. Ed. by David Rhoads and
               Kari Syreeni. 153-179. Sheffield: Sheffield Academic Press.
McBride, Maureen
1996   "Power." – An A to Z to Feminist Theology.Ed. By Lisa
               Isherwood and Dorothea McEwan. 182-183. Sheffield:
               Sheffield Academic Press.
McGinn, Sheila
1995   "Not Counting Women. A Feminist Reading of Matthew 26-
               28." – SBL Seminar Papers 34, 168-176.
Meeks, Wayne
1983   First Urban Christians. The Social World of Apostle Paul. New
               Haven: Yale University Press.
Melzer-Keller, Helga
1997   Jesus und die Frauen. Eine Verhältnisbestimmung nach den
               synoptischen Überlieferungen. Freiburg:Herder.
Merenlahti, Petri and Hakola, Raimo
1999   "Reconceiving Narrative Criticism." – Characterization in the
               Gospels. Reconceiving Narrative Criticism. Ed. by David
               Rhoads and Kari Syreeni. 13-48. Sheffield: Sheffield Academic
               Press.
Middleton, Deborah F.
1990   "Feminist Interpretation." – A Dictionary of Biblical
               Interpretation. Ed.by R.J. Coggins and J.L. Houlden. 231-234.
               London: SCM Press.
Minear, P.
1974   "The Disciples and the Crowds in the Gospel of Matthew." –
               ATR Supp Series 56, 28-44.
Moi, Toril
1989   "Feminist, Female, Feminine." – The Feminist Reader: Essays
               in gender and politics of literary criticism. Ed. by Catherine
               Belsey and Jane Moore. 117-132. Basingstoke: MacMillan.
Moltmann-Wendel, Elisabeth
1991   Ein Eigener Mensch werden. Frauen um Jesus. 7. Auflage.
               Gütersloh:Gütersloher Verlagshaus Gerd Mohn.
Morris, Pam
1997   Kirjallisuus ja Feminismi. Johdatus feministiseen
               kirjallisuudentutkimukseen. Toimittaen suomentanut Päivi
               Lappalainen. Helsinki: Suomalaisen Kirjallisuuden Seura.
Nau, Arlo J.
1992   Peter in Matthew. Discipleship, Diplomacy, and Dispraise.
               Collegeville, Minnesota: The Liturgical Press.
Niditch, Susan
1979   "The Wrong Woman Righted. An Analysis of Genesis 38." –
               HTR 72, 143-149.

Nineham, Dennis Eric
1992   The Gospel of St Mark. Reprinted. London: Penguin Books.
Okure, Teresa
1994   "Feminist Interpretation in Africa." – Searching the Scriptures
                     I: A Feminist Introduction. Ed.by Elisabeth Schüssler Fiorenza.
                     77-85. London: SCM Press.
Osiek, Carolyn
1985   "The Feminist and the Bible: Hermeneutical Alternatives." –
                     Feminist Perspectives on Biblical Scholarship. Ed. by Adela
                     Yarbro Collins. 93-105. Chico, CA: Scholars Press.
Osiek, Carolyn and Balch, David
1997   Families in the New testament World. Households and House
                     Churches. Louisville, Kentucky: Westminster John Knox Press.
Parvikko, Tuija
1997   "Politiikkaa ihmisten välissä. Hannah Arendtin maailma." –
                     Tiede ja Edistys 1, 14-22.
Pilch, John J.
1981   "Biblical Leprosy and Body Symbolism." – BTB 11, 108-113.
1986   "The Health care System in Matthew." – BTB 16, 102-106
1992   "Understanding Healing in the Social World of early
                     Christianity." BTB 1, 26-33.
Plaskow, Judith
1994   "Anti-Judaism in feminist Christian Interpretation." Searching
                     the Scriptures I: A Feminist Introduction. Ed. by Elisabeth
                     Schüssler Fiorenza. 117-129. London: SCM Press.
Perrin, Norman
1976   Jesus and the Language of the Kingdom. Symbol and Metaphor
                     in New Testament Interpretation.London: SCM Press.
Powell, Mark Allan
1992(1)   "Toward a narrative-Critical Understanding of Matthew." – Int
                     46, 341-346.
1992(2)   "The Plot and Sublots of Matthew's Gospel. – NTS 38, 198-
                     202.
1993   What is Narrative Criticism? A New Approach to the Bible.
                     London: SPCK
Quinn, Jerome
1982   "Is RAXAB in MT 1,5 Rahab of jericho? – Bib 62, 225-228.
Radforf Ruether, Rosemary
1978   Nächstenliebe und Brudermord. Die Theologischen Wurzeln
                     des Antisemitismus. München: Kaiser.
1983   Sexism and God-Talk. Toward a Feminist Theology. Boston:
                     Beacon Press.
1985   "Feminist Interpretation: A Method of Correlation" – Feminist
                     Interpretation of the Bible. Ed. by Letty M. Russell. 111-124.
                     Oxford: Blackwell.
1996   "Patriarchy." – An A to Z of Feminist Theology. Ed. by Lisa
                     Isherwood and Dorothea McEwan. 173-174. Sheffield:
                     Sheffield Academic Press.

1998   Women and Redemption. A Theological History. London:
                       SCM Press.
Räisanen, Heikki
1969   Die Mutter Jesu im Neuen Testament. Helsinki: Suomalainen
                       Tiedeakatemia.
1992   "Maria, Jeesuksen Äiti." – Naisia Raamatussa: Viisaus ja
                       Rakkaus. Ed.by Raija Sollamo and Ismo Dunderberg. 39-58.
                       Helsinki: Yliopistopaino.
2001   "Tradition, Experience, Interpretation. A Dialectical Model for
                       Describing the Development of Religious Thought." –
                       Challenges to Biblical Interpretation: Collected Essays 1991-
                       2001.252-262. Leiden-Boston-Köln:Brill.
Reinhartz, Adele
1988   "The New Testament and Anti-Judaism. A Literary-Critical
                       Approach." – Journal of Ecumenical Studies 25, 524-537.
Ricci, Carla
1994   Mary Magdalene and Many Others. Women who followed
                       Jesus. Minneapolis: Fortress Press.
Rimmon-Kenan, Shlomith
1983   Narrative Fiction: Contemporary Poetics. London and New
                       York: Methuen.
Ringe, Sharon H.
1985   "A Gentile Woman's Story" – Feminist Interpretation of the
                       Bible. Ed.by Letty M. Russell. 65-72. Oxford: Blackwell.
1992   "When Women Interpret the Bible." – The Women's Bible
                       Commentary. Ed. by Carol A. Newsom and Sharon H. Ringe.
                       London: SPCK
Russell, Letty M.
1985(1)   "Introduction: Liberating the Word." – Feminist Interpretation
                       of the Bible. Ed.by Letty M. Russell. 11-18. Oxford: Blackwell.
1985(2)   "Authority and Challenge of Feminist Interpretation." –
                       Feminist Interpretation of the Bible. ED. by Letty M. Russell.
                       137-146. Oxford:Blackwell.
Sakenfeld, Katharine Doob
1985   "Feminist Uses of Biblical material."– Feminist Interpretation
                       of the Bible. Ed. by Letty M. Russell. 55-64. Oxford:
                       Blackwell.
Saldarini, Anthony J.
1994   Matthew's Christian-Jewish Community. Chigaco: The
                       University of Chigaco Press.
Sanders, E.P.
1985   Jesus and Judaism. London: SCM Press.
Schaberg, Jane
1990   The Illegitimacy of Jesus. A Feminist Theological
                       Interpretation of the Infancy Narratives. Reprint. New York:
                       Crossroad.

1996   "The Foremothers and the Mother of Jesus." – A Feminist Companion to the Hebrew Bible in the New Testament. Ed. by Athalya Brenner. Sheffield: Sheffield Academic Press

Schneiders, Sandra M.

1989   "Feminist Ideology Criticism and Biblical Hermeneutics." – BTB vol 19, 3-10.

Schottroff, Luise

1990   Befreiungserfahrungen: Studien zur Sozialgeschichte des Neuen Testaments. München: Kaiser Verlag.

1993   Let the Oppressed go Free. Feminist Perspectives on the New Testament. Louisville, Kentucky: Westminster/John Knox Press.

1995   Lydia's Impatient Sisters. A feminist Social History of early Christianity. London: SCM Press.

Schottroff, Luise/Schroer, Silvia/Wacker, Marie-Theres

1995   Feministische Exegese. Forschungserträge zur Bibel aus der Perspektive von Frauen. Darmstadt: Wissenschaftliche Buchgesellschaft.

Schottroff, Luise and Wacker, Marie-Theres (eds.)

1995   Von der Wurzel getragen. Deutschsprachiche christlich-feministische Exegese in Auseinandersetzung mit Antijudaismus. Leiden: Brill.

Schüssler Fiorenza, Elisabeth

1983   In Memory of Her. A Feminist Theological Reconstruction of Christian Origins. New York: Crossroads.

1985(1)   "The Will to Choose or Reject. Continuing Our critical Work." – Feminist Interpretation of the Bible. Ed.by Letty M. Russell. 125-136. Oxford: Blackwell

1985(2)   "Remembering the Past in Creating the Future. Historical-Critical Scholarship and Feminist Biblical Interpretation." – Feminist Perspectives on Biblical Scholarship. Ed.by Adela Yarbro Collins. 43-63. Chico, CA: Scholars Press.

1990   Bread Not Stone. The Challenge of Feminist Biblical Interpretation. Edinburgh: T&T Clark.

1992   But She Said. Feminist Practices of Biblical Interpretation. Boston: Beacon Press.

1993   Discipleship of Equals. A Critical Feminist Ekklesia-logy of Liberation. London: SCM Press.

1994   Jesus Miriam's Child Sophia's Prophet. Critical Issues in Feminist Christology. London: SCM Press.

Schweizer, Eduard

1974   Matthäus und seine Geneinde. Stuttgart: KBW Verlag

1981   Das Evangelium nach Matthäus. 15. durchgesehene Auflage. NTD 2. Göttingen: Vandenhoeck & Ruprecht.

Segal, Alan

1991   "Matthew's Jewish Voice." – Social History of the Matthean Community. Ed.by David L. Balch. 3-37. Minneapolis: Fortress Press.

Segovia, Fernando F.
1985   "Introduction. Call and Discipleship. Toward a re-examination
                          of the Shape and Character of Christian Experience in the New
                          Testament." – Discipleship in the New Testament. Ed. by
                          Fernando F. Segovia. 1-23. Philadelphia: Fortress Press.
Seim, Turid Karlsen
1994   The Double Message. Patterns of Gender in Luke-Acts.
                          Nashville: Abingdon Press.
Selvidge, Marla J.
1984   "Mark 5:25-34 and Leviticus 15:19-20. A Reaction to
                          restrictive purity regulations." – JBL 103, 619-623.
Senior, Donald P.
1975   The Passion narrative according to Matthew. A Redactional
                          Study. Leuven.
1998   Matthew. Abingdon New Testament Commentaries. Nashville:
                          Abingdon Press.
Smith, Christopher R.
1997   "Literary Evidences of a Fivefold Structure in the Gospel of
                          Matthew." – NTS 43, 540-551.
Sollamo, Raija and Dunderberg, Ismo (eds.)
1992   Naisia Raamatussa. Viisaus ja Rakkaus. Helsinki:
                          Yliopistopaino.
Stambaugh, John E. and Balch, David. L.
1986   The New Testament in Its Social Environment. Philadelphia,
                          PA: Westminster Press.
Stanton, Graham N.
1992   "The Communities of Matthew." – Int 46, 379-391
1993   A Gospel for a New People: Studies in Matthew. Reprinted:
                          Edinburgh: T&T Clark.
1996   "Ministry in Matthean Christianity." – Call to Serve. Essays on
                          Ministry in Honour of Bishop Penny Jamieson. Ed. by Douglas
                          A. Campbell. 142-160. Sheffield: Sheffield Academic Press.
Starhawk
1990   Truth or Dare. Encounters with Power, Authority, and Mystery.
                          San Francisco: Harper.
Staumberger, Christine
1991   "Patriarchat als feministischer Begriff." – Wörterbuch der
                          feministischen Theologie. 321-323. Güterloh: Mohn.
Stenström, Hanna
1999   The Book of Revelation. A Vision of the Ultimate Liberation
                          or the Ultimate Backlash. A Study in 20th century
                          interpretations of Rev 14:1-5, with special emphasis on
                          feminist exegesis. Uppsala University.
Stock, Augustine
1987   "Is Matthew's Presentation of Peter Ironic?" – BTB 17, 64-69.
Strack, H. and Billerbeck, P.
1922   Das Evangelium nach Matthäus. Kommentar zum neuen
                          Testament aus Talmud und Midrash I. München.

Strecker, Georg
1971   Das Weg der Gerechtigkeit. Untersuchungen zur Theologie des
               Matthäus. FRLANT 82. Dritte, durchgesehene Auflage.
               Göttingen: Vandenhoeck & Ruprecht.
1983   "The Concept of History in Matthew." – The Interpretation of
               Matthew. IRT 3. Ed. by G. Stanton. 67-84. London: SPCK
Struthers Malbon, Elisabeth
1983   "Fallible Followers. Women and men in the Gospel of Mark."
               – Semeia 28, 29-48.
Struthers Malbon, Elisabeth and Anderson, Janice Capel
1994   "Literary-Critical Methods." – Searching the Scriptures I. A
               Feminist Introduction. Ed. by Elisabeth Schüssler Fiorenza.
               241-254. London:SCM Press.
De Swarte Gifford, Carolyn
1985   "American Women and the Bible. The nature of Woman as
               Hermeneutical Issue." – Feminist Perspectives on Biblical
               Scholarship. Ed. by Adela Yarbro Collins. 11-33. Chico, CA:
               Scholars Press.
1994   "Politizicing the Sacred Texts. Elisabeth cady Stanton and the
               Woman's Bible." – Searching the Scriptures I. A Feminist
               Introduction. Ed. by Elisaberh Schüssler Fiorenza. 52-63.
               London: SCM Press.
Syreeni, Kari
1987   The Making of the Sermon on the Mount. A procedural
               analysis of Matthew's redactional activity. Part I: Methodology
               & Compositional Analysis. Helsinki: Suomalainen
               Tiedeakatemia.
1999   "Peter as Character and Symbol in the Gospel of Matthew." –
               Characterization in the Gospels. Reconceiving Narrative
               Criticism. 106-152. Sheffield: Sheffield Academic Press.
Syreeni, Kari and Luomanen Petri
1997   "Matteuksen evankeliumi." – Varhaiskristilliset evankeliumit.
               Ed. by Matti Myllykoski ja Arto Järvinen. 183-235. Helsinki:
               University Press.
Tamez, Elsa
1988   "Women's Re-reading of the Bible." – With Passion and
               Compassion. Third World Women Doing Theology. Ed.by
               Virginia Fabella, M.M. and mercy Amba Oduyoye. 173-180.
               Maryknoll, NY: Orbis Book.
Theissen, Gerd
1983   The Miracle Stories of Early Christian Tradition. (Original
               Urchristliche Wundergaschichten, transl. By Francis
               McDonagh). Edinburgh: T&T Clark.
Thiede, Carsten P.
1986   Simon Peter. From Galilee to Rome. Exeter: The Paternoster
               Press.
Thiemann, Ronald F.
1973   "The Unnamed Woman at Bethany." – Ttod 44, 179-188.

Tolbert, Mary Ann
1983   "Defining the Problem. The Bible and Feminist Hermeneutics."
             – Semeia 28, 113-126.
Trible, Phyllis
1983   God and the Rhetoric of Sexuality. Reprinted. Philadelphia:
             Fortress Press.
1984   Texts of Terror. Literary Feminist Readings of Biblical
             Narratives. Philadelphia: Fortress Press.
Trilling, Wolfgang
1959   Das wahre Israel. Studien zur Theologie des
             Matthäusevangelium. Erfurter Theologische Studien 7. Leipzig.
Van Unnik, Willem C.
1974   "The Death of Judas in Saint Matthew's Gospel." – ATRSup
             3, 44-57.
Uro, Risto
1996   "Apocalyptic Symbolism and Social Identity in Q." – Symbols
             and Strata. Essays on the sayings Gospel Q. Ed. by Risto Uro.
             67-118. Helsinki: Finnish Exegetical Society.
Viviano, Benedict T.
1979   "Where was the Gospel according to St Matthew written?" –
             CBQ 41, 533-540.
Wacker, Marie-Theres
1995   "Geschichtliche, hermeneutische und methodologische
             Grundlagen." – Luise Schottroff/Silvia Schroer/Marie-Theres
             Wacker: Feministische Exegese. Forschungserträge zur Bibel
             aus der Perspektive von Frauen. 3-79. Darmstadt:
             Wissenschaftliche Buchgesellschaft.
Waetjen, Herman C.
1976   "The Genealogy as the key to the Gospel according to
             Matthew." – JBL 95, 205-230.
Wainwright, Elaine Mary
1991   Towards a Feminist Critical Reading of the Gospel according
             to Matthew. BZNW 60. New York: Walter de Gruyter.
1995   "The Gospel of Matthew." – Searching the Scriptures II. A
             Feminist Commentary. Ed. by Elisabeth Schüssler Fiorenza.
             635-677. London: SCM Press.
Weder, Hans
1992   "Disciple, Discipleship." – ABD vol 2, 207-210.
Weren, Wim J.C.
1997   "The Five Women in Matthew's Genealogy." – CBQ 59, 288-
             305.
Wilkins, Michael J.
1988   The Concept of disciple in Matthew's gospel as reflected in the
             use of the term μαθητής. SNT. Leiden:Brill.
Williams, James G.
1982   Women Recounted. Narrative Thinking and the God of Israel.
             BL 6. Sheffield: Almond.

Wire, Antoinette
1978   "The Structure of the Gospel Miracle Stories and their Tellers."
                – Semeia 11, 83-113.
1991   "Gender Roles in Scribal Community." – Social History of the
                Matthean Community. Ed.by David L. Balch. Minneapolis:
                Fortress Press.
1994   "1 Corinthians." – Searching the Scriptures II. A Feminist
                Commentary. Ed. by Elisabeth Schüssler Fiorenza. 153-195.
                London: SCM Press.
Witherington III, Ben
1991   Women in the Ministry of Jesus. A Study of Jesus' Attitudes to
                Women and their Roles as Reflected in His Earthly Life.
                Reprinted. Cambridge: Cambridge University Press.

ABBREVIATIONS

AB	Anchor Bible
ABD	David Noel Freedman (ed.), Anchor Bible Dictionary (New York: Doubleday 1992)
ATRSup	Anglican Theological Review Supplementary series
Bib	Biblica
BL	Bible and Literature
BNTC	Black's New Testament Commentaries
BTB	Biblical Theology Bulletin
BZNW	Beiheft zur Zeitschrift für die neutestamentliche Wissenschaft
CBQ	Catholic Biblical Quartely
EKKNT	Evangelisch-Katholischer Kommentar zum Neuen Testament
FRLANT	Forschungen zur Religion und Literatur des Alten und Neuen Testaments
HTR	Harvard Theological Review
ICC	International Critical Commentary
Int	Interpretation
IRT	Issues in Religion and Theology
JBL	Journal of Biblical Literature
JR	Journal of Religion
JSNT	Journal for the Study of the New Testament
JSNTSup	Journal for the Study of the New Testament, Supplement Series
JSOT	Journal for the Study of the Old Testament
JTS	Journal of Theological Studies
MSSNTS	Monograph Series; Society for New Testament Studies
NCB	New Century Bible
NTD	Das Neue Testament Deutsch
NTS	New Testament Studies
SUTS	Suomalainen Uuden Testamentin selitys
TA	Teologinen Aikakauskirja
TDNT	Gerhard Kittel and Gerhard Friedrich (eds.) Theological Dictionary of the New Testament (transl. Geoffrey W. Bromiley; 10 vols.; Grand Rapids: Eerdmans, 1964–)
TTod	Theology Today
WBC	Word Biblical Commentary
WMANT	Wissenschaftliche Monographien zum Alten und Neuen Testament

ABSTRACT
Talvikki Mattila:
Citizens of the Kingdom. Followers in Matthew from a Feminist Perspective

In this thesis, I have sketched an alternative for the idea of following in Matthew's narrative, making use of a feminist interpretation of power, the idea of the kingdom of God and the character groups in Matthew's narrative.

The characters are analysed with the main focus on the text in its final form, but still anchored in history by taking advantage of redaction critical observations as well as the results from social science. My main interest has centred around feminist ideology and especially the different power relationships between the characters in the narrative. The patriarchal concept of power-over is contrasted with the feminist view of relational power-with, which excludes hierarchies.

The women characters in Matthew s patriarchal environment do not transcend their conventional social status in their encounter with Jesus. Still, they fulfil a symbolic task as the ones who prove faithful: They understand the true meaning of the kingdom, serve, follow, and are the messengers of Jesus' resurrection. These women are part of the new kind of following that includes women as well as male disciples, Jews and Gentiles, leaders and servants, rich and poor.

The central theme in Matthew s narrative is the kingdom, with its non-hierarchical power relationships instead of patriarchal hierarchy. The different character groups in Matthew – the disciples, the Twelve, the crowd, and the women – need different lessons for inner transformation, which is the core of being a citizen of the kingdom. The powerless people in the patriarchal society need empowerment while leaders and masters need to learn the new power models of the kingdom. Matthew uses the different character groups in his narrative to convey this.